ISBN 978-1-330-97843-6
PIBN 10129008

1 MONTH OF
FREE
READING

at

www.ForgottenBooks.com

By purchasing this book you are eligible for one month membership to ForgottenBooks.com, giving you unlimited access to our entire collection of over 700,000 titles via our web site and mobile apps.

To claim your free month visit:

www.forgottenbooks.com/free129008

English
Français
Deutsche
Italiano
Español
Português

www.forgottenbooks.com

Mythology Photography **Fiction**
Fishing Christianity **Art** Cooking
Essays Buddhism Freemasonry
Medicine **Biology** Music **Ancient
Egypt** Evolution Carpentry Physics
Dance Geology **Mathematics** Fitness
Shakespeare **Folklore** Yoga Marketing
Confidence Immortality Biographies
Poetry **Psychology** Witchcraft
Electronics Chemistry History **Law**
Accounting **Philosophy** Anthropology
Alchemy Drama Quantum Mechanics
Atheism Sexual Health **Ancient History**
Entrepreneurship Languages Sport
Paleontology Needlework Islam
Metaphysics Investment Archaeology
Parenting Statistics Criminology
Motivational

INTO

BOKHARA;

BEING THE ACCOUNT OF

A JOURNEY FROM INDIA TO CABOOL, TARTARY,
AND PERSIA;

ALSO, NARRATIVE OF

A VOYAGE ON THE INDUS,

FROM THE SEA TO LAHORE,

WITH PRESENTS FROM THE KING OF GREAT BRITAIN,

PERFORMED UNDER THE ORDERS OF THE SUPREME GOVERNMENT
OF INDIA, IN THE YEARS 1831, 1832, AND 1833.

BY

LIEUT. ALEXr BURNES, F.R.S.

OF THE EAST INDIA COMPANY'S SERVICE;
AS POLITICAL RESIDENT IN CUTCH, AND LATE ON A MISSION TO
THE COURT OF LAHORE.

——— " Per syrtes iter æstuosas,
.   .   .   .   per inhospitalem
Caucasum, vel quæ loca fabulosus
    Lambit Hydaspes." Hor.

IN THREE VOLUMES.

VOL. III.

LONDON:
JOHN MURRAY, ALBEMARLE STREET.
MDCCCXXXIV.

NARRATIVE

OF A

VOYAGE BY THE RIVER INDUS,

FROM THE SEA TO

THE COURT OF LAHORE IN THE PUNJAB,

WITH PRESENTS FROM THE KING OF GREAT BRITAIN,

COMPRISING

AN ACCOUNT OF THE PROCEEDINGS OF THE MISSION,

AND A

MEMOIR OF THE RIVER INDUS,

WITH CURSORY REMARKS ON THE REMAINS OF ANTIQUITY NEAR THAT
CLASSICAL AND CELEBRATED STREAM.

A 4

INTRODUCTION.

I was employed as an officer of the Quarter-master-general's department, for several years, in the province of Cutch. In the course of enquiries into its geography and history, I visited the eastern mouth of the Indus, to which the country adjoins, as well as that singular tract called the " Run," into which that river flows. The extension of our knowledge in that quarter served only to excite further curiosity, in which I was stimulated by Lieut-General Sir Thomas Bradford, then Commander-in-Chief of the Bombay army. That officer directed his views, in a most enlightened manner, to the acquisition of every information regarding a frontier so important to Britain as that of north-western India. Encouraged by such approbation, for which I am deeply grateful, I volunteered my services, in the year 1829, to traverse the deserts between India and, the Indus, and finally, endeavour to descend that river to the sea. Such a journey involved matters of political moment; but the government of Bombay was then held by an individual distinguished above all others, by zeal in the cause of Asiatic geography and literature. Sir John Malcolm despatched me at once, in prosecution of the design, and was pleased to remove me to the political branch of the service, observing, that I should be then invested " with " influence with the rulers, through whose " country I travelled, that would tend greatly " to allay that jealousy and alarm, which might " impede, if they did not arrest, the progress of " my enquiries."

In the year 1830, I entered the desert, accompanied by Lieut. James Holland, of the Quartermaster-general's department, an officer ably qualified to assist me. After reaching Jaysulmeer, we were overtaken by an express from the Supreme Government of India, desiring us to return, since at that time " it was deemed

" inexpedient to incur the hazard of exciting
" the alarm and jealousy of the rulers of Sinde,
" and other foreign states, by the prosecution of
" the design." This disappointment, then most
acutely felt, was dissipated in the following year,
by the arrival of presents from the King of Great
Britain for the ruler of Lahore, coupled, at the
same time, with the desire that such an opportunity for acquiring correct information of the
Indus should not be overlooked. The following
work contains the narrative of that mission,
which I conducted by the Indus to Lahore.
The information which I collected, relative to
Jaysulmeer and the countries on the N. W. frontier of India, has just been published in the
Transactions of the Royal Geographical Society
of London.

London, June 7. 1834.

CONTENTS

OF

THE THIRD VOLUME.

MEMOIR ON THE INDUS AND ITS TRIBUTARY RIVERS IN THE PUNJAB.

CHAPTER I.

CHAP. X.

THE INDUS FROM MITTUN TO ATTOK.

CHAP. XI.

THE CHENAB, OR ACESINES, JOINED BY THE SUTLEGE, OR HESUDRUS.

CHAP. XII.

ON BHAWUL KHAN'S COUNTRY.

CHAP. XIII.

THE PUNJAB.

CHAP. XIV.

THE CHENAB, OR ACESINES, JOINED BY THE RAVEE, OR HYDRAÖTES.

CHAP. XV.

THE RAVEE, OR HYDRAÖTES, BELOW LAHORE.

CHAP. XVI.

A MEMOIR ON THE EASTERN BRANCH OF THE INDUS, AND THE RUN OF CUTCH.

NARRATIVE.

CHAPTER I.

In the year 1830, a ship arrived at Bombay, with a present of five horses from the King of Great Britain to Maharaja Runjeet Sing, the Seik chieftain at Lahore, accompanied by a letter of friendship from his majesty's minister * to that prince. At the recommendation of Major-General Sir John Malcolm, then governor of Bombay, I had the honour of being nominated by the Supreme Government of India to proceed on a mission to the Seik capital, with these presents, by way of the river Indus. I held at that time a political situation in Cutch, the only portion of the British dominions in India which borders on the Indus.

Arrival of presents from the King of England for Runjeet Sing at Lahore.

The authorities, both in England and India, contemplated that much information of a political and geographical nature might be acquired in such a journey. The knowledge which we possessed of the Indus was vague and unsatis-

Information on the Indus desiderated.

---

* Lord Ellenborough, then President of the India Board.

factory, and the only accounts of a great portion
of its course were drawn from Arrian, Curtius,
and the other historians of Alexander's expedition.   Sir John Malcolm thus minuted in the
records of government, in August, 1830 : —

" The navigation of the Indus is important in
" every point of view ; yet we have no inform-
" ation that can be depended upon on this sub-
" ject, except of about seventy miles from Tatta
" to Hyderabad.   Of the present state of the
" Delta we have native accounts, and the only
" facts which can be deduced are, that the dif·
" ferent streams of the river below Tatta, often
" change their channels, and that the sands of
" all are constantly shifting ; but, notwithstand-
" ing these difficulties, boats of a small draft of
" water can always go up the principal of them.
" With regard to the Indus above Hyderabad,
" there can be no doubt of its being, as it has
" been for more than two thousand years, navi-
" gable far up."

Arrange-
ments.

In addition therefore to the complimentary
mission on which I was to be employed, I had
my attention most specially directed to the acquisition of full and complete information regarding the Indus.   This was a matter of no
easy accomplishment, as the Ameers, or rulers
of Sinde, had ever evinced the utmost jealousy
of Europeans, and none of the missions which

visited the country had been permitted to proceed beyond their capital of Hyderabad. The river Indus, likewise, in its course to the ocean, traverses the territories of many lawless and barbarous tribes, from whom both opposition and insult might be dreaded. On these matters much valuable advice was derived from Lieutenant-Colonel Henry Pottinger, political resident in Cutch, and well known to the world for his adventurous travels in Beloochistan. He suggested that it might allay the fears of the Sinde government, if a large carriage were sent with the horses, since the size and bulk of it would render it obvious that the mission could then only proceed by water. This judicious proposal was immediately adopted by government; nor was it in this case alone that the experience of Colonel Pottinger availed me, as it will be seen that he evinced the most unwearied zeal throughout the difficulties which presented themselves, and contributed, in a great degree, to the ultimate success of the undertaking.

That a better colour might also be given to my deputation by a route so unfrequented, I was made the bearer of presents to the Ameers of Sinde, and at the same time charged with communications of a political nature to them. These referred to some excesses committed by their subjects on the British frontier; but I was in-

The escort.

formed that neither that, nor any other negotiation, was to detain me in my way to Lahore.
The authorities in England had desired that a
suitable escort might accompany the party; but
though the design was not free from some degree of danger, it was evident that no party of
any moderate detail could afford the necessary
protection.   I preferred, therefore, the absence
of any of our troops, and resolved to trust to the
people of the country; believing that, through
their means, I might form a link of communication with the inhabitants.   Sir John Malcolm
observed, in his letter to the Governor General,
that " the guard will be people of the country
" he visits, and those familiar with it.   Lieut.
" Burnes prefers such, on the justest grounds, to
" any others; finding they facilitate his pro-
" gress, while they disarm that jealousy which
" the appearance of any of our troops excites."
Nor were my sentiments erroneous; since a
guard of wild Beloochees protected us in Sinde,
and allayed suspicion.

Appointed
to conduct
the mission
to Lahore.
When these preliminary arrangements had
been completed, I received my final instructions
in a secret letter from the chief secretary at
Bombay.   I was informed that " the depth of
" water in the Indus, the direction and breadth
" of the stream, its facilities for steam navigation,
" the supply of fuel on its banks, and the con-

" dition of the princes and people who possess
" the country bordering on it, are all points of
" the highest interest to government; but your
" own knowledge and reflection will suggest to
" you various other particulars, in which full
" information is highly desirable; and the slow
" progress of the boats up the Indus will, it is
" hoped, give you every opportunity to pursue
" your researches."   I was supplied with all the
requisite surveying instruments, and desired to
draw bills on honour for my expenses. In a
spirit also purely characteristic of the distinguished individual who then held the government, I received the thanks of Sir John Malcolm
for my previous services; had my attention
drawn to the confidence now reposed in me;
and was informed that my knowledge of the
neighbouring countries and the character of
their inhabitants, with the local impressions by
which I was certain to be aided, gave me advantages which no other individual enjoyed, and
had led to my selection; nor could I but be
stimulated by the manner in which Sir John
Malcolm addressed the Governor General of
India : — " I shall be very confident of any
" plan Lieut. Burnes undertakes in this quarter
" of India; provided a latitude is given him to
" act as circumstances may dictate, I dare
" pledge myself that the public interests will be

" promoted. Having had my attention much
" directed, and not without success, during
" more than thirty years, to the exploring and
" surveying countries in Asia, I have gained
" some experience, not only in the qualities and
" habits of the individuals by whom such enter-
" prises can be undertaken, but of the pretexts
" and appearances necessary to give them suc-
" cess."   A young active and intelligent officer,
Ensign J. D. Leckie, of the 22d Regiment N. I.,
was also nominated to accompany me ; a surveyor, a native doctor, and suitable establish-
ments of servants were likewise entertained.

Departure
from Cutch.
We sailed from Mandivee in Cutch with a
fleet of five native boats, on the morning of the
21st of January, 1831.   On the day succeeding
our departure, we had cleared the Gulf of Cutch.
The danger in navigating it has been exaggerated.   The eddies and dirty appearance of the
sea, which boils up and bubbles like an effer-
vescing draught, present a frightful aspect to a
stranger, but the natives traverse it at all seasons.
It is tolerably free from rocks, and the Cutch
shore is sandy with little surf, and presents in-
ducements for vessels in distress to run in upon
the land.   We passed a boat of fifty tons, which
had escaped shipwreck, with a very valuable
cargo from Mozambique, the preceding year, by
this expedient.

Among the timid navigators of the East, the mariner of Cutch is truly adventurous ; he voyages to Arabia, the Red Sea, and the coast of Zanguebar in Africa, bravely stretching out on the ocean after quitting his native shore. The " moallim" or pilot determines his position by an altitude at noon or by the stars at night, with a rude quadrant. Coarse charts depict to him the bearings of his destination, and, by long-tried seamanship, he weathers, in an undecked boat with a huge lateen sail, the dangers and tornadoes of the Indian Ocean. This use of the quadrant was taught by a native of Cutch, who made a voyage to Holland in the middle of last century, and returned, " in a green old age," to enlighten his country with the arts and sciences of Europe. The most substantial advantages introduced by this improver of his country were the arts of navigating and naval architecture, in which the inhabitants of Cutch excel. For a trifling reward, a Cutch mariner will put to sea in the rainy season, and the adventurous feeling is encouraged by the Hindoo merchants of Mandivee, an enterprising and speculating body of men.

On the evening of the 24th we had cleared the Gulf of Cutch, and anchored in the mouth of the Koree, the eastern, though forsaken, branch of the Indus, which separates Sinde from

Cutch. The Koree leads to Lueput, and is the largest of all the mouths of the river, having become a branch of the sea as the fresh water has been turned from its channel. There are many spots on its banks hallowed in the estimation of the people. Cotasir and Narainseer are places of pilgrimage to the Hindoo, and stand upon it and the western promontory of Cutch. Opposite them lies the cupola of Rao Kanoje, beneath which there rests a saint, revered by the Mahommedans. To defraud this personage of frankincense, grain, oil, and money, in navigating the Koree, would entail, it is superstitiously believed, certain shipwreck. In the reverence we recognise the dangers and fear of the mariner. There is a great contrast between the shores of Sinde and Cutch; the one is flat and depressed, nearly to a level with the sea, while the hills of Cutch rise in wild and volcanic cones, which meet the eye long after the coast has faded from the view. We gladly exchanged this grandeur for the dull monotony of the shores of Sinde, unvaried, as it is, by any other signs of vegetation than stunted shrubs, whose domain is invaded by each succeeding tide.

Coast of
Sinde.

We followed the Sinde coast for four or five days, passing all the mouths of the Indus, eleven in number, the principal of which we entered and examined, without even the observation of the

NATIVES OF CUTCH.

Lith for Burnes Travels into Bokhara ___ by Day & Haghe Lith to the King

John Murray Albemarle St 1834

inhabitants. There was little indication of our being near the estuary of so great a river, for the water was only fresh a mile off shore from the Gora, or largest mouth of the Indus; and the junction of the river water with that of the sea was formed without violence, and might be now and then discovered by a small streak of foam and a gentle ripple. The number and subdivision of the branches diminish, no doubt, the velocity as well as the volume of the Indus; but it would be supposed that so vast a river would exercise an influence in the sea far from its embouchure; and, I believe, this is really the case in the months of July and August, during the inundation. The waters of the Indus are so loaded with mud and clay, as to discolour the sea for about three miles from the land. Opposite its different mouths numberless brown specks are to be seen, called "pit" by the natives. I found them, on examination, to be round globules, filled with water, and easily burst. When placed on a plate, they were about the size of a shilling, and covered by a brown skin. These specks are considered by the pilots to denote the presence of fresh water among the salt; for they believe them to be detached from the sand banks, by the meeting of the sea and the river. They give a particularly dirty and oily appearance to the water.

At night-fall on the 28th, we cast anchor in the western mouth of the Indus, called the Pittee. The coast of Sinde is not distinguishable a league from the shore. There is not a tree to be seen, though the mirage sometimes magnifies the stunted shrubs of the Delta, and gives them a tall and verdant appearance; a delusion that vanishes with a nearer approach. From our anchorage, a white fortified tomb, in the Bay of Curachee, was visible north-west of us; and beyond it lay a rocky range of black mountains, called Hala, the Irus of Nearchus. I here read from Arrian and Quintus Curtius the passages of this memorable scene in Alexander's expedition, the mouth from which his admiral, Nearchus, took his departure from Sinde. The river did not exceed 500 yards in width, instead of the 200 stadia (furlongs) of Arrian, and the twelve miles, which more modern accounts had assigned to it, on the authority of the natives. But there was still some resemblance to the Greek author; for the hills over Curachee form with the intervening country a semicircular bay, in which an island and some sand-banks might lead a stranger to believe, that the ocean was yet distant. " Alex-
" ander sent two long galleys before the fleet,
" towards the ocean, to view a certain island,
" which they called Cillutas, where his pilots

" told him he might go on shore before he en-
" tered the main ocean ; and when they assured
" him that it was a large island, and had commo-
" dions harbours, besides plenty of fresh water,
" he commanded the rest of the fleet to put in
" there, while he himself passed out to sea."
The island, as it now exists, is scantily covered
with herbage, and destitute of fresh water.   In
vain I sought an identity of name in the Indian
dialect, for it was nameless ; but it presented a
safe place of anchorage ; and, as I looked upon
it, I could not but think it was that Cillutas
where the hero of Macedon, " drawing up his
" fleet under a promontory, sacrificed to the
" gods, as he had received orders from Ammon."
Here it was, too, that Nearchus caused " a canal
" to be dug, of about five stadia in length, where
" the earth was easiest to remove ; as soon as
" the tide began to rise they got their whole
" fleet safe through that passage into the ocean."
The Greek admiral only availed himself of the
experience of the people ; for it is yet customary
among the natives of Sinde to dig shallow
canals, and leave the tides or river to deepen
them ; and a distance of five stadia, or half a
mile, would call for no great labour.   It is not
to be supposed that sand-banks will continue
unaltered for centuries ; but I may observe, that
there was a large bank contiguous to the island,

between it and which a passage like that of
Nearchus might have been dug with the greatest advantage. " Having sailed from the mouth
" of the Indus, Nearchus came to a sandy island,
" called Crocola, and proceeded on his voyage,
" having the mountain Irus on his right hand."
The topography is here more accurate : two
sandy islands, called Andry, lie off Curachee,
at a distance of eighteen miles from the Indus ;
and it is worthy of remark, that that portion of
the Delta through which the Pittee runs, is yet
denominated " Crocola" by the natives.

Ebb and
flow of the
tides.
But the ebb and flow of the tides were an
object of the greatest surprise to Alexander's
fleet, and we could soon discover the cause of
their astonishment, for two of our boats stranded
at a spot where, half an hour previously, there
had been abundance of water. The tides inun-
date the country with great impetuosity, and re-
cede as rapidly, so that if a vessel be not in the
channel, she will be left on shore. Arrian ob-
serves, that " while they continued in that sta-
" tion, an accident happened which astonished
" them ; namely, the ebbing and flowing of the
" waters, like as in the great ocean, inasmuch
" that the ships were left upon dry ground,
" which Alexander and his friends never having
" perceived before, were so much the more
" surprised. But what increased their astonish-

" ment was, that the tide returning a short
" while after began to heave the ships, so that
" * * * some of them were swept away by
" the fury of the tide, and dashed to pieces,
" and others driven against the bank, and de-
" stroyed." *

A graphic and animated description of these
disasters of the Greeks has been likewise given
by Quintus Curtius, and is nowhere more remarkable than in the allusion to the " knolls"
rising above the river like " little islands," for
at full tide the mangrove shrubs present exactly
that appearance ; but let the author speak in his
own words : —

" About the third hour, the ocean, according
" to a regular alternation, began to flow in furi-
" ously, driving back the river. The river, at
" first, resisted ; then impressed with a new
" force, rushed upwards with more impetuosity
" than torrents descend a precipitous channel.
" The mass on board, unacquainted with the na-
" ture of the tide, saw only prodigies and symbols
" of the wrath of the gods.   Ever and anon the
" sea swelled ; and on plains, recently dry, de-
" scended a diffused flood. The vessels lifted
" from their stations, and the whole fleet dis-
" persed ; those who had debarked, in terror
" and astonishment at the calamity, ran from all

marginal note: Quintus Curtius's description of Alexander's disasters.

* Arrian, lib. vi. c. 19.

" quarters towards the ships. But tumultuous
" hurry is slow. *   *   * Vessels dash together,
" and oars are by turns snatched away, to impel
" other galleys. A spectator would not imagine
" a fleet carrying the same army; but hostile
" navies commencing a battle. *   *   *   * Now
" the tide had inundated all the fields skirting
" the river, only *tops of knolls* rising above it
" like little islands; to these, from the evacuated
" ships, the majority swam in consternation.
" The dispersed fleet was partly riding in deep
" water, where the land was depressed into
" dells; and partly resting on shoals, where the
" tide had covered elevated ground; suddenly
" breaks on the Macedonians a new alarm more
" vivid than the former. The sea began to ebb;
" the deluge, with a violent drain, to retreat
" into the frith, disclosing tracts just before
" deeply buried. Unbayed, the ships pitched
" some upon their prows, others upon their
" sides. The fields were strewed with baggage,
" arms, loose planks, and fragments of oars. The
" soldiers scarcely believed what they suffered
" and witnessed. Shipwrecks on dry land, the
" sea in a river. Nor yet ended their unhappi-
" ness; for ignorant that the speedy return of
" the tide would set their ships afloat, they pre-
" dicted to themselves famine and death. Ter-
" rifying monsters, too, left by the waves, were

" gliding about at random."   Our little fleet did
not encounter such calamity and alarm as that
of Nearchus ; for, in Q. Curtius's words, —
" by a gradual diffusion, the inundation began
" to raise the ships, presently flooding all the
" fields, set the fleet in motion."

I shall not now dwell on these subjects, Reflec-
though eminently interesting ; but, in the course tions.
of my narrative, I shall endeavour to identify
the modern Indus with the features of remoter
times. If successful in the enquiry, we shall
add to our amusement, and the interest of the
chronicles themselves. It is difficult to describe
the enthusiasm one feels on first beholding the
scenes which have exercised the genius of Alexander. That hero has reaped the immortality
which he so much desired, and transmitted the
history of his conquests, allied with his name, to
posterity. A town or a river, which lies on his
route, has acquired a celebrity that time serves
only to increase ; and, while we gaze on the
Indus, we connect ourselves, at least in as-
sociation, with the ages of distant glory. Nor
can I pass over such feelings without observing,
that they are productive of the most solid advantages to history and science. The Scamander
has an immortality which the vast Mississippi
itself can never eclipse, and the descent of the
Indus by Alexander of Macedon is, perhaps, the

most authentic and best attested event of pro-
fane history.

The jealousy of the Sinde government had
been often experienced, and it was therefore
suggested that we should sail for the Indus,
without giving any previous information. Immediately on anchoring, I despatched a communication to the agent of the Ameers at Darajee, signifying my plans; and, in the meanwhile,
ascended the river with caution, anchoring in
the fresh water on the second evening, thirty-
five miles from the sea. Near the mouth of
the river we passed a rock stretching across the
stream, which is particularly mentioned by Nearchus, who calls it a "dangerous rock," and is
the more remarkable, since there is not even
a stone below Tatta in any other part of the
Indus. We passed many villages, and had much
to enliven and excite our attention, had we not
purposely avoided all intercourse with the people
till made acquainted with the fate of our in-
timation to the authorities at Darajee. A day
passed in anxious suspense; but, on the following morning, a body of armed men crowded
round our boats, and the whole neighbourhood
was in a state of the greatest excitement. The
party stated themselves to be the soldiers of the
Ameer, sent to number our party, and see the
contents of all the boats, as well as every box

that they contained. I gave a ready and immediate assent; and we were instantly boarded by about fifty armed men, who wrenched open every thing, and prosecuted the most rigorous search for cannon and gunpowder. Mr. Leckie and myself stood by in amazement, till it was at length demanded that the box containing the large carriage should be opened; for they pretended to view it as the Greeks had looked on the wooden horse, and believed that it would carry destruction into Sinde. A sight of it disappointed their hopes; and we must be conjurors, it was asserted, to have come without arms and ammunition.

When the search had been completed, I entered into conversation with the head man of the party, and had hoped to establish, by his means, a friendly connection with the authorities; but after a short pause, this personage, who was a Reis of Lower Sinde, intimated, that a report of the day's transactions would be forthwith transmitted to Hydrabad; and that, in the meanwhile, it was incumbent on us to await the decision of the Ameer, at the mouth of the river. The request appeared reasonable; and the more so, since the party agreed to furnish us with every supply while so situated. We therefore weighed anchor, and dropped down the

Retire to the mouth of the Indus.

VOL. III.   C

river; but here our civilities ended. By the way we were met by several " dingies" full of armed men, and at night were hailed by one of them, to know how many troops we had on board. We replied, that we had not even a musket. " The evil is done," rejoined a rude Belooche soldier, " you have seen our country; " but we have four thousand men ready for ac- " tion!" To this vain-glorious observation suc- ceeded torrents of abuse; and when we reached the mouth of the river, the party fired their matchlocks over us; but I dropped anchor, and resolved, if possible, to repel these insults by personal remonstrance. It was useless; we were surrounded by ignorant barbarians, who shouted out in reply to all I said, that they had been or- dered to turn us out of the country. I protested against their conduct in the most forcible lan- guage; reminded them that I was the represent- ative, however humble, of a great Government, charged with presents from Royalty; and added, that, without a written document from their master, I should decline quitting Sinde. An hour's delay served to convince me that per- sonal violence would ensue, if I persisted in such a resolution; and as it was not my object to risk the success of the enterprise by such col-

Quit the country.

lision, I sailed for the most eastern mouth of the Indus, from which I addressed the authorities in Sinde, as well as Colonel Pottinger, the Resident in Cutch.

I was willing to believe that the soldiers had exceeded the authority which had been granted them; and was speedily put in possession of a letter from the Ameer, couched in friendly terms, but narrating, at great length, the difficulty and impossibility of navigating the Indus. " The boats are so small," said his Highness, " that only four or five men can embark in one " of them; their progress is likewise slow; they " have neither masts nor sails; and the depth of " water in the Indus is likewise so variable as " not to reach, in some places, the knee or waist " of a man." But this formidable enumeration of physical obstacles was coupled with no refusal from the Ruler himself; and it seemed expedient, therefore, to make a second attempt, after replying to his Highness's letter.

Communications with the Ameer.

On the 10th of February we again set sail for Sinde; but at midnight, on the 14th, were overtaken by a fearful tempest, which scattered our little fleet. Two of the vessels were dismasted; we lost our small boat, split our sails, sprung a leak; and, after being buffeted about for some days by the fury of the winds and waves, succeeded in getting an observation of the sun, which enabled us to steer our course, and finally conducted us in safety to Sinde. One of the

Return to Sinde.

other four boats alone followed us. We now anchored in the Pieteanee mouth of the Indus, and I forthwith despatched the following document, by a trustworthy messenger, to the agents at Darajee.

1. " Let it be known to the Government agent " at Darajee, that this is the memorandum of " Mr. Burnes (sealed with his seal, and writ-" ten in the Persian language in his own hand-" writing), the representative (vakeel) of the " English to the Ameer of Sinde, and like-" wise the bearer of presents to Maharaja Run-" jeet Sing from the King of England.

2. " I came to the Indus a few days ago ; and " you searched my baggage, that you might re-" port the contents thereof to your master.   I " have now returned, and await an answer.

3. " You may send any number of armed men " that you please ; my life is in your power; but " remember that the Ameer will hold every one " responsible who molests me.   Remember, too, " that I am a British officer, and have come " without a musket or a soldier (as you well " know); placing implicit reliance on the protec-" tion of the ruler of Sinde, to whose care my " Government have committed me.

4. " I send this memorandum by two of my " own servants, and look to you for their being " protected."

This remonstrance drew no reply from the
agent at Darajee; for the individual who had
held the situation on our first visit to Sinde, had
been dismissed for permitting us to ascend the
river; and our servants brought us notice that
we should not be permitted to land, nor to
receive either food or water.   We observed,
therefore, the greatest possible economy in the
distribution of our provisions, and placed pad-
locks on the tanks, in the hope of reason yet
guiding the councils of the Ameer.   When our
supply of water failed, I despatched a small boat
up the river to procure some; but it was
seized, and the party detained; which now rendered us hopeless of success, and only anxious
to quit the inhospitable shores of Sinde.

On the 22d of February we weighed our an- Imminent
chor, at daylight; and when in the narrow mouth danger on
                                                 the Indus.
of the river, the wind suddenly changed.   The QuitSinde.
tide, which ran with terrific violence, cast us on
the breakers of the bar; the sea rolled over us,
and we struck the ground at each succeeding
wave.   In despair, the anchor was dropped; and
when we thought only of saving our lives, we
found our vessel had rubbed over the breakers
of the bank, and floated.   I admired the zeal
and bravery of our crew; and was much struck
with their pious ejaculations to the tutelar saint
of Cutch, Shah Peer, when they found themselves

beyond the reach of danger. " Oh! holy and
" generous saint," shouted the whole crew,
" you are truly good." Frankincense was forthwith burned to his honour; and a sum of money
was collected, and hallowed by its fragrance, as
the property of the saint. The amount sub-
scribed testified the sincerity of the poor men's
gratitude; and if I believed not the efficacy of
the offering, I refused not, on that account, to
join, by their request, in the manifestations of
their duty and gratitude. Our other vessel, not
so fortunate as ourselves, was cast on shore,
though on a less dangerous bank. We rendered
her assistance, and sailed for Cutch, and anchored in Mandivee roads after a surprising run
of thirty-three hours.

Negoti-
ations with
the Ameer.
It could not now be concealed that the conduct of the Ameer of Sinde was most unfriendly;
but he yet betrayed no such feeling in his letters.
He magnified the difficulties of navigating the
Indus, and arrayed its rocks, quicksands, whirl-
pools, and shallows, in every communication;
asserting that the voyage to Labore had never
been performed in the memory of man. It was
evident that he viewed the expedition with the
utmost distrust and alarm; and the native agent,
who resides at Hydrabad on the part of the
British Government, described, not without some
degree of humour, the fear and dread of this

jealous potentate. In his estimation, we were
the precursors of an army; and did he now desire to grant us a passage through Sinde, he was
at a loss to escape from the falsehoods and con-
tradictions which he had already stated in his
epistles. One letter went on to say, that " the
" Ameer of Sinde avoids giving any reply, lest
" he should be involved in perplexity; and he
" has stopped his ears with the *cotton* of *ab-*
" *surdity,* and taken some silly notions into his
" head, that if Captain Burnes should now come,
" he will see thousands of boats on the Indus,
" and report the same to his Government, who
" will conclude that it is the custom of the
" Ameer of Sinde to deceive on all subjects,
" and that he has no sort of friendship." At
length, after a remonstrance from Colonel Pottinger, both he and myself received letters
from Hydrabad, offering a road through Sinde
by land. As this might be fairly deemed the
first opening which had presented itself during
the whole negotiation, with the advice of Colonel
Pottinger I set out a third time for the Indus.
That officer in the meanwhile intimated my departure to the Ameer, and pointed out the impossibility of my proceeding by land to Lahore.
He also intimated, in no measured language,
that the vacillating and unfriendly conduct of
the Ameer of Sinde would not pass unnoticed;

the more particularly, since it concerned the passage of gifts, which had been sent by his most gracious Majesty the King of Great Britain.

Third voyage to the Indus.

On the 10th of March we once more set sail for the Indus ; and reached the Hujamree, one of the central mouths of the river, after a prosperous voyage of seven days. We could hire no pilot to conduct us across the bar, and took the wrong and shallow mouth of the river, ploughing up the mud as we tacked in its narrow channel. The foremost vessel loosened her red ensign when she had fairly reached the deep water ; and, with the others, we soon and joy-fully anchored near her. We were now met by an officer of the Sinde Government, one of the favoured descendants of the Prophet, whose enor-mous corpulence bespoke his condition. This personage came to the mouth of the river ; for we were yet refused all admittance to the fresh water. He produced a letter from the Ameer, and repeated the same refuted arguments of his master, which he seemed to think should receive credit from his high rank. It would be tiresome to follow the Sindians through the course of chi-canery which they adopted, even in this stage of the proceedings. An embargo was laid on all the vessels in the Indus ; and we ourselves were confined to our boats, on a dangerous shore, and even denied fresh water. The officer urged the propriety of our taking a route by land; and, as a last resource, I offered to accompany him to the capital, and converse with the Ameer in person, having previously landed the horses. I made known this arrangement by a courier, which I despatched to the Court; and on the following morning quitted the boats, along with Syud Land in Sinde. Jeendul Shah, who had been appointed our Mihmandar.* No sooner had we reached Tatta, than the required sanction for the boats to ascend by the Indus was received, provided we ourselves took the land route; but I immediately declined to advance another step without my charge; and ultimately effected, by a week's negotiation at Tatta, the desired end. At the expense of being somewhat tedious, I will give an abstract of these proceedings as a specimen of Sindian policy and reasoning.

A few hours after reaching Tatta, Syud Zoolf- Negotiations at Tatta. kar Shah, a man of rank, and engaging manners, waited on us on the part of the Ameer. He was accompanied by our Mihmandar, and met us very politely. He said that he had been sent by his Highness to escort us to Hydrabad; to which I laconically replied, that nothing would now induce me to go, since the Ameer had conceded the request which I had made of him. The Syud here marshalled all his eloquence; asked

* An officer who receives a guest.

me if I wished to ruin the Mihmandar, by making
him out a liar, after I had promised to accompany him to the Court, and he had written so
to the Ameer; if I had no regard for a promise;
that the capital was close at hand, and I could
reach it in two marches; that, if I did not now
go, it could only be inferred that I had been
practising delusion, from a desire to see Tatta;
for I had even been allowed to choose the route
by that city, contrary to orders; and that I was
not, perhaps, aware of the high character of the
Syud, who was a descendant of the holy Prophet, and honourable in this land; whose dignity,
the Christians, who preserved even the relic of
Jesus Christ's nail, could well understand; and
that it was not the part of a wise man to cavil
like a moollah, since the Ameer had sanctioned
the advance of the mission by water, if we embarked at Hydrabad, and would be answerable
for the safety of the horses to that place; and,
finally, that if I persisted in taking the route by
water, he was desired to say that it was a violation
of the treaty between the states.

I heard with attention the arguments of Zoolf-
kar Shah; nor did I forget that the praises and
respect which he claimed for his friend, as a
descendant of the Prophet, likewise included
himself. I replied, that there had existed a
long standing friendship between Sinde and the

British Government; that I had been despatched
by a well frequented route, to deliver the presents of our gracious Sovereign to Runjeet
Sing at Lahore; that, on reaching Sinde, I had
been insulted, abused, starved, and twice turned
out of the country by low persons, whom I
named; that my Government, which was ever
considerate, had attributed this unheard-of inso-
lence, not to their *friend*, the Ameer of Sinde,
but to the ignorance of mean individuals, and
had despatched me a third time to Sinde : when
I reached it, I found Syud Jeendul Shah ready
to receive me ; but although thoroughly satisfied
that the presents of which I was in charge could
never be forwarded by land, he offered me that
route, and detained me on board ship for eleven
days, till necessity had driven me to make a proposal of repairing in person to the presence of
the Ameer, in hopes of persuading that personage.   The case was now altered; the water
route had been granted, which rendered my
visit to Hydrabad unnecessary; and I could
only view the present procedure in the light of
jealousy, which it was unbecoming in a Government to entertain.   I continued, that I had
chosen the route by Tatta, because my bills were
payable at that city; and the sooner the Syud
got his master to meet my wishes, the better; for
the floods of the Indus were at hand, the hot

season approached, and delay would increase the
hazard ; while no arguments but force would
now induce me to visit the Court, or permit the
horses to be moved without my presence.   In
fine, if it were not the intention of the Ameer to
act a friendly part, he had only to say so, and
I would forthwith quit the country when I received a letter to that effect; and finally, that he
had formed a very erroneous opinion of the British
character, if he considered that I had been sent
here in breach of a treaty, for I had come to
strengthen the bonds of union ; and, what was
further, that the promise of an officer was sacred.

Address the
Ameer.
An interview in the following morning, brought
a repetition of the whole arguments ; and as we
could not convince each other, we both agreed
to address his Highness.   After the style of
Asiatic diplomacy, I informed the Ameer, " that
" he had acted the part of a friend, in first point-
" ing out the difficulties of navigating the Indus,
" and now assisting me through them by giving
" his sanction to the water route ; but since I
" was so thoroughly acquainted, through his
" Highness's kindness, with the dangers of the
" river, I dared not trust such royal rarities, as the
" gifts of the King of Great Britain, to the care
Success.
" of any servant."   In three days I received a
full and unqualified sanction to advance by water
from the mouth of the Indus.   I gladly quit the

detail of occurrences which have left few pleasing reflections behind, except that success ultimately attended our endeavours, and that they elicited the approbation of Government. The Ameer of Sinde had sought to keep us in ignorance of the Indus; but his treatment had led to another and opposite effect; since we had entered, in the course of our several voyages, *all* the mouths of the river, and a map of them, as well as of the land route to Tatta, now lay before me. Our dangers on the banks and shoals had been imminent; but we looked back upon them with the pleasing thought, that our experience might guide others through them.

CHAP. II.

TATTA TO HYDRABAD.

Tatta. A WEEK's stay was agreeably spent in examining
Tatta and the objects of curiosity which surround
it. The city stands at a distance of three miles
from the Indus.   It is celebrated in the history
of the East.   Its commercial prosperity passed
away with the empire of Delhi, and its ruin has
been completed since it fell under the iron
despotism of the present rulers of Sinde.   It
does not contain a population of 15,000 souls ;
and of the houses scattered about its ruins,
one half are destitute of inhabitants.   It is
said, that the dissentions between the last and
present dynasties, which led to Sinde being over-
run by the Afghans, terrified the merchants of
the city, who fled the country at that time, and
have had no encouragement to return.   Of the
weavers of " loongees " (a kind of silk and cotton
manufacture), for which this place was once so
famous, but 125 families remain.   There are not
forty merchants * in the city.   Twenty money-
changers transact all the business of Tatta ; and

* Banians.

its limited population is now supplied with animal food by five butchers.   Such has been the gradual decay of that mighty city, so populous in the early part of last century, in the days of Nadir Shah.   The.country in its vicinity lies neglected, and but a small portion of it is brought under tillage.

The antiquity of Tatta is unquestioned.   The *Its antiquity.* Pattala of the Greeks has been sought for in its position, and, I believe, with good reason ; for the Indus here divides into two great branches ; and these are the words of the historian : — " Near Pattala, the river Indus divides itself " into two vast branches." *   Both Robertson and Vincent appear to have entertained the opinion of its identity with Tatta.   The Hindoo Rajas named it Sameenuggur, before the Mahommedan invasion ; which I believe to be the Minagur of the Periplus.   There is a ruined city, called Kullancote, to be yet seen, four miles S.W. of Tatta.   It was also named Brahminabad, and ruled by one brother, while another held Hydrabad, then called Nerancote ; the Arabs called it Dewul Sindy.   Nuggur Tatta (by which it is now familiarly known) is a more modern name. Till the Talpoors secured their present footing in Sinde, it was always the capital of the country. It is an open town, built on a rising ground in a

* Arrian, lib. 6.

low valley. In several wells I found bricks im-
bedded in earth, at a depth of twenty feet from
the surface ; but there are no remains of a
prior date to the tombs, on a remarkable ridge
westward of the town, which are about 200 years
old. The houses are formed of wood and wicker-
work, plastered over with earth ; they are lofty,
with flat roofs, but very confined, and resemble
square towers ; their colour, which is of a greyish
murky hue, gives an appearance of solidity to
the frail materials of which they are constructed.
Some of the better sort have a base of brick-
work ; but stone has only been used in the
foundations of one or two mosques, though it
may be had in abundance. There is little in
modern Tatta to remind one of its former greatness. A spacious brick mosque, built by Shah
Jehan, still remains, but is crumbling to decay.

Hinglaj,
a famous
pilgrim-
age.

Tatta stands on the high road from India to
Hinglaj, in Mekran, a place of pilgrimage and
great celebrity, situated under the barren mountains of Hala (the Irus of the ancients), and
marked only by a spring of fresh water, without
house or temple. The spot is believed to have
been visited by Ramchunder, the Hindoo demi-
god, himself; an event which is chronicled on
the rock, with figures of the sun and moon
engraven as further testimony! The distance
from Tatta exceeds 200 miles; and the road

passes by Curachee, Soumeeanee, and the province of Lus, the country of the Noomrees, a
portion of the route of Alexander the Great. A
journey to Hinglaj purifies the pilgrim from his
sins ; a cocoa-nut, cast into a cistern,, exhibits
the nature of his career : if the water bubbles
up, his life has been, and will continue, pure ; but
if still and silent, the Hindoo must undergo
further penance, to appease the deity. The
tribe of Goseins, who are a kind of religious
mendicants, though frequently merchants and
most wealthy, frequent this sequestered place,
and often extend their journey to an island called
Seetadeep, not far from Bunder Abbass, in Persia.
They travel in caravans of an hundred, or even
more, under an " agwa," or spiritual guide. At
Tatta they are furnished by the high-priest with
a rod, which is supposed to partake of his own
virtues, and to conduct the *cortège* to its destination. In exchange for its talismanic powers, each
pilgrim pays three rupees and a half, and faithfully
promises to restore the rod on his return ; for no
one dares to reside in so holy and solitary a spot.
The " agwa" receives with it his reward ; and
many a Hindoo expends in this pilgrimage the
hard-earned wealth of a whole life. On his
arrival at Tatta from Hinglaj, he is invested
with a string of white beads, peculiar to that
city, and only found on the rocky ridge near it,

They resemble the grains of pulse or juwaree; and the pilgrim has the satisfaction of believing that they are the petrified grain of the Creator, left on earth to remind him of his creation. They now form a monopoly and source of profit to the priests of Tatta.

Climate.
Return to
the mouth
of the In-
dus.

We quitted Tatta on the morning of the 10th of April, and retraced our steps to Meerpoor; a distance of twenty-four miles, over roads nearly impassable from rain. I observe, in Hamilton's India," that there is frequently a dearth of it here for three years at a time; but we had very heavy showers and a severe fall of hail, though the thermometer stood at 86°. The dews and mists about Tatta make it a disagreeable residence at this season; and the dust is described as intolerable in June and July.

Our road lay through a desert country along the " Buggaur;" one of the two large branches of the Indus, which separate below Tatta. It has its name from the destructive velocity with which it runs, tearing up trees in its course. It has been forsaken for a few years past, and had only a width of 200 yards where we crossed it, below Meerpoor. The Indus itself, before this division takes place, is a noble river; and we beheld it at Tatta with high gratification. The water is foul and muddy; but it is 2000 feet wide, two fathoms and a half deep, from shore to shore. When I

first saw it, the surface was agitated by a violent
wind, which had raised up waves, that raged
with great fury; and I no longer felt wonder at
the natives designating so vast a river by the
name of " durya," or the Sea of Sinde.

On our return, we saw much of the people, Notions of
the people.
who were disposed from the first to treat us more
kindly than the government.   Their notions
regarding us were strange : some asked us why
we allowed dogs to clean our hands after a meal,
and if we indiscriminately ate cats and mice, as
well as pigs.   They complained much of their
rulers, and the ruinous and oppressive system of
taxation to which they were subjected, as it
deterred them from cultivating any considerable
portion of land.   Immense tracts of the richest soil
lie in a state of nature, between Tatta and the
sea, overgrown with tamarisk shrubs, which
attain, in some places, the height of twenty feet,
and, threading into one another, form impervious
thickets.   At other places, we passed extensive
plains of hard-caked clay, with remains of ditches
and aqueducts, now neglected.   We reached the
sea in two days.

Arrian informs us, that, after Alexander re- Alexander's
journey.
turned from viewing the right branch of the
Indus, he again set out from Pattala, and descended the other branch of the river, which
conducted him to a " certain lake, joined either

" by the river spreading wide over a flat country,
" or by additional streams flowing into it from
" the adjacent parts, and making it appear like a
" bay in the 'sea." There, too, he commanded
another haven to be built, named Xylenopolis.
The professed object of this second voyage to
the sea was to seek for bays and creeks on the
sea-coast, and to explore which of the two
branches would afford the greatest facilities for
the passage of his fleet; for Arrian says, " he
" had a vast ambition of sailing all through the
" sea, from India to Persia, to prove that the
" Indian Gulf had a communication with the
" Persian." In this bay Alexander landed, with
a party of horse, and travelled along the coast,
to try if he could find bays and creeks to
secure his fleets from storms; " *causing wells to*
" *be dug, to supply his navy with water.*" I
look upon it, therefore, as conclusive that Alexander the Great descended by the Buggaur and
Sata, the two great branches below Tatta, and
never entered Cutch, as has been surmised, but
that his three days' journey, after descending the
eastern branch, was westward, and between the
two mouths, in the direction his fleet was to sail.

Embark on   On the 12th of April, we embarked in the
the Indus.
Boats.   flat-bottomed boats, or " doondees," of Sinde,
and commenced our voyage on the Indus, with
no small degree of satisfaction. Our fleet con-

sisted of six of these flat-bottomed vessels, and a small English-built pinnace, which we had brought from Cutch.   The boats of the Indus are not unlike China junks, very capacious, but most unwieldy.   They are floating houses; and with ourselves we transported the boatmen, their wives and families, kids and fowls.   When there is no wind, they are pulled up against the stream, by ropes attached to the mast-head, at the rate of a mile and a half an hour; but with a breeze, they set a large square-sail, and advance double the distance.   We halted at Vikkur, which is the first port; a place of considerable export for grain, that had then fifty " doondees," besides sea-vessels, lying near it.

On the 13th, we threaded many small creeks *Wanyanee branch.* for a distance of eight miles, and then entered the Wanyanee, or principal branch of the Indus, which is a fine river, 500 yards broad and 24 feet deep.   Its banks were alternately steep and flat, the course very crooked, and the different turnings were often marked by branches running from this trunk to other arms of the delta.   We had nothing but tamarisk on either bank, and the reed huts of a few fishermen, alone indicated that we were in a peopled country.

As we ascended the river, the inhabitants *A holy man.* came for miles around to see us.   A Syud stood on the water's edge, and gazed with astonish-

ment. He turned to his companion as we
passed, and, in the hearing of one of our party,
said, " Alas! Sinde is now gone, since the En-
" glish have seen the river, which is the road to
" its conquest." If such an event do happen, I
am certain that the body of the people will hail
the happy day ; but it will be an evil one for the
Syuds, the descendants of Mahommed, who are
the only people, besides the rulers, that derive
precedence and profit from the existing order of
things.

Strictness
of religious
observ-
ances.

Nothing more arrests the notice of a stranger,
on entering Sinde, than the severe attention of
the people to the forms of religion, as enjoined
by the Prophet of Arabia. In all places, the
meanest and poorest of mankind may be seen, at
the appointed hours, turned towards Mecca,
offering up their prayers. I have observed a
boatman quit the laborious duty of dragging the
vessel against the stream, and retire to the shore,
wet and covered with mud, to perform his genu-
flexions. In the smallest villages, the sound of
the " mowuzzun," or crier, summoning true be-
lievers to prayers, may be heard, and the Mahommedans within reach of the sonorous sound
suspend, for the moment, their employment, that
they may add their " Amen" to the solemn sen-
tence when concluded. The effect is pleasing
and impressive ; but, as has often happened in

other countries at a like stage of civilisation, the moral qualities of the people do not keep pace with this fervency of devotion.

On the evening of the 15th, we anchored at Tatta, after a prosperous voyage, that afforded a good insight into the navigation of the Indus; which, in the Delta, is both dangerous and dif· ficult.   The water runs with impetuosity from one bank to another, and undermines them so, that they often fall in masses which would crush a vessel.   During night they may be heard tumbling with a terrific crash and a noise as loud as artillery.   In one place, the sweep of the river was so sudden that it had formed a kind of whirlpool, and all our vessels heeled round, on passing it, from the rapidity of the current.   We had every where six fathoms of water, and in these eddies the depth was sometimes threefold; but our vessels avoided the strength of the current, and shifted from side to side, to choose the shallows.

We ascended the Indus in the season of the " pulla," a fish of the carp species, as large as the mackerel, and fully equalling the flavour of salmon.   It is only found in the four months that precede the swell of the river from January to April, and never higher than the fortress of Bukkur.   The natives superstitiously believe the fish to proceed there on account of Khaju

Navigation of the Indus.

Pulla fish.

Khizr, a saint of celebrity, who is interred there, from whence they are said to return without ever turning their tails on the sanctified spot, — an assertion which the muddy colour of the Indus will prevent being contradicted. The mode of catching this fish is ingenious, and peculiar, I believe, to the Indus. Each fisherman is provided with a large earthen jar, open at the top, and somewhat flat. On this he places himself, and, lying on it horizontally, launches into the stream, swimming or pushing forward like a frog, and guiding himself with his hands. When he has reached the middle of the river, where the current is strongest, he darts his net directly under him, and sails down with the stream.   The net consists of a pouch attached to a pole, which he shuts on meeting his game ; he then draws it up, spears it, and, putting it into the vessel on which he floats, prosecutes his occupation. There are some vessels of small dimensions, without any orifice, and on these the fishermen sail down, in a sitting posture. Hundreds of people, old and young, may be seen engaged in catching pulla, and the season is hailed with joy by the people, as furnishing a wholesome food while it lasts, and an abundant supply of dry fish for the remaining part of the year, as well as for exportation to the neighbouring countries.

On the morning of the 18th, we moored op- Reach the capital.
posite Hydrabad, which is five miles inland,
having had a strong and favourable breeze from
Tatta, that brought us against the stream, at the
rate of three miles an hour.   The dust was intolerable every where, and a village might always
be discovered by the dense clouds which ho-
vered over it.   This part of Sinde is well
known: the country is devoted to sterility by
the Ameers, to feed their passion for the chase.
The banks are enclosed to the water's edge,
and the interior of these hunting-thickets is
overgrown with furze, brushwood, and stunted
babool trees, which always retain a verdant
hue, from the richness of the soil.   One or
two solitary camels were to be seen raising
water to fill the pools of these preserves, as the
Ameer and his relatives had announced a hunting excursion, and the deer * would be drawn by
thirst to drink at the only fountain, and shot by
an Ameer from a place of concealment.   It is
thus that the chiefs sport with their game and
their subjects.

Immediately on our arrival, four different de- Deputation from the Ameer.
putations waited on us, to convey the congra-
tulations of Meer Moorad Ali Khan, and his
family, at our having reached the capital of

* The species hunted in Sinde is called " hotapuchu: " it
is a kind of hog deer.

Sinde, and at the same time to tender the strongest professions of friendship and respect for the British government; to all of which I returned suitable answers.   In the evening we were conducted to Hydrabad, and alighted at the house, or " tanda," of Nawab Wulee Mahommed Khan, the Vizier of Sinde, whose son, in the father's absence, was appointed our mihmandar.   Tents were pitched, and provisions of every description sent to us; and it would, indeed, have been difficult to discover that we were the individuals who had so long lingered about the shores of Sinde, now the honoured guests of its jealous master.   Great and small were in attendance on us : khans and Syuds, servants and chobdars brought messages and enquiries, till the night was far spent; and it may not be amiss to mention, as a specimen of conducting business in Sinde, that the barber, the water-cooler, and the prime minister were sent indiscriminately with errands on the same subject.

Prepara-
tions for
reception at
court.

The ceremonial of our reception was soon adjusted, but not without some exhibition of Sindian · character.   After the time had been mutually fixed for the following afternoon, our mihmandar made his appearance at *daybreak*, to request that we would then accompany him to the palace.   I spoke of the arrangements that had been made; but he treated all explanation with indifference, and eulogised, in extravagant language, the great condescension of his master in giving us an interview so early, while the Vakeels, or representatives of other states, often waited for weeks. I informed the Khan that I entertained very different sentiments regarding his master's giving us so early a reception, and assured him that I viewed it as no sort of favour, and was satisfied that the Ameer himself was proud in receiving, at any time, any agent of the British Government. The reply silenced him, and he shortly afterwards withdrew, and sent an apology for this importunity, which, he stated, had originated in a mistake. The pride of the Sindian must be met by the same weapons; and, however disagreeable the line of conduct, it will be found, in all matters of negotiation, to carry along with it its own reward: altercations that have passed will be succeeded by civility and politeness, and a shade of oblivion will be cast over all that is unpleasant.

In the evening we were presented to the Presentation. Ameer of Sinde by his son, Nusseer Khan, who had previously received us in his own apartments, to inform us of his attachment to the British Government, and the state secret of his having been the means of procuring for us a passage through Sinde. We found the Ameer

seated in the middle of a room, attended by his
various relatives: they all rose on our entrance,
and were studiously polite. His Highness addressed me by name ; said I was his friend, both
on public and private grounds ; for my brother
(Dr. Burnes) had cured him of a dangerous dis-
ease. At the same time he caused me to be
seated along with him on the cushion which he
occupied : he begged that I would forget the dif·
ficulties and dangers encountered, and consider
him as the ally of the British Government, and
my own friend. The long detention which
had occurred in our advance, he continued,
had arisen from his ignorance of political concerns, as he considered it involved a breach of
the treaty between the states; for he was a
soldier, and knew little of such matters, and
was employed in commanding *the three hundred
thousand Beloochees,* over whom God had appointed him to rule! We had now, however,
arrived at his capital, and he assured us that
we were welcome : his own state barge should
convey us to his frontier; his subjects should
drag our vessels against the stream. Elephants
and palanqueens were at our disposal, if we
would accept them; and he would vie in exertion with ourselves, to forward, in safety, the
presents of his Most Gracious Majesty the King
of Great Britain, and had nominated the son of

his Vizier to accompany us to the limits of his territories. I did not deem it necessary to enter into any explanation with his Highness, nor to give him in return the muster-roll of our mighty army. I thanked him for his marks of attention to the Government and ourselves, and said, that I was glad to find that the friendship between the states, which had led to my taking the route through his dominions, had not been underrated; for it would be worse than folly in an unprotected individual to attempt a passage by the Indus without his cordial concurrence. With regard to the dangers and difficulties which had been already encountered, I assured his Highness, that the prevailing good fortune of the British Government had predominated; and though it was not in the power of man to avert calamities by sea, we had by the favour of God happily escaped them all, and I doubted not that the authorities I served would derive as much satisfaction from the manner in which he had now received us as I myself did. The interview here terminated; his Highness previously fixing the following morning for a second meeting, when I would communicate some matters of a political nature with which I had been charged by the Government.

I shall not enter on a description of the Court Court of Sinde.

of Sinde, as it may be found in Lieut. Col. Pottinger's work, and in a narrative lately published by my brother * Its splendour must have faded, for though the Ameer and his family certainly wore some superb jewels, there was not much to attract our notice in their palace or durbar: they met in a dirty hall without a carpet; they sat in a room which was filled by a rabble of greasy soldiery, and the noise and dust were hardly to be endured. The orders of the Ameer himself to procure silence, though repeated several times, were ineffectual, and some of the conversation was inaudible on that account. We were, however, informed that the crowd had been collected to display the legions of Sinde; and they certainly contrived to fill the alleys and passages every where, nor could we pass out of the fort without some exertion on the part of the nobles, who were our conductors.

Presents.

I followed up the interview by sending the government presents which I had brought for his Highness : they consisted of various articles of European manufacture,—a gun, a brace of pistols, a gold watch, two telescopes, a clock, some English shawls and cloths, with two pair of elegant cut glass candlesticks and shades. Some Persian works beautifully lithographed in

* Narrative of a Visit to the Court of Sinde. Edin. 1831.

Bombay, and a map of the World and Hindoostan, in Persian characters, completed the gift.
The principal Ameer had previously sent two
messages, begging that I would not give the
articles to any person but himself; and the pos-
sessor of fifteen millions sterling portioned, with
a partial hand, among the members of his family,
the gifts that did not exceed the value of a few
hundred pounds. His meanness may be imagined, *Sindian meanness.*
when he privately deputed his Vizier to beg
that I would exchange the clock and candlesticks
for some articles among the presents, which
I doubtless had for other chiefs, as they formed
no part of the furniture of a Sindian palace. I
told the Vizier that the presents which I had
brought were intended to display the manufactures of Europe, and it was not customary to
give the property of one person to another.
This denial produced a second message; and,
as a similar occurrence happened, in 1809, to a
mission at this court, we gather from the coincidence how little spirit and feeling actuate the
cabinet of Hydrabad.   Some score of trays,
loaded with fruit and sweetmeats adorned with
gold-leaf, and sent by the different members of
the family, closed the day.

Early in the morning, we were conducted to *Parting in-*
the durbar by Meer Ismaeel Shah, one of the *terview.*
Viziers, and our mihmandar: on the road the

Vizier took occasion to assure me how much I
would please the Ameer by changing the clock!
There was more order and regularity in our
second interview, which was altogether very
satisfactory; for the Ameer gave a ready assent to the wishes of Government when they
were communicated to him. The conversation
which ensued was of the most friendly description. His Highness asked particularly for
my brother, looked attentively at our dress, and
was much amused with the shape and feather of
the cocked hat I wore. Before bidding him
adieu, he repeated, in even stronger language, all
his yesterday's professions; and, however ques-
tionable his sincerity, I took my departure with
much satisfaction at what had passed, since it
seemed he would no longer interrupt our advance to Lahore. Meer Nusseer Khan, the son
of the Ameer, presented me with a handsome
Damascus sword, which had a scabbard of red
velvet ornamented with gold; his father sent
me a purse of fifteen hundred rupees, with an
apology, that he had not a blade mounted as he
desired, and begged I would accept the value of
one. After all the inconvenience to which we
had been subjected, we hardly expected such a
reception at Hydrabad. Next morning we left
the city, and encamped on the banks of the
Indus near our boats.

The scenery near the capital of Sinde is varied and beautiful: the sides of the river are lined with lofty trees; and there is a background of hill to relieve the eye from the monotony which presents itself in the dusty arid plains of the Delta. The Indus is larger, too, than in most places lower down, being about 830 yards wide; there is a sand-bank in the middle, but it is hidden by the stream. The island on which Hydrabad stands is barren, from the rocky and hilly nature of the soil, but even the arable parts are poorly cultivated.

On the capital itself, I can add little to the accounts which are already on record. It does not contain a population of twenty thousand souls, who live in houses, or rather huts, built of mud. The residence of the chief himself is a comfortless miserable dwelling. The fort, as well as the town, stands on a rocky hillock; and the former is a mere shell, partly surrounded by a ditch, about ten feet wide and eight deep, over which there is a wooden bridge. The walls are about twenty-five feet high, built of brick, and fast going to decay. Hydrabad is a place of no strength, and might readily be captured by escalade. In the centre of the fort there is a massive tower, unconnected with the works, which overlooks the surrounding country. Here are deposited a great portion of the riches of

Sinde.   The Fulailee river insulates the ground
on which Hydrabad stands; but, though a
considerable stream during the swell, it was
quite dry when we visited this city in April.
The view of Hydrabad, prefixed to this volume,
and for which I am indebted to Captain M.
Grindlay, faithfully represents that capital and
the country which surrounds it.

CHAP. III.

VOYAGE TO BUKKUR.

O<small>N</small> the morning of the 23d of April, we
embarked in the state barge of the Ameer,
which is called a " jumtee" by the natives of the
country. They are very commodious vessels,
of the same build as the other flat-bottomed
boats of the Indus, and sadly gainsayed the
beggarly account which his Highness had, in his
correspondence, so often given of the craft in
the river. It was about sixty feet long, and had
three masts, on which we hoisted as many sails,
made of alternate stripes of red and white cloth.
There were two cabins, connected with each
other by a deck; but, contrary to the custom
in other countries, the one at the bows is the
post of honour. It was of a pavilion shape,
covered with scarlet cloth, and the eyes of
intruders were excluded on all sides by silken
screens. The jumtee was further decorated by
variegated flags and pendants, some of which
were forty feet long. We hoisted the British
ensign at the stern of our pinnace, the first time,
I suppose, it had ever been unfurled on the
Indus; and the little vessel which bore it out-

sailed all the fleet. I hope the omen was
auspicious, and that the commerce of Britain
may soon follow her flag. We moved merrily
through the water, generally with a fair wind,
anchoring always at night, and pitching our
camp on the shore, pleased to find ourselves
beyond the portals of Hydrabad.

Sehwun.   We reached Sehwun on the 1st of May, a
distance of 100 miles, in eight days. There
was little to interest us on the banks of the
river, which are thinly peopled, and destitute of
trees or variety to diversify the scene. The
Lukkee mountains, a high range, came in sight
on the third day, running in upon the Indus at
Sehwun. The stream itself, though grand and
magnificent, was often divided by sand-banks,
and moved sluggishly along at the rate of two
miles and a half an hour. One of our boats had
nearly sunk from coming in contact with a pro-
truding stump; an accident of frequent occurrence on the Indus, as well as on the American
rivers, and sometimes attended with fatal results, particularly to vessels descending the
stream. Our escape from calamity gave the
Sindians a topic for congratulation, and we
daily heard the greatness of our fortune proclaimed. Every trivial incident, a slight breeze
or any such occurrence, they did not hesitate to
ascribe to our destiny.

Our crew consisted of sixteen men; and a Crew of the boat. happy set of beings they were: they waded through the water all day, and swam and sported about, as they passed along, with joyous hearts, returning occasionally to the boat to indulge in the hooka, and the intoxicating " bang," or hemp, to which they are much addicted. They prepare this drug by straining the juice from the seeds and stalks through a cloth: when ready for use, it resembles green putrid water. It must be very pernicious. I do not know if I can class their pipes among the movables of the ship; for their stands were formed of a huge piece of earthenware, too heavy to be lifted, which remains at the stern, where the individuals retire to inhale the weed, made doubly noxious by its being mixed with opium. The sailors of Sinde are Mahommedans. They are very superstitious, the sight of a crocodile below Hydrabad is an evil omen which would never be forgotten; and in that part of the Indus these monsters certainly confined themselves to the deep.

In the songs and chorus which the Sindians A Sindian song. use in pulling their ropes and sails, we discover their reverence for saints. Seafaring people are, I believe, musical in all countries; and, though in a strange dialect, there is simplicity and beauty in some of the following rhymes: —

E 3

Original.

Hulam hulam hyl,	Joomba lanee,
Leenlanee,	Hewa qila,
Mudud peeran.	Dawa fuqueeran
Dawa jee nalee.	Beree chale :
Beree ranee,	Surung sookhanee.
Oono panee,	
Lumba kooa,	Sulamut hooa,
Wujun dumana	Acbar Shah ja.

Translation.

Pull, oh! pull!	Use your strength,
Raise your shoulders,	By the favour of God,
Press your feet.	By the Saint's assistance
The boat will sail,	She is a pretty boat:
The steersman's a warrior.	The water is deep,
The mast is tall.	She will reach in safety.
Beat the drum	Of King Acbar,
The port is attained	By the favour of God.

Another specimen runs thus : —

Peer Putta!	Jug ditta,
Nuggur Tatta!	Panee mitta.
Julla kejye,	Tanee lejge,
Tan tumasha:	Bunder khasa,
Bundur koochee.	Murd Beloochee.
Bundur maryo,	Rub dekkaryo.
Moolk Hubeebee.	Rub a rubbee.

Translation.

Hail, Peer Putta!	Who has seen the world,
Hail, city of Tatta!	The water is sweet.
Pull together,	Pull at once,
Pull for joy.	The port is good,
Tho' the harbour is small.	The men are Beloochees.
Behold the harbour tower,	Which God has shown us.
The country is God's,	By God we came.

As we discovered the mosques of Sehwun, the boatmen in their joy beat a drum, and chanted many of these verses, which had a pleasing sound on passing the base of the Lukkee mountains, that present a rocky buttress to the Indus on approaching Sehwun.

The town of Sehwun stands on a rising ground, at the verge of a swamp, two miles from the Indus, close to a branch of that river called Arul, which flows from Larkhanu. It has a population of about 10,000 souls, and is commanded on the north side by a singular castle or mound of earth. Sehwun is sometimes called Sewistan, and is a place of antiquity. There are many ruined mosques and tombs which surround it, and proclaim its former wealth; but it has gradually gone to decay since it ceased to be the residence of a governor, who here held his court in the days of Moghul splendour. As it stands near the Lukkee mountains, I believe it may be fixed on as the city of Sambus, Raja of the Indian mountaineers, mentioned by Alexander. The Sindomanni cannot refer to the inhabitants of Lower Sinde, which is always called Pattala, and its ruler the " prince " of the Pattalans." Sindee is the modern term for the aboriginal inhabitants.

Sehwun has considerable celebrity and sanctity from the tomb of a holy saint of Khorasan,

Sehwun, its antiquity.

Pilgrimage of Sehwun.

E 4

by name Lal Shah Baz, who was interred
here about 600 years ago. The shrine stands
in the centre of the town, and rests under
a lofty dome at one end of a quadrangular
building, which is handsomely ornamented by
blue painted slabs, like Dutch tiles, that give it
a rich appearance. A cloth of gold, with two
other successive palls of red silk, are suspended
over the sepulchre, and on the walls which surround it are inscribed in large Arabic letters
the praises of the deceased, and extracts from
the Koran. Ostrich eggs, peacocks' feathers,
beads, flowers, &c. complete the furniture of this
holy spot; and pigeons, the emblems of peace,
are encouraged to perch on the cloths which
shade the remains of departed virtue. The
miracles of Lal Shah Baz are endless, if you
believe the people. The Indus is subject to his
commands, and no vessel dares to pass his shrine
without making a propitiatory offering at his
tomb. Thousands of pilgrims flock to the con-
secrated ·spot, and the monarchs of Cabool and
India have often visited the sanctuary. The
drums which proclaim the majesty of the saint
are a gift from the renowned persecutor Alla-o-
deen, who reigned A. D. 1242; and the gate,
which is of silver, attests the homage and devotion of a deceased Ameer of Sinde. The
needy are daily supplied with food from the

charity of the stranger ; but the universal bounty
has corrupted the manners of the inhabitants,
who are a worthless and indolent set of men.
The Hindoo joins with the Mahommedan in his
veneration of the saint, and artfully insinuates
" Lal " to be a Hindoo name, and that the
Mahommedans have associated with the faith
of their prophet the god of an infidel creed.   A
tiger, once the tenant of the neighbouring hills,
partakes of the general bounty in a cage near
the tomb.

By far the most singular building at Sehwun, and perhaps on the Indus, is the ruined
castle which overlooks the town, and is in all
probability as old as the age of the Greeks.   It
consists of a mound of earth sixty feet high,
and surrounded from the very ground by a brick
wall.   The shape of the castle is oval, about
1200 feet long by 750 in diameter.   The interior
presents a heap of ruins, and is strewed with
broken pieces of pottery and brick.   The gateway is on the town side, and has been arched :
a section through it proves the whole mound
to be artificial.   At a distance this castle resembles the drawings of the Mujilebe tower at
Babylon, described by Mr. Rich in his interesting Memoir.

Castle of Sehwun, its antiquity.

The natives afford no satisfactory account of
this ruin, attributing it to the age of Budur-ool-

Jamal, a fairy, whose agency is referred to in
every thing ancient or wonderful' in Sinde.   It
is to be observed, that the Arul river passes close
to this castle; and we are informed by Quintus
Curtius that, in the territories of Sabus Raja,
(which I imagine refers to Sehwun,) "Alexander
" took the strongest city by a tunnel formed by
" his miners."   A ruin of such magnitude,
standing, as it therefore does, on such a site,
would authorise our fixing on it as the very city
" where the barbarians, untaught in engineer-
" ing, were confounded when their enemies
" appeared, almost in the middle of the city,
" rising from a subterraneous passage of which
" no trace was previously seen."   So strong a
position would not, in all probability, be ne-
gleeted in after-times; and in the reign of the
Emperor Humaioon, A.D. 1541, we find that
monarch unable to capture Sehwun, from which
he fled on his disastrous journey to Omercote.
His son Acbar also invested Sehwun for seven
months, and after its capture seems to have
dismantled it.   There are many coins found in
the castle of Sehwun; but among thirty I could
find no trace of the Greek alphabet.   They were
Mahommedan coins of the sovereigns of Delhi.

Mound of
Amree.   About eighteen miles below Sehwun, and on
the same side of the river, is the village of
Amree, believed to have been once a large city,

and the favourite residence of former kings. It is said to have been swept into the Indus. Near the modern village, however, there is a mound of earth, about forty feet high, which the traditions of the country point out as the halting-place of a king, who ordered the dung of his cavalry to be gathered together, and hence the mound of Amree! There are some tombs near it, but they are evidently modern.

We halted four days at Sehwun. The climate was most sultry and oppressive: the thermometer stood at 112°, and did not fall below 100° at midnight, owing to scorching winds from the west, where the country is bleak and mountainous. The lofty range which runs parallel with the Indus from the sea-coast to the centre of Asia, is joined by the Lukkee mountains south of Sehwun, and thus excludes the refreshing breezes of the ocean.

We quitted Sehwun on the 4th with difficulty, for we could not procure men to drag our boats. The mihmandar, though he was the vizier's son, and acted under the seal of the Ameer, could not prevail on the Calendar, or priest of the tomb, who said that no such order had been ever given, and he would not now obey it. Some persons were seized: his people drew their swords, and said that, when no longer able to wield them, they might go.

We knew nothing of the matter till it was over, as it was entirely a private arrangement of Syud Tukkee Shah, the mihmandar.   When the men heard they were to be remunerated for their trouble, they came of their own accord before we sailed.   Every thing in Sinde being effected by force under despotism, the watermen of Sehwun fled the town, or took up their abode in the sanctuary, when they saw the "jumtee" approach, believing, as usual, that services would be required of them gratuitously.

Congratu-
lations from
Khyrpoor.
On the day after quitting Sehwun, we were met by Mahommed Gohur, a Belooche chief, and a party, the confidential agents of Meer Roostum Khan, the Ameer of Khyrpoor, who had been sent to the frontier, a distance of eighty miles, to congratulate us on our arrival, and declare their master's devotion to the British Government.   We hardly expected such a mark of attention in Sinde, and were therefore gratified.   The deputation brought an abundant supply of sheep, flour, fruit, spices, sugar, butter, ghee, tobacco, opium, &c. &c., on which our people feasted.   Sheep were slain and cooked; rice and ghee were soon converted into savoury viands; and I believe all parties thanked Meer Roostum Khan as heartily as we did, nor did I imagine that this was but the commencement of a round of feasting which was daily repeated

so long as we were in his country, a period of
three weeks. Mahommed Gohur was a decrepit
old man, with a red beard. He wore a very
handsome loongee round his waist. He did not
recover from his surprise throughout the interview, for he had never before seen an European.

In return for Meer Roostum Khan's kindness, Address the
I addressed to him a Persian letter in the follow- Ameer of
Khyrpoor.
ing terms, which will serve as a specimen of the
epistolary style used by the people of this country, which I imitated as closely as possible. : —

(After compliments:) " I hasten to inform your
" Highness that I have reached the frontiers of
" your country in company with the respectable
" Syud Tukkee Shah, who has accompanied me
" on the part of Meer Morad Ali Khan from
" Hydrabad. As I have long since heard of
" your Highness from those who pass between
" Cutch and Sinde, it forms a source of con-
" gratulation to me that I have arrived in your
" dominions, and brought along with me in
" safety the presents which have been graciously
" bestowed on Maha Raja Runjeet Sing by His
" Majesty the King of England, mighty in rank,
" terrible as the planet Mars, a monarch great
" and magnificent, of the rank of Jemshid, of
" the dignity of Alexander, unequalled by Da-
" rius, just as Nousherwan, great as Fureedoon,

" admired as Cyrus, famed as the Sun, the de-
" stroyer of tyranny and oppression, upright
" and generous, pious and devout, favoured
" from above, &c. &c.: may his dominion endure
" for ever!

" It is well known that when a friend comes
" to the country of a friend it is a source of
" much happiness, and I have therefore written
" these few lines; but when I have the pleasure
" of seeing you, my joy will be increased.

" I had written thus far, when the respectable
" Mahommed Gohur, one of those enjoying your
" Highness's confidence, arrived at this place,
" to acquaint me with your professions of respect
" and friendship for the British Government,
" bringing along with him many marks of your
" hospitality.   Need I say I am rejoiced? Such
" civilities mark the great."

Character of the people.

A voyage of ten days brought us to Bukkur;
but we landed a few miles from that fortress, to
prepare for a visit to Khyrpoor and its chief,
who had made us so welcome in his country.
We saw much of the Sindians on our way up
the river, and did every thing to encourage
their approach by granting free admission on
board to the commonest villager who wished to
view the horses. The body of the people are
little better than savages, and extremely ignorant; their spiritual guides and Synds, or the

followers of the prophet, however, showed knowledge and independence. I happened to ask a party of Syuds to what Ameer they were subject: they replied, " We acknowledge no " master but God, who gives us villages and all " we desire." I was struck with the family likeness that prevails throughout this class in Sinde; for it is not to be supposed that a tribe so numerous has lineally descended from the prophet of Arabia. The beggars of Sinde are most importunate and troublesome. They practise all manner of persuasion to succeed in their suit for alms; tear up grass and bushes with their mouths, and chew sand and mud to excite compassion.

With the better orders of society we had frequent intercourse and conversation. Some of them felt interested about the objects of our mission to Lahore. They did not give us much credit for sincerity in sending it by a route which they believed never to have been passed since the time of Noah. They were full of enquiries regarding our customs. Our Khyrpoor friend, Mahomed Gohur, was particularly horrified at our arrangements for getting a wife, and begged me in future to let my beard grow. The knowledge of this individual I may describe, when he asked me if London were under Calcutta: he was, however, a pleasant

man; I delighted to hear him sing the praises
of the soldiers of Sinde, who, he said, differed
from all the world in thinking it an honour to
fight on foot.   The feelings of pity which some
of the people displayed for us were amusing:
they were shocked to hear that we cleaned our
teeth with hogs' bristles.   I was frequently asked
to lay aside the English saddle, which they considered quite unworthy, and worse than a seat
on the bare back of the horse.

The Indus:
names for
it.

The Indus in this part of its course is called
Sira, in distinction from Lar, which is its appellation below Sehwun.   These are two Belooche
words for north and south; and of the name of
Sirae, or Khosa, a tribe inhabiting the desert on
the east, we have thus a satisfactory explanation;
as these people originally spread from Sira, in
the upper course of the Indus.   Mehran, a name
of this river, familiar to the Indians and
foreigners, is not used by the natives of the
country.   The water of the Indus is considered
superior, for every purpose of life, to that drawn
from the wells of Sinde.   When taken from the
river it is very foul; but the rich keep it till the
mud with which it is loaded subsides.   There
are few ferry-boats on the Indus; and it is a
curious sight to see the people crossing it on
skins and bundles of reeds.   A native will often
float down to a distance of fifteen or twenty

miles, accompanied by a whole herd of buffaloes, preferring this mode of travelling to a journey on the banks. From Sehwun upwards they kill the "pulla" fish by nets suspended from the bow of small boats, which are, at the same time, the habitations of the fisherman and his family. The wife, who is generally a sturdy dame, pulls the stern oar to keep the vessel in the middle of the stream, often with a baby in her arms, while the husband kills the fish. One would not have expected to find porpoises so far from the sea; but they are to be observed sporting in the river as high as Bukkur; they are more grey than those in the salt water.

I should have mentioned, that before reach- Visited by the Vizier of Sinde. ing Bukkur, we were visited by the Nawab Wulee Mahomed Khan Lugharee, one of the viziers of Sinde, who had travelled from Shikarpoor to meet us. We found him a decrepit old man of seventy-two, on the verge of the grave. He treated us with particular kindness, and quite won our hearts by his attentions. He gave me a horse and a rich loongee. He said in the plainest terms that the Ameer had had evil counsel to detain us so long in Sinde, and that he had written urgently to his Highness not to commit himself by such a step. We had now a good opportunity of seeing a Belooche chief on his native soil. He came with a

splendid equipage of tents and carpets, accompanied by three palankeens, and about 400
men.   A set of dancing girls were among his
suite ; and in the evening we were compelled,
against our inclination, to hear these ladies squall
for a couple of hours, and, what added to the
disgust of the scene, they drank at intervals of
the strongest spirits, to *clear their voices*, as they
said, until nearly intoxicated.   It was impossible
to express any displeasure at this exhibition,
since the gala, however much out of taste, was
got up in the hope of adding to our amusement.
The people with us, who now amounted to 150,
were sumptuously entertained by the Nawab,
who kept us with him for two days.

Vizier of
Khyrpoor.

On the morning of the 14th we disembarked
near the small village of Alipoor, and were met
by the vizier of Meer Roostum Khan, who had
come from Khyrpoor to receive us.   His name
was Futteh Khan Ghoree, an aged person of
mild and affable manners, and of peculiar appearance from a snow white beard and red hair.
Our reception was cordial and kind ; the vizier
assured us of the high satisfaction with which
his master had heard of our arrival, for he had
long desired to draw closer to the British government, and had never yet had the good
fortune to meet any of its agents.   He said that
Meer Roostum Khan did not presume to put

himself on an equality with so potent and great a nation, but hoped that he might be classed among its wellwishers, and as one ready to afford his services on all occasions. Futteh Khan added that Khyrpoor formed a separate portion of Sinde from Hydrabad, a fact which he begged I would remember. I was not altogether unprepared for this communication, for I judged from his previous efforts to please that the ruler had some object in view. I assured the vizier of my sense of his master's attentions, and promised to talk on these matters after our interview. He brought a palankeen to convey me in state to Khyrpoor, a distance of fourteen miles, to which city we marched on the following day.

After what I have already stated, our interview with Meer Roostum Khan may be well imagined : he received us under a canopy of silk, seated on a cushion of cloth of gold. He was surrounded by the members of his family, forty of whom (males), descended in a right line from his father, are yet alive. There was more state and show than at Hydrabad, but as little attention to order or silence. We exchanged the usual complimentary speeches of like occasions. I thanked his Highness for the uniform attention and hospitality which we had received. Meer Roostum Khan is about fifty;

Ameer of Khyrpoor.

his beard and hair were quite white, and the expression of his countenance, as well as his manners, were peculiarly mild. He and his relatives were too much taken up with our uniforms and faces to say much; and he begged us to return in the evening, when there would be less bustle and confusion, to which we readily assented. I gave him my watch before leaving, and sent him a brace of pistols and a kaleidescope, with various articles of European manufacture, with which he was highly delighted. The crowd was hardly to be penetrated, but very orderly: they shouted as we approached; and nothing seemed to amuse them so much as the feathers of our hats. " Such cocks!" was literally the expression. For about 200 yards from the palace (if I can use such a term for the mud buildings of Sinde) there was a street of armed men, and among them stood thirty or forty persons with halberds, the foresters or huntsmen of the household.

Audience of leave.

In the evening we again visited the Ameer, and found him seated on a terrace spread with Persian carpets, and surrounded, as before, by his numerous relatives. He made a long address to me regarding his respect for the British government, and said that I had of course learned his sentiments from his vizier. He looked to our Mihmandar from Hydrabad, who I found

had been doing every thing in his power to prevent our meeting at all, and then changed the
conversation.   The Ameer asked innumerable
questions about England and its power, remark-
ing that we were not formerly so military a
nation; and he had heard that a few hundred
years ago we went naked and painted our
bodies.   On our religion he was very inquisitive; and when I informed him that I had read
the Koran, he made me repeat the " Kuluma,"
or creed, in Persian and Arabic, to his inex-
pressible delight.   He said that our greatness
had risen from a knowledge of mankind, and
attending to other people's concerns as well as
our own.   He examined my sword, a small
cavalry sabre, and remarked that it would not
do much harm; but I rejoined, that the age of
fighting with this weapon had passed, which
drew a shout and a sigh from many present.
There was so much mildness in all that the
Ameer said that I could not believe we were in
a Belooche court.   He expressed sorrow that we
could not stay a month with him; but since we
were resolved to proceed, we must take his state
barge, and the son of his vizier, to the frontier,
and accept the poor hospitality of a Belooche
soldier, meaning himself, so long as we were in
the Khyrpoor territory.   I must mention that
the hospitality, which he so modestly named,

consisted of eight or ten sheep, with all sorts of provisions for 150 people daily, and that while at Khyrpoor he sent for our use, twice a day, a meal of seventy-two dishes. They consisted of pillaos and other native viands. The cookery was rich, and some of them delicious. They were served up in silver. We quitted Khyrpoor with regret, after the attentions which we had received. Before starting, the Ameer and his family sent to us two daggers, and two beautiful swords with belts ornamented by large masses of gold. The blade of one of them was valued at 80l. To these were added many cloths and native silks; also a purse of a thousand rupees, which I did not accept, excusing myself by the remark that I required nothing to make me remember the kindness of Meer Roostum Khan.

Sindian rule.

Mr. Elphinstone has remarked, " that the " chiefs of Sinde appear to be barbarians of the " rudest stamp, without any of the barbarous " virtues," and I fear that there is too much truth in the character, though the Khyrpoor family exhibited little to show themselves deserving of the stigma; but the chiefs of this country live entirely for themselves. They wallow in wealth, while their people are wretched. Professing an enthusiastic attachment to the religion of Mahommed, they have not even a substantial mosque in their territories; and at Hydrabad, where the town stands on rock, and indeed every where, they pray in temples of mud, and seem ignorant of elegance or comfort in all that concerns domestic arrangement. The Beloochees are a particularly savage race of people, but they are brave barbarians. From childhood they are brought up in arms; and I have seen some of the sons of chiefs who had not attained the age of four or five years strutting about with a shield and a sword of small size, given by the parents to instil into them, at that early period, the relish for war. This tribe composes but a small portion of the Sindian population; and while they are execrated by the peaceable classes of the community for their imperious conduct, they, on the other hand, hate the princes by whom they are governed. It would be difficult to conceive a more unpopular rule, with all .classes of their subjects, than that of the Ameers of Sinde: nor is the feeling disguised; many a fervent hope did we hear expressed, in every part of the country, that we were the forerunners of conquest, the advance-guard of a conquering army. The persons of the Ameers are secure from danger by the number of slaves which they entertain around their persons. These people are called " Khaskelees," and enjoy the confidence of their masters, with a considerable share of power: they are hereditary slaves, and a distinct class of the community, who marry only among themselves.

We marched to Bukkur on the morning of the 19th, which is a fortress fifteen miles from Khyrpoor, situated on an insulated rock of flint on the Indus, with the town of Roree on one side and Sukkur on the other. It was not to be supposed that the Ameer would give us permission to visit this fancied bulwark of his frontier, and I did not press a demand which I saw was far from agreeable; but we had good opportunities of examining the place while passing it, both on shore and on the river. The island is about 800 yards long, of an oval shape, almost entirely occupied by the fortification, which looks more European than most Indian works: it is a beautiful object from the banks of the Indus; its towers are mostly shaded by large full grown trees, and the tall date drops its weeping leaves on the mosques and walls. There are several other islets near it, on one of which stands the shrine of Khaju Khizr, a holy Mahommedan, under a dome that contributes to the beauty of the scene. The Indus rolls past Bukkur in two streams, each of 400 yards wide, and the waters lash the rocks which confine them with noise and violence. During the swell, the navigation of this part of the river is dangerous, though the boatmen of·Bukkur are both expert and daring.   The town of Roree, which faces Bukkur, stands on a precipice of flint forty feet high, and some of its houses, which are lofty, overhang the Indus.   The inhabitants of these can draw up water from their windows; but a cut road in the rock supplies the citizens with this necessary of life without risking their lives. The opposite bank of Sukkur is not precipitous like that of Roree.   A precious relic, the lock of Mahommed's hair, enclosed in a golden box, attracts the Mahommedan pilgrim to Bukkur, though the inhabitants are chiefly Hindoos.

On the banks of the Indus we had a curious interview in the evening after our arrival with the Vizier from Khyrpoor, who had been sent by Meer Roostum Khan to escort us thus far, and see that we were furnished with boats.   After requesting to be received privately, he renewed the subject of our first conversation, and said that he had been instructed by his master to propose a solemn treaty of friendship with the British government on any terms that might be named : he then ran over the list of neighbouring states which owed their existence to an alliance, — the Chief of the Daodpootras, the Rawul of Jaysulmeer, and the Rajah of Beecaneer, &c. &c. and then concluded with a peroration full of gravity,

Grave predictions.

that it was foretold by astronomers, and recorded
ın his books, that the English would in time
possess all India, a prediction which both Meer
Roostum and himself felt satisfied would come
to pass, when the British would ask why the
chiefs of Khyrpoor had not come forward with
an offer of allegiance. I tried to remove, but
without effect, the sad prognostications of the
minister, and declared my incompetency to enter
on such weighty matters as a treaty between the
states, without authority and before receiving a
written statement under the Ameer's seal. I
said that I would make known the wishes that
had been expressed to my government, which
would be gratified to hear they had such
friends, which seemed to please the diplomatist;
he begged that I would bear in mind what had
passed, and exacted a promise that I would
write to him when gone, and so water the tree
of friendship, that the object might be ultimately
effected,—" for the stars and heaven proclaimed
" the fortune of the English !"

Amusing
incident.

This was not the only incident of interest that
occurred at Bukkur: we had a visit from an
Afghan nobleman of rank, who had been on a
mission to the Governor-General from the late
Shah Mahmood of Herat, and was now on his
return to his native country, by the way of
Sinde and Mekran, the dissensions of dismem-

bered Cabool preventing his passing by the usual route. He was one of the finest natives I ever saw, and had a flowing beard reaching to his waist : he was full of Calcutta and its wonders, and had adopted many of our customs. He rode on an English saddle ; but said he had just found out that it was partly made of hog's skin, and brought it to beg my acceptance of it, for he dared not take such a thing to his country, and would not again use it. I civilly declined the offer, and regretted that the information regarding the materials of the saddle had been traced to me ; for, as he liked our fashions, it was a pity he could not carry them to his own country. Previous to the envoy's leaving us, he begged I would give him an English brush, which I did with pleasure ; but I did not consider it necessary to add that, in addition to the skin of the unclean beast, he would now have the bristles. He went away in great good humour with his gift, for which he offered me his palankeen.

I was sorry that I should have been the means Mihman-dar. of giving uneasiness to the Afghan; for it seems that he acquired his knowledge regarding the construction of his saddle from our Sindian Mihmandar, Tukkee Shah, who had taunted him with uncleanness. This person was a Syud, one of the strictest Mahommedans I ever met.

He was a son of Meer Ismael Shah, and of Persian descent. We found him intelligent and learned, and his polished manners made us regret the loss of so agreeable a companion. He left us at Bukkur, to take temporary charge of the Shikarpoor district during the absence of his brother, the Nawab. The character of this person was singularly disfigured by Mahommedan bigotry and superstition; while sceptical and dispassionate on all other topics, there was no miracle too absurd for his credence in religion. Among other fables, he assured me that when the Imam Hoosein had been beheaded by the Yezeedees, and a Christian reproached them for murdering their Prophet, one of them fell on him; the man, instantly seizing the head of the Imam, placed it on his breast, and it pronounced the well-known words, " There is no " God but one God, and Mahommed is his " prophet;" which immediately silenced this Mahommedan Judas!

Alore, or Arore, the ancient capital.

While at Bukkur, I visited the ruins of Alore, which is said to have been once the capital of a mighty kingdom, ruled by the Dulora Rae, and on which Roree, Bukkur, and Sukkur, have risen. It extended from the ocean to Cashmeer, from Candahar to Kanoje, and was divided into four vast viceroyalties: the harbour of Diu, in Kattywar, is expressly mentioned as one of its sea-ports. It sunk under the Mahommedan arms so early as the seventh century of the Christian era, when subdued by the lieutenant of the Caliph of Bagdad, Mahommed bin Cassim, who invaded India, according to a Persian manuscript, in search of ornaments for the seraglio of the Caliph.

The particulars of its history are to be found at great length in the Chuchnama, a history of Sinde in Persian believed to be authentic, and so called from the ruler of Alore, a Brahmin, by name Duhr bin Chuch. The ruins of Alore are yet to be discovered in a rocky ridge four miles south-east of Bukkur, and are now marked by an humble hamlet, with some ruined tombs. A low bridge with - three arches, named the " Bund of Alore or Arore," constructed of brick and stone, alone remains of all its greatness. It is thrown across a valley, which in by-gone years formed the bed of a branch of the Indus, from which the waters fertilised the desert, and reached the sea by Omercote and Lucput,—a channel through which they still find egress in a great inundation.

The description of the battle which overwhelmed the city of Alore, and terminated the life and reign of the Dulora Rae, affords some clue to the manners of the age. The Brahmin appeared with a train of elephants, on one of

which he was seated, with two females of ex-
quisite beauty to supply him with wine and the
betel nut. The Mahommedans, unable to oppose
these animals, retired from the field to provide
themselves with combustibles : they filled their
pipes, and returned with them to dart fire at the
elephants, which fled in dismay and disorder *
The Raja fell in the action, and his two virgin
daughters, " more beautiful than the morn,"
were despatched to Bagdad as fit ornaments for
the seraglio of the vicegerent of the Prophet.
The story of these ladies deserves mention.
On their arrival at the holy city, they averred
that the General had dishonoured them in the
fever of victory, and the mandate for his death
was forthwith despatched by the Caliph. The
innocent Moslem, sewed up in a raw hide, was
transported from the East to Arabia; and when
his bones were produced in the seraglio, the
daughters of Duhr bin Chuch freely confessed
the falsehood of their accusation, and expressed
their readiness to die, having avenged their
father's murder. They were dragged to death
in the streets of Bagdad.

Alore the kingdom of Musicanus. We have recorded the splendour of Alore,
ruled by Brahmins so late as the seventh century

* It would appear from this, that they smoked in that
age: it must have been *bang*, or hemp, since tobacco was
unknown till the discovery of America.

of our era; and history, I think, identifies it with the kingdom of Musicanus, which Alexander found to be governed by Brahmins, and the richest and most populous in India. Here it was that that conqueror built a fort, as " the " place was commodiously situated for bridling " the neighbouring nations," and where Mahommed bin Cassim a thousand years afterwards subdued the Brahmins who revolted from the Macedonians. Its prosperity at this late period confirms the probability of its former wealth. Bukkur is the ancient Munsoora*, and has likewise been supposed to be Minagur, which I believe is erroneous. The second Arrian, in his Periplus, speaks of that city as the metropolis of Sinde, to which the cargo of the ships was carried up by the river " from Barbarike, a " port in the middle branch of the Indus." It has apparently escaped notice, that Minagur is to be identified with Tatta, as proved by a singular but convincing fact. The Jhareja Rajpoots of Cutch, who trace their lineage from Tatta, invariably designate it in these days by the name of Sa-Minagur, of which Minagur is evidently an abbreviation. I look upon the identity of Tatta and Minagur as conclusive, though the author of the Periplus never mentions Pattala. In Reechel we may also have

Larkhanu, of Oxycanus. Minagur as Tatta, not Bukkur.

Ayeen Acbaree.

the harbour of Barbarike.   The historians of
Alexander do not inform us of the name of the
country of Musicanus, but only of its ruler.
The position of Larkhanu, on the opposite side
of the Indus, is well marked as the country of
Oxycanus, which was famed for its fertility, since
Alexander despatched from hence his superan-
nuated soldiers, by the country of the Archoti
and Drangi, to Carmania, or Kerman.   The great
road westward branches from Larkhanu, and
crosses the mountains to Kelat by the pass of
Bolan, which is the route to Kerman.   The
modern inhabitants of the Indus have no traditions of the conquest of the Macedonians to
assist the enquirer in a subject that excites among
civilised nations such intense curiosity.

CHAP. IV.

THE COUNTRY OF BHAWUL KHAN.

O<small>N</small> the 21st of May we set sail from Bukkur, Quit Buk-
kur. having exchanged our boats for another description of vessel, called " zohruk," not in use in Lower Sinde. They are of an oblong square shape, rounded fore and aft, and built of the *talee* tree, clamped with pieces of iron instead of nails, an operation which is performed with great neatness. Some of the vessels exceed eighty feet ın length, and twenty in breadth. They are flat-bottomed, and pass quicker through the water than the *doondee,* though they have but one mast. By the description of boats in which Alexander transported his cavalry, I understand the " zohruk," which is well suited for the transport of troops. Arrian describes it " as of a round form," and says that they received no injury on leaving the Hydaspes, when the long vessels were wrecked. Their peculiar build has doubtless arisen from the occurrence of such rapids as the Macedonians experienced at the junction of the Acesines and Hydaspes.

The curiosity of the people on the banks of Curiosity
of the
people. the Indus was intense. One man in the crowd

demanded that we should stop and show ourselves, since there had never been a *white-
face* in this country before, and we were bound
to exhibit, from the welcome which we had
received: he had seen Shah Shooja, he said (the
ex-king of Cabool), but never an Englishman.
Need I say we gratified him and the crowd, of
which he was the spokesman? " Bismilla," " in
" the name of God," was their usual exclama-
tion when we appeared, and we daily heard ourselves styled kings and princes.   The ladies
were more curious than their husbands.   They
wear ear-rings of large dimensions, with tur-
quoises suspended or fixed to them; for these
stones are of little value in the vicinity of Khorasan.   Among the women, I should note the
Syudanees, or Bebees, the female descendants of
Mahommed : they go about veiled, or rather with
a long white robe thrown over their entire body,
having netted orifices before the eyes and mouth.
They are all beggars, and very vociferous in
their demands for alms: one set of them, (for
they go about in troops,) when they found I did
not readily meet their demands, produced a
written paper from the shrine of Lal Shah Baz,
at Sehwun, to hasten my charity! Father Man-
rique, in his journey by the Indus some centuries ago, complains " of the frail fair ones"
who molested him by the way.   In the present

age, the dress of the courtezans, who are to be met in every place of size in the country, would give a favourable idea of the wealth of Sinde; and it is one of the few, if not the only, amusements of the inhabitants to listen to the lascivious songs of these people. They are a remarkably handsome race, and carry along with them a spirit of enthusiasm in their performance unknown to the ladies of Hindoostan.

Three days after quitting Bukkur, we came in sight of the mountains of Cutch Gundava, distant about a hundred miles from the right bank of the Indus; the most remarkable peak was named Gendaree. We here entered a country inhabited by various Beloche tribes, long addicted to piracy and plunder; but their spirit has been destroyed by the growing power of the Khyrpoor chiefs. They offered no opposition or insult; and many came to pay us a friendly visit. Their manner of saluting each other, which indeed prevails among all the Beloochees, is somewhat peculiar. On approaching, they seize the stranger's hand, and touch the right breast with the right shoulder, and the left with the left, and follow up the words " welcome" with half a dozen such sentences as, " Are " you happy? Is every thing right? Are all " well, great and small, children and horses? " You are welcome."

Beloochees of Sinde.

G 2

A very few days brought us beyond the reach
of these Beloochees, and the dominions of Sinde ;
for we anchored thirty miles north of Subzulcote,
the frontier town, on the evening of the 26th,
on the line of boundary between the Khan of
the Daoodpootras and the Ameers of Sinde.
Our progress had been exceedingly rapid ; for
we had a favourable breeze, and often followed
the lesser branches of the Indus to escape the
violence of the stream.   The boats sailed with
celerity ; for we came one hundred and twenty
miles by the course of the river in six days
against the stream.   We here had a farewell feast
from the Khyrpoor Ameer and Meer Nusseer
Khan, the son of the principal Ameer, who had
shown us marked civility throughout the journey.
After the people had fared sumptuously, our
boats were crowded like sheepfolds.   I addressed
valedictory letters to both the Ameers and their
chief ministers, besides several replies to other
persons; for the " *cacoethes scribendi*" seemed to
have beset the nobles of the land; and I had received, in one day, no less than six letters.   These
productions were full of metaphor and over-
strained expressions of anxiety for our health
and safety, with trite sayings about the advantages of friendship, and a letter being half an
interview.   There is no difference between the
manners of Europe and Asia so striking as in

correspondence. The natives of the East commit the writing and diction of their compositions
to a native secretary, simply telling him to write
a letter of friendship, congratulation, or whatever may be the subject, to which he affixes his
seal, sometimes without a perusal. If the signet
is not legible, one may often try in vain to find
out his correspondent; for he never names himself in his letter. In my epistles, I told the
Khyrpoor chief that his friendship and kindness
had brought us without an accident, and with
unprecedented speed, against the mighty stream
of the Indus; and I thought it as well, for the
edification of the Hydrabad Ameer, to add, that
the Indus was a navigable river from the ocean,
and had abundance of water every where ! I did
not quit Sinde favourably impressed, either with
his character or policy; but we should not try
such a man by an European standard, and he
doubtless opposed our choice of the route by the
Indus on sufficiently good grounds.   I parted
from our Khyrpoor friends really with reluctance ;
for their hospitality and kindness had been great,
and it was with difficulty that I was permitted
to reward the boatmen.   The Mihmandar said
that he had been ordered to prohibit it; and his
master only desired to please the British Government.   This person was very inferior to our
former companion the Syud; but, if less learned

G 3

and intelligent, he had the more sterling qualities
of sincerity and honesty : his name was Inayut
Khan Ghoree.

We here dismissed, and with regret, our
Sindian escort, which had followed us from the
mouths of the Indus. They seemed to have
become attached to us, and followed us in our
walks and rides with unusual alacrity; as we
were leaving, they accompanied us to the water's
edge, with loud cries of thanks for our kindness
and prayers for our welfare. They consisted of
twenty-four men; twelve of whom were Beloochees and the rest Jokeeas, a tribe of mountaineers near Curachee. We had not, I am sure,
done much to deserve such gratitude; for they
had only received an additional month's pay
(eight rupees each) to take them back to their
country, a distance of three hundred and fifty
miles. Some of them begged to accompany us
to Lahore; but, on the same principle that they
had been hired in Sinde, it would be proper to
enlist natives of the new country we were entering, and I civilly declined their request. These
men used to kill game for us; and were ever
ready to anticipate our wishes. Their honesty
we found unimpeachable; and we never lost
any thing in our progress through a strange
country, protected by strangers on whom we had
no tie, and who had been brought from the fields
to enter our service.

NATIVES OF SINDE.

Lith.d for Burnes' Travels into Bokhara — by Day & Haghe Lith.rs to the King

John Murray Albemarle St. 1834

The natives of the neighbouring countries, Fish diet. and the higher class of people in Sinde, have a singular notion regarding the fish diet of the inhabitants.   They believe it prostrates the understanding; and, in palliation of ignorance in any one, often plead that " he is but a fish-" eater."   The lower order of the Sindians live entirely on fish and rice; and the prevailing belief must be of an old date, as they tell an anecdote of one of the Emperors of Delhi who addressed a stranger in his court with the question from whence he came; he replied, from Tatta, and the king turned away his head. The stranger, recollecting the prejudice against his country, immediately rejoined, that he was not a " fish-eater."   I am not prepared to state how far a fish diet may affect the intellect of the Sindian, but I certainly remarked the prolific nature of the food in the number of children on the banks of the Indus.   The greatest fault Manners, which an European would find with the people tume. &c. Cos- of Sinde is their filthy habits.   They always wear dark-coloured garments from religious motives; but the ablutions of the Prophet are little attended to.   People must be in easy circumstances, I believe, or cease to feel want before they adopt habits of cleanliness.   The change of costume in the people, announced already a change of country.   Since leaving

Bukkur, we had met many Afghans and natives of the kingdom of Cabool.   The boots of some of these strangers, made of variegated leather, ribbed, in some instances, not unlike the skin of the tiger, formed an extraordinary dress for a long-bearded old man.

Quit Sinde. Bhawul Khan's country.

In the evening of the 27th we quitted Sinde, and ascended the river for a few miles, where we were met by Gholam Kadir Khan, a Nuwab and person of high rank, who had been sent to welcome us by Bhawul Khan, the chief of the Daoodpootras, in whose country we had now arrived.   He was a little, pot-bellied old man, with a happy expression of countenance ; and he said that he was sent to communicate the delight with which his master hailed our approach. He brought a most kind message — that a fleet of fifteen boats had been collected, and was now in readiness to convey us through the Daoodpootra country, while the Khan had fitted up a boat expressly for our accommodation.   He brought likewise a purse of a hundred rupees, which he said he had been desired to send me daily : this I declined, saying, that money was useless where every necessary and luxury of life was furnished by his master's hospitality. We soon got on easy terms with our new hosts, and weighed anchor next evening for the frontier village, where we halted.   Many Daoodpootras came to see us; they differ in appearance from the Sindians, ¹and wear turbans formed of tight and round folds of cloths.

On the 30th of May our fleet, now swelled to eighteen boats, quitted the Indus at Mittuncote, where it receives the united waters of the Punjab rivers; and, as if to remind us of its magnitude, the stream was here wider than in any other part of its course, and exceeded 2000 yards. We took a last farewell of its waters, and entered the Chenab or Acesines of the Greeks. Alexander sailed down this river to the Indus; but no tradition of that event is preserved on its banks. The Sindians point to Cabool as the theatre of his exploits, where Sikunder the Persian achieved many memorable deeds. In the East, as in the West, there have not been wanting ages of darkness to draw a mist over truth, and substitute, in poetical language, the fables of an Eastern country for one of the most authentic facts in ancient history — the voyage of Alexander on the Indus. Mittun is a small town, about a mile distant from the Indus, and occupies, I imagine, the site of one of the Grecian cities, since the advantage of its position for commerce attracted the attention of Alexander.

Quit the Indus.

In Lower Sinde the pastoral tribes live in reed houses, and rove from one place to an-

Elevated houses of Sinde.

other.   In these parts of the Indus they dwell
in habitations elevated eight or ten feet from
the ground, to avoid the damp and the insects
occasioned by it.   These are also built of reeds,
and entered by a ladder.   They are small neat
cottages, and occupied by wandering tribes, who
frequent the banks of the river till the season
of inundation.   Herodotus mentions that the
Egyptians slept in turrets during the rise of the
Nile.   The inhabitants have strange notions
regarding the influence of the Indus on the
climate.   They believe that it gives out a per-
petual breeze; and they, therefore, seek a habit-
ation near it, for the heat of Sinde is most
oppressive.   The father of history expressed
his belief that such also was the case with the
Nile; and it is curious that a similar opinion
should be entertained by the people of Sinde.
I can readily understand that a vast volume of
running water would cool the banks of a river:
the heat is said to increase on receding from the
Indus.

Effects of the Indus on the climate.

We reached Ooch, where the joint streams
of the Sutlege and Beas, here called the Garra,
fall into the Chenab.   The name of Punjnud,
or Five Rivers, is unknown to the natives;
and we now navigated the Chenab or Acesines of the Greeks, the name of the five rivers
being lost in that of the greater stream.   It

Chenab or Acesines.

is curious to observe that this fact is expressly
mentioned by Arrian : — " The Acesines retains
" its name till it falls at last into the Indus,
" after it has received three other rivers." The
Sutlege, or Hesudrus, is not mentioned by Alexander's historians.   These united rivers form a
noble stream ; and the banks of the Chenab are
free from the thick tamarisk jungles of the
Indus.   They were studded with innumerable
hamlets, particularly towards the Indus ; for the
rich pasture attracts the shepherd.

Our arrival at Ooch had been so much earlier   Incident.
than was anticipated as to give rise to an in-
eident which might have proved serious.   The
troops of Bhawul Khan were encamped on the
banks of the river, and in a dusky day our
numerous fleet was mistaken for the Seik army,
which had been threatening to invade his territories.   A discharge of a cannon and some mus-
quetry arrested the progress of our advanced
boat.   The mistake was readily discovered, and
the chagrin and vexation that followed afforded
us some amusement.   I thought that apologies
and regrets would never have ceased.

The town of Ooch stands on a fertile plain at   Ooch.
a distance of four miles from the Acesines, beautifully shaded by trees.   It is formed of three
distinct towns, a few hundred yards apart from
each other, and each has been encompassed by

a wall of brick, now in ruins. The population amounts to 20,000. The streets are narrow, and covered with mats as a protection from the sun; but it is a mean place. We were accommodated in a garden well stocked with fruit trees and flowers, which was an agreeable change from our confined boats. When preparing for a journey to visit the Khan,— who was absent at Dirawul, in the desert,— we were surprised by the arrival of a messenger, with the information that he had reached Ooch from a distance of sixty miles, that he might save us the trouble of coming to him, and evince his respect for the British Government. The messenger brought us a deer, which the Khan had shot, and of which he begged our acceptance, with forty vessels of sherbet, and as many of sweetmeats and preserves; also a bag containing 200 rupees, which he requested I would distribute in charity, to mark the joyful event of our arrival.

Arrival of Bhawul Khan.

Interview with him.

On the morning of the 3d of June we visited Bhawul Khan, who had alighted at a large house outside the town, a mile distant : he sent an escort of his regular troops, with horses, palankeens, and various other conveyances, — one of which deserves description. It was a sort of chair, covered with a red canopy of cloth, supported by two horses, one in front and the other behind, and the most awkward vehicle

that can be imagined; for it could be turned
with difficulty, and the horses did not incline to
such a burden.   We passed a line of soldiers,
about 600 in number, dressed in uniforms of
red, blue, white, and yellow; and then entered the court yard, under a salute of eighty
guns.   The passages were lined with officers
and chiefs; and we found the Khan seated in
an area spread with carpets, attended only by
about ten persons: he rose and embraced us.
He made particular enquiries regarding Mr.
Elphinstone, who, he said, had been the means
of raising up a sincere and lasting friendship
between his family and the British Government.

Bhawul Khan is a handsome man, about
thirty years of age, somewhat grave in his demeanour, though most affable and gentlemanlike; during the interview he held a rosary in
his hand, but the telling of the beads did not interrupt his conversation.   He dilated at length
on the honour which Runjeet Sing had had conferred upon him in receiving presents from the
King of Great Britain; nor did he, in any way,
betray his feelings towards the Lahore chief,
though they are far from friendly.   The Khan,
unlike most natives, seemed to avoid all political
subjects.   He produced his matchlock, and explained to us his manner of hunting deer, his
favourite sport; and expressed a strong wish

that we should accompany him to his residence
in the desert.   We left him quite charmed with
his kindness, and the sincere manner in which
he had shown it.   In the evening the Khan
sent for our perusal the testimonials that had
been given to his grandfather by Mr. Elphinstone, which are preserved with great pride and
care in the archives of his government.   For my
own part, I felt equal satisfaction to find the
English character stand so high in this remote
corner of India, and the just appreciation of the
high-minded individual who had been the means
of fixing it.

Merchants
at Bhawul-
poor.

During our stay at Ooch, we were visited by
some of the principal merchants of Bhawulpoor,
who had followed the Khan.   The intelligence
of these people, and extent of their travels, surprised me.   Most of them had traversed the
kingdom of Cabool, and visited Balkh and Bokhara : some had been as far as Astracan ; and
they used the names of these towns with a
familiarity as if they had been in India.   They
had met Russian merchants at Bokhara, but
assured me that they never came to the eastward
of that city.   The intervening countries they
represented as perfectly safe, and bestowed the
highest commendations on Dost Mahommed, of
Cabool, and the Uzbeks, who encouraged commercial communication.   These merchants are

chiefly Hindoos, whose disposition peculiarly
adapts them for the patient and painstaking
vocation of a foreign merchant. Some of them
are Jews, who retain the marks of their nation
in all countries and places.*

We continued at Ooch for a week. The place History of
is ancient, and highly celebrated in the surrounding countries from the tombs of two saints of
Bokhara and Bagdad. The Ghorian emperors
expelled the Hindoo Rajas of Ooch, and con-
signed the surrounding lands to pious Mahommedans. The tombs of the two worthies I have
named are handsome, and held in much reverence by the people; they are about five hundred
years old, and tradition is silent regarding the
history of the place beyond that period. The
posterity of these saints enjoy both spiritual and
temporal power to the present day; but, instead
of ministering to the wants of the inhabitants,
who are needy and poor, they waste their
fortunes in the chase, and retain hounds and
horses for their amusement. An inundation of
the Acesines, some years back, swept away one
half of the principal tomb, with a part of the
town; and, though the return of the river to its
original bed is attributed to the miraculous

---

* It was my conversation with these men which made me
decide on undertaking the journey to Central Asia, which I
afterwards performed.

interference of the deceased saint, the people
have, as yet, failed to testify their gratitude by
repairing his tomb.   The town of Ooch stands
on a mound of earth or clay, like the city of
Tatta, which I judge to have been formed by
the ruins of houses.   The Chenab has swept
away a portion of the mound; and the section
of it which has been thus exposed seems to
support the conjecture which I have stated.

Visit from
Bhawul
Khan.

On the 5th of June we had a visit from
Bhawul Khan.   He insisted on coming in person
to see us; and sent a large tent to be pitched
by our garden, in which we received him.   He
sat for about an hour; and put numerous
questions regarding the manufactures of Europe.
The chief is of a mechanical turn of mind; he
produced a detonating gun, which had been
made under his directions from an European
pattern, and certainly did credit to the artificer;
he had also manufactured the necessary caps
and fulminating powder.   He expressed, at
this interview, much satisfaction with the presents which we had sent him; they consisted of
a brace of pistols, a watch, and some other
articles.   The Khan came in an open sort of
chair, to which we conducted him on his departure.   He was attended by about a thousand
persons; and I observed that he distributed
money as he passed along.   After the visit, our

Mihmandar brought us presents from the Khan; they consisted of two horses richly caparisoned with silver and enamel trappings, a hawk, with shawls and trays of the fabrics made at Bhawulpoor, some of which were very rich; to these were added a purse of 2000 rupees, and a sum of 200 for the servants; and, last of all, a beautiful matchlock, which had its value doubled by the manner in which it was presented. "The " Khan," said the messenger, " has killed many " a deer with this gun; and he begs you will " accept it from him, and, when you use it, " remember that Bhawul Khan is your friend."

In the evening we had a parting interview with Bhawul Khan. I gave him a handsome percussion gun; and assured him, what I felt most sincerely, that we should long remember his kindness and hospitality. He embraced us on our leaving him; and intreated us to write to him and command his services. The courtiers and people were as polite as their chief.

We left Ooch on the following morning, and pitched our camp at the junction of the Chenab with the Garra, or united streams of the Beas and Sutlege.

The country about Ooch is flat and exceedingly rich; there are many signs of inundation between the town and the river. The dust was

Audience of leave.

Mountains of Sooliman.

most intolerable; but it always cleared up
towards evening, and we saw the sun set in
splendour behind the mountains of Sooliman
across the Indus, eighty miles distant. They
did not appear high, and were not distinguished by any remarkable peaks. It is a
little below the latitude of Ooch that they
assume a direction parallel to the Indus, which
they afterwards preserve. We lost sight of the
range on our voyage to Mooltan the day after
leaving Ooch.

Embou-
chure of the
Sutlege.

On the morning of the 7th we passed the
mouth of the Sutlege, and continued our voyage
on the Chenab to the frontiers of Bhawul Khan,
which we reached on the evening of the 8th.
The Chenab receives the Sutlege without
turmoil, and appears quite as large above as
below the conflux. The waters of either river
are to be distinguished some miles below the
junction by their colour: that of the Chenab
is reddish; and, when joined by the Sutlege,
the waters of which are pale, the contrast is
remarkable. For some distance the one river
keeps the right, and the other the left, bank;
the line of demarcation between the two being
most decided. The nature of the soil through
which the Chenab flows, no doubt, tinges its
waters. This peculiarity is well known to the
natives, who speak of the " red water;" but

none of the ancient authors allude to the circumstance. The nature of the country between Ooch and the Indus has been mistaken, as it is never flooded. Several decayed canals, if cleared, would yet lead the water of the Chenab to the Indus, and may account for Major Rennell's conducting that river into the great stream, so many miles above the true point of union, until the geographical error was rectified by the mission to Cabool.

We parted with our Mihmandar, Gholam The Mih-
Cadir Khan, before passing into the Seik ter- mandar.
ritory. We had seen a great deal of him, and found him well informed on all such subjects as he could be supposed to know. He carried four or five historical works with him, among which was the Chuchnamu, or History of Sinde, to which I have alluded, one or two books on medicine, and some volumes of poetry: yet he made a most particular request, at our last interview, that I would tell him the secret of magic, which he was certain we possessed. I assured him of the error under which he laboured: "But," said he, "how is it that you "have had a favourable wind ever since I met "you, and performed a twenty days' voyage in "five, when a breath of air does not sometimes "stir in this country for months?" I told him that such was the good fortune of the English.

When the Nawaub found me wanting in the black
art, he whispered that he himself was a dealer
in spells and magic ; but very sensibly added,
that he had no faith in his own incantations,
high as they stood in the opinion of others;
though it was not his part to say so.   He begged
I would give him some medicine to prevent
him growing fatter ; but neither regular exercise, nor vinegar, which I prescribed, seemed to
suit his taste.   What a whimsical creature man
is.   In Sinde, every person of rank seeks for
rotundity to support his dignity ; and but a few
miles from that country, the " martyr to obesity"
is considered unfortunate.

There is little cordiality subsisting between
the Seiks and Bhawul Khan ; and it was with
the utmost difficulty that I prevailed on the
Nawaub to let us proceed to the Seik camp, a
distance of six miles, in the boats belonging
to his master.   " The Seiks," he said, " are
" my master's enemies, and no boat of ours
" shall cross their frontier."   He at last assented,
on my becoming answerable for the return of
the vessels.

Runjeet
Sing's
country.
A few hours' sail brought us to the place of
rendezvous late at night, and the fires of the
soldiers blazing in the darkness only increased
our anxiety to meet our new friends.   It was
the camp of the party which had been sent from

Lahore to await our arrival, and had long expected us. Immediately on landing, we were received by Sirdar Lenu Sing, who came with considerable state on an elephant, and was attended by a large retinue. The Sirdar was richly dressed, and had a necklace of emeralds, and armlets studded with diamonds. In one hand he held a bow, and in the other two Persian letters in silken bags. He congratulated us, in the name of Maharajah Runjeet Sing, on our arrival, and had been desired by his Highness to communicate that he was deeply sensible of the honour conferred upon him by the King of England, and that his army had been for some time in readiness on the frontier, to chastise the barbarians of Sinde, who had so long arrested our progress. He then delivered to me the letters which appointed himself as our Mihmandar, in conjunction with two other persons; presenting at the same time a bow, according to the custom of the Seiks. On the ceremony being terminated, the Sirdar and several others placed bags of money at my feet, amounting to about 1400 rupees, and then withdrew.

The first intercourse with a new people can never be destitute of interest, and the present was far from being so.

These Seiks are tall and bony men, with a very martial carriage: the most peculiar part of their

dress is a small flat turban, which becomes them
well; they wear long hair, and from the knee
downwards do not cover the leg. When the
deputation had withdrawn, an escort of regular
troops attended to receive orders, and sentries
were planted round our camp. It was novel to
hear the words of command given in the French
language.

Exhibition
of the dray
horses.

No sooner had the day broke, than the Maharajah's people evinced much anxiety to view
the dray horses, and we had them landed for
exhibition. Their surprize was extreme; for
they were little elephants, said they, and not
horses. Their manes and tails seemed to please,
from their resemblance to the hair of the cow of
Thibet; and their colour, a dappled grey, was
considered a great beauty. It was not without
difficulty that I replied to the numerous questions
regarding them; for they believed that the
presents of the King of England must be extraordinary in every way; and for the first time, a
dray horse was expected to gallop, canter, and
perform all the evolutions of the most agile
animal. Their astonishment reached its height
when the feet of the horses were examined; and
a particular request was made of me to permit
the despatch of one of the shoes to Lahore, as it
was found to weigh 100 rupees, or as much as
the four shoes of a horse in this country. The

curiosity was forthwith despatched by express, and accompanied by the most minute measurement of each of the animals, for Runjeet Sing's special information.   The manner in which this rarity was prized, will be afterwards seen, when it is gravely recorded, that the new moon turned pale with envy on seeing it!

Our own comforts were not forgotten among their wonder and admiration, for the attentions of the people were of the most marked description.   Our Mihmandar said that he had the strictest injunctions regarding our reception; and he rigidly acted up to the spirit of the following document, which will best show the distinguished and kind manner we were treated in the territories of Maharajah Runjeet Sing. *Civilities.*

COPY OF THE MAHARAJAH'S " PURWANU," OR COMMAND TO HIS OFFICERS. *Purwanu of Runjeet Sing.*

" Be it known to Dewan Adjoodia Pursad,
" Monsieur Chevalier Ventura, and the great
" and wise Sirdar Lenu Sing, and Lalla Sawun
" Mull, Soobadar of Mooltan, that when Mr.
" Burnes reaches the frontier, you are imme-
" diately to attend to all his wants, and pre-
" viously despatch 200 infantry and the lancers,
" under Tajee Sing, to Julalpoor, that they
" may be ready on his arrival as an honorary

H 4

" escort ; and you are at the same time to make
" known your own arrival in the neighbourhood.
" When Mr. Burnes approaches, you are imme-
" diately to despatch an elephant, with a silver
" houda, in charge of the Dewan, who is to
" state that the animal has been sent for his
" own express use, and then ask him to be
" seated thereon, which will be gratifying, as
" the friendship between the states is great.

" When Mr. Burnes has mounted the ele-
" phant, then shall the Sirdar Lenu Sing, and
" Sawun Mull, seated on other elephants, ap-
" proach, and have an interview with that gentle-
" man, paying him every manner of respect and
" attention in their power, and congratulating
" him in a hundred ways on his safe arrival
" from a long and distant journey, distributing
" at the same time 225 rupees among the poor.
" You are then to present a handsome bow, and
" each of you eleven gold Venetians, and con-
" duct the gentleman to the halting-place, and
" there set before him 1100 rupees, and fifty
" jars of sweetmeats. You are then to supply
" the following articles : grass, grain, bran,
" milk, eggs, fowls, sheep (doombus), curds,
" vegetables, fruit, roses, spices, water-vessels,
" beds, and every other thing that may be ne-
" cessary, in quantities without bounds, and be
" neglectful and dilatory in nothing. When

" you visit, you are to parade the two com-
" panies and the horse, and salute, and then
" place guards according to Mr. Burnes' plea-
" sure.

" When you reach Shoojuabad, you are to
" fire a salute of eleven guns, and furnish every
" thing as before directed, and present 1100
" rupees, with sweetmeats and fruits, and attend
" to every wish that is expressed.   If Mr.
" Burnes desires to look at the fort of Shoo-
" juabad, you are to attend on him and show it,
" and see there is no obstruction, and that no
" one even raises his voice.

" On reaching Mooltan, you are to conduct
" Mr. Burnes with great respect, and pitch his
" camp in whatever garden he shall select; the
" Huzooree, the Begee, the Shush Muhl, or
" the Khass wu Am, or any other.   You are
" then to present him with a purse of 2500
" rupees, and 100 jars of sweetmeats, and fire a
" salute of eleven guns from the ramparts of
" the fortress.   When you have complimented
" him on his arrival, you are to suggest for his
" consideration, whether he would not like to
" halt at Mooltan for five or six days after his
" long journey, and act entirely as he desires;
" if he wishes to view the fort, you three per-
" sons are to attend him, and allow no one to

" make a noise, and take most particular care
" that the Nihungs, and such other wrong-
" headed people, are kept at a distance.

" In quitting Mooltan, you are to load 100
" camels with provisions for the supply of Mr.
" Burnes to Lahore, and Soobadar Sawan Mull
" is to attend him in person for the first stage,
" and after taking leave, repair to the camp of
" Monsieur Chevalier Ventura.   Sirdar Lenu
" Sing and Dewan Adjoodia Pursad, together
" with Futih Sing Ramgurree, accompanied by
" an escort of two companies and the lancers,
" shall attend Mr. Burnes, and proceed by easy
" stages to Lahore, despatching daily notice of
" his approach.   At Dehra, Syudwulla the Kardar
" is to present 1100 rupees, with the usual
" sweetmeats; and you are all directed to re-
" member, in every instance, and at all times,
" the great friendship which subsists between
" the two states."

There is at all times much display and hyper-
bole in affairs of this description throughout the
East; but in the present instance it will be
observed, that the Maharajah not only evinced
his liberality in other matters, but in throwing
open to our inspection the strong holds of his
country, which can be duly appreciated by those
only who have experienced the extreme jealousy

of most Indian governments.   The Seik Sirdars
in attendance on us were likewise most communicative ; and this is the more remarkable, as it
could not have escaped the Maharajah, that in
taking the unfrequented tract we had followed
on the Indus we were seeking for new information, after the spirit of our country.

108

CHAPTER V.

Voyage in
the Seik
country. By the 12th of June, our preparations for the
voyage were completed, and we again embarked
on the Chenab. The boats here were of a very
inferior description, still called " zohruq ;" they
had no sails, and hoist a mat on a low mast
instead; their waists are scarcely a foot above
water, and those which they could collect for us,
were but the different ferry boats of the river.
There is no trade carried on by water in this
country, and there are in consequence no boats.
A sail of a few hours brought us to the ferry
opposite Shoojuabad, where we halted. The
country is of the richest and most fertile description, and its agricultural resources are much
increased, by conducting water to the remoter
parts, in large canals and aqueducts.

Shoojua-
bad. In the evening of the 13th we visited the
town of Shoojuabad, which stands four miles
eastward of the river. It is a thriving place,
surrounded by a fine wall of brick, about thirty
feet high. The figure of the place is that of an
oblong square, and the wall is strengthened by
octagonal towers, at equal distances. The in-

terior is filled up with houses, which are built in streets, at right angles to one another; and a suburb of huts surrounds the walls. Shoojuabad fort was built by the Nuwab of Mooltan in the year 1808, and the public spirit of that person raised it, in the course of ten years, to great opulence. It is situated in a most beautiful country, and is watered by two spacious canals for many miles, both above and below the town. It was captured by the Seiks, along with Mooltan, and now forms the frontier fortress of the Lahore chief. We were accompanied to Shoojuabad by our Mihmandar, who appeared in state for the occasion; he sat on an elephant in a chair of silver, — two horses were led before him, with saddles of red and yellow velvet, — his bow and quiver were borne by one menial, and his sword by another; while he himself was decorated with precious jewels. At the palace of the town, we were met by many of the respectable inhabitants, before whom the "zyafut," or money gift, and sweetmeats of the Maharajah, were presented to us. We afterwards were conducted through the principal street, and welcomed in a gratifying manner, wherever we went. On quitting the fortress the garrison fired a salute.

On the 15th we came in sight of the domes Mooltan. of Mooltan, which look well at a distance; and

alighted in the evening at the Hoozooree Bagh,
a spacious garden enclosed by a thin wall of
mud, a mile distant from the city. The ground
is laid out in the usual native style; two spacious
walks crossed each other at right angles, and
are shaded by large fruit trees, of the richest
foliage. In a bungalow, at the end of one of
these walks, we took up our quarters, and were
received by the authorities of the city in the
same hospitable manner as at Shoojuabad. They
brought a purse of 2500 rupees, with 100
vessels of sweetmeats, and an abundant supply
of fruit: we felt happy and gratified at the
change of scene, and civilities of the people.

The city of Mooltan, is described in Mr.
Elphinstone's work on Cabool, and it may appear
foreign to my purpose to mention it; but his
mission was received here with great jealousy,
and not permitted to view the interior of the
town, or the fort. I do not hesitate, therefore,
to add the following particulars, drawn up after
a week's residence. The city of Mooltan is
upwards of three miles in circumference, surrounded by a dilapidated wall, and overlooked
on the north by a fortress of strength. It
contains a population of about 60,000 souls, one
third of whom may be Hindoos; the rest of the
population is Mahommedan, for though it is
subject to the Seiks, their number is confined to

the garrison, which does not exceed 500 men.
The Afghans have left the country, since they
ceased to govern. Many of the houses evidently
stand on the ruins of others : they are built of
burnt brick, and have flat roofs : they sometimes
rise to the height of six stories, and their loftiness
gives a gloomy appearance to the narrow streets.
The inhabitants are chiefly weavers and dyers
of cloth. The silk manufacture of Mooltan is
called " kais," and may be had of all colours,
and from the value of 20 to 120 rupees : it is
less delicate in texture than the " loongees" of
Bhawulpoor. Runjeet Sing has with much propriety encouraged their manufacture, since he
captured the city ; and by giving no other cloths
at his court, has greatly increased their consumption, and they are worn as sashes and scarfs
by all the Seik Sirdars. They are also exported
to Khorasan and India, and the duties levied
are moderate. To the latter country, the route
by Jaysulmeer and Beecaneer is chosen in preference to that by Sinde, from the trade being
on a more equitable footing. The trade of
Mooltan is much the same as at Bhawulpoor,
but is on a larger scale, for it has forty Shroffs,
(money changers) chiefly natives of Shikarpoor.
The tombs of Mooltan are celebrated : one of
them, that of Bawulhuq, who flourished upwards
of 500 years ago, and was a contemporary of

Sadee the Persian poet, is considered very holy; but its architecture is surpassed by that of his grandson, Rookn-i-Allum, who reposes under a massy dome sixty feet in height, which was erected in the year 1323, by the Emperor Toogh-luck, as his own tomb. Its foundation stands on higher ground than the summit of the fort wall; there is also a Hindoo temple of high antiquity, called Pyladpooree; mentioned by Thevenot in 1665.

Fort of
Mooltan.
The fortress of Mooltan merits a more par-ticular description; it stands on a mound of earth, and is an irregular figure of six sides, the longest of which (towards the north-west) ex-tends for about 400 yards. The wall has up-wards of thirty towers, and is substantially built of burnt brick, to the height of forty feet outside; but in the interior, the space between the ground and its summit does not exceed four or five feet, and the foundations of some of the buildings overtop the wall, and are to be seen from the plain below. The interior is filled with houses, and till its capture by the Seiks in 1818, was peopled, but the inhabitants are not now permitted to enter, and a few mosques and cupolas, more substantially built than the other houses, alone remain among the ruins. The fortress of Mooltan has no ditch; the nature of the country will not admit of one being constructed; and Runjeet

Sing has hitherto expended great sums without effect. The inundation of the Chenab, and its canals, together with rain, render the vicinity of Mooltan a marsh, even in the hot weather, and before the swell of the river has properly set in, the waters of last year remain. The walls of the fortress are protected in two places by dams of earth ; the modern fort of Mooltan was built on the site of the old city, by Moorad Bukhsh, the son of Shah Jehan, about the year 1640, and it subsequently formed the Jagheer of that prince's brothers, the unfortunate Daro Shikoh, and the renowned Aurungzebe   The Afghans seized it in the time of Ahmed Shah, and the Seiks wrested it from the Afghans, after many struggles, in 1818. The conduct of its governor during the siege, deserves mention ; when called on to surrender the keys, and offered considerate treatment, he sent for reply, that they would be found in his heart, but he would never yield to an infidel ; he perished bravely in the breach. His name, Moozuffur Khan, is now revered as a saint, and his tomb is placed in one of the holiest sanctuaries of Mooltan. The Seiks threw down the walls of the fort in many places, but they have since been throughly renewed or repaired ; they are about six feet thick, and could be easily breached from the mounds that have been left in baking

the bricks, which are within cannon range of
the walls.

Antiquity
of Mooltan
supposed
Capital of
the Malli.
Mooltan is one of the most ancient cities in
India.   We read of its capture by Mahommed-
bin-Cassim, in the first century of the Hejira,
and its wealth afterwards attracted the Ghiznian,
Ghorian, and Moghul emperors of Hindoostan.
But we have little reason to doubt its being the
capital of the Malli of Alexander: Major Rennell
has supposed that metropolis to have been higher
up, and nearer the banks of the Ravee, because
Arrian states, that the inhabitants fled across
that river.   This is high authority, but Mooltan
is styled "Malli than," or "Malitharun" the place
of the Malli, to this day, and we have no ruins
near Tolumba, the site pointed at by Rennell to
fix on as the supposed capital.   It is expressly
stated that Alexander crossed the Ravee, and
after capturing two towns, led his forces to the
capital city of the Malli.   As the distance from
the river is but thirty miles, and Mooltan is considered a place of high antiquity, I do not see
why we should forsake the modern capital when
in search of the ancient : had we not the earliest
assurances of the age of Mooltan, its appearance
would alone indicate it.   The houses are piled
upon ruins, and the town stands on a mound of
clay, the materials of former habitations which
have gradually crumbled, an infallible proof of

antiquity, as I have remarked of Tatta and Ooch. The late Nawab of Mooltan, in sinking a well in the city, found a war drum, at a depth of sixty feet from the surface; and several other articles have been from time to time collected, but no coins have been hitherto seen. Mooltan may, in some degree, be considered to answer the description of the Brahmin city and its castle, which Alexander captured, before attacking the capital of the Malli; but in that case, we should have no site to fix on as the capital. The manufactures of Mooltan and Bhawulpoor, the "kais" and "loungee," seem to assist in fixing the country of the Malli, for Quintus Curtius informs us that the ambassadors of the Malli and Oxydracæ (Mooltan and Ooch) "wore garments of cotton, lawn or muslin (lineæ vestes), interwoven with gold, and adorned with purple," and we may safely translate "lineæ vestes," into the stuffs of Mooltan and Bhawulpoor, which are interwoven with gold, and most frequently of a purple colour.

During our stay at Mooltan, we were freely conducted to view the lions of this decayed Viceroyalty of the Mogul empire. In the interior of the fort there is the Hindoo temple, before alluded to, which its votaries believe to be of boundless antiquity, and with it couple

Buildings of Mooltan Superstitions.

the following tradition.   One Hurnakus, a giant, despised God, and worshipped himself; he desired his son Pylad to follow his steps, and was about to murder him for his contumacy, when the youth was miraculously saved by an incarnation of the Deity, who appeared in a shape of half lion and man.   Hurnakus had given out that his death could never be effected in earth or air, in fire or water, by sword or bow, by night or day; and it happened without an infringement of these conditions, for Nursingavater (the name of the incarnation) seized him at dusk, and placing him on his knee, tore Hurnakus to pieces, and took his son under protection.   This Hindoo temple, which goes by the name of Pyladpooree, is a low building, supported by wooden pillars, with the idols Hooneeman and Guneesa as guardians to its portal. It is the only place of Hindoo worship in Mooltan; we were denied entrance to it.

There is a shrine of some celebrity, near the walls of Mooltan, where rest the remains of Shumsi-Tabreezee, a saint from Bagdad, who is believed to have performed many miracles, and even raised the dead.   This worthy, as the story is told, was flayed alive for his pretensions.   He had long begged his bread in the city, and in his hunger caught a fish, which he held up to the sun, and brought that luminary near enough to

roast it; this established his memory and equi-
vocal fame on a firmer basis. The natives to
this day attribute the heat of Mooltan, which is
proverbial, to this incident.

In the ready belief which the inhabitants of Mooltan grant to such absurdities, we see little
to exalt them in the scale of reasonable beings;
but it seems inherent in the people to propagate
and uphold such delusions, for there are tales
equally improbable regarding every tomb in the
city. Rookn-i-alum, the son of Bhawul Huq,
removed to his present sepulchre when dead.

At Mooltan we first saw the practice of religion amongst the Seiks. In a veranda of
the tomb of Shumsi-Tabreezee, a "Gooroo,"
or priest of that persuasion, had taken up his
abode since the conquest of the city. We
found him seated on the ground, with a huge
volume in front of him; and a place covered
with cloth, like an altar, at one end of the apartment: he opened the book at my request, and
repeating the words " wa gooroojee ka futteh," *
touched the volume with his forehead, and all
the Seiks in attendance immediately bowed to
the ground: he then read and explained the
first passage that he turned up, which was as fol-

*Reflec-
tions.*

*Religion of
the Seiks.*

* " May the Gooroo be victorious," the national war-cry of
the Seiks.

I 3

lo — "All of you have sinned ; endeavour
" therefore to purify yourselves : if you neglect
" the caution, evil will at last overtake you."   I
need hardly mention that the volume was the
"Grinth," or holy book of the Seiks : their reverence for it amounts to veneration, and the
priest waves a " *choury*," or a Tibet cow's tail,
over it, as if he were fanning an emperor.   The
Gooroo was free from pomp and pride, and gave
a willing explanation to our enquiries : he opened
his holy book to acknowledge the gift of a few
rupees, that I made in due form, and requested
my acceptance of some confections in return.

Intoler-
ance.

The presence of a Seik priest, and the para-
phernalia of his order, under the roof of a
Mahommedan tomb, will furnish a good com-
mentary on the state of that religion in this
country ; it is barely tolerated.   In this city,
which held for upwards of 800 years, so high
a Mahommedan supremacy, there is now no
public "*numaz ;*" the true believer dare not lift
his voice in public.   The " *Eeds*" and the
Mohurum pass without the usual observances ;
the " *Ullaho Acbar*" of the priest is never
heard ; the mosques are yet frequented, but the
pious are reduced to offering up their orisons in
silence.   Such has been the state of things since
Mooltan fell, in 1818, and yet the number of
Seiks is confined to that of the garrison, from

four to five hundred men. The Mahommedans, who amount to about 40,000 souls, suffer no other inconvenience from their new masters, who afford every protection to their trade. The Seiks excuse themselves, by alleging, that they have not inflicted, in retribution, one fourth of their own sufferings at the hands of the Mahommedans. They are, I believe, correct in the averment, but religious persecution is always revolting, and exercises a baneful influence in every age and country.

The climate of Mooltan differs from that of the countries lower down the Indus; showers of rain are common at all seasons, and yet the dust is intolerable. For nine successive evenings, we had a tornado of it from the westward, with lightning, and distant thunder. Such storms are said to be frequent; they appear to set in from the Sooliman mountains, between which and the Indus the sand or dust is raised. The heat and dust of Mooltan have grown into a proverb, to which have been added, not unmeritedly, the prevalence of beggars, and the number of the tombs, in the following Persian couplet: — Climate.

> " Chuhar cheez hust, toohfujat-i-Mooltan.
> " Gird, guda, gurma wu goristan."

As far as I could judge, the satire is just: the dust darkened the sun : the thermometer rose in

June to 100° of Fahrenheit, in a bungalow artifi-
cially cooled : the beggars hunted us every where ;
and we trod on the cemeteries of the dead, in
whatever direction we rode.

The country around Mooltan is highly cultivated ; the Acesines sends the water of its
inundation to the very walls of the city, and
there is a large canal, that extends it, at other
seasons, through Mooltan itself. The plain that
intervenes between the river and city has the
appearance of a rich meadow, and is overgrown
with date trees, which form here a productive
source of revenue. It is a popular belief in the
country, that this tree was introduced from
Arabia by the army of Mahommed-bin-Cassim,
who brought the fruit as a provision for his army.
It is a curious fact that they are principally
found in the track of that invader, who marched
from Aloré to Mooltan. If the tradition be
true, the destroying Moslem compensated in
some degree for the evils and scourge of his
inroad. There are many ruined hamlets around
Mooltan, the remains of Jagheers, held by the
Afghans, but though these are deserted their
inhabitants have only changed their residence,
and occupy houses in the city.

We removed our camp on the 20th to the
banks of the Acesines, which is four miles
distant. The river is about 650 yards wide,

but at the ferry itself, it is expanded to 1000 at this season.   We here found ten boats, laden with mineral salt, from Pind Dadun Khan ; they exceeded eighty feet in length. These boats drop down to Mooltan in twelve days, from the mines, when fully laden.

We embarked on the 21st of June, on a boat which the Maharajah had fitted up for our reception with two wooden bungalows ; and, along with the rest of our fleet, prosecuted our voyage.   We did not again exchange our boats, in the way to Lahore.   On quitting the ferry at Mooltan, we came in sight of the desert that lies between the Chenab and the Indus.   It does not commence so low as Ooch, as has been represented in our maps, but near the latitude of Mooltan, and runs parallel with the river, at a distance of about two miles, leaving a stripe of cultivated land.   The sand-hills resemble those of the sea shore, and have a scanty covering of bushes, I cannot call it verdure : they do not exceed twenty feet in elevation, but from refraction often appeared much higher.   There is a great contrast between the sterile tract, and the champaign plains of the eastern bank, which we found every where irrigated.   The villages lie at a distance of about two miles from the river, and have their fields fertilised from canals, by the Persian wheel.   On the banks of the Indus,

Quit Mooltan.

Desert.

wells are common, but on the Chenab they are only to be seen on the verge of canals that branch from it,

There is a shrub called " peeloo *," which is to be found in this neighbourhood, and in all tracts of saline soil that border on the Indus and Punjab Rivers. It produces a red and white berry, which has but a poor flavour; the taste of its seeds resembles watercresses: this is the season of the fruit, and it was exposed for sale in the bazars of Mooltan. I observed this shrub in greatest abundance in the delta, and lower parts of Sinde; and, as I am satisfied that it is only to be found in the particular soil described, I believe we recognise it in Arrian's Indian History. " The leaves resemble those of the " laurel; they grow *chiefly* in places where the " tide flows among them, and where they are " again left dry at low water. Their flower is " white, and in shape like a violet, but much ex- " celling it in sweetness."

The arrangements made for our progress through the Seik territories were very complete. We sailed from sunrise to sunset; and found thirty or forty villagers alongside by day-break to drag each boat. The fatigue and exertion which these people underwent in a hot sun was

* Salvadora Persica.

excessive. When they passed a field of melons, but few were left to the owner; and many an old lady scolded loudly as they invaded her property. The people of this country are treated with little consideration by the government; they are not oppressed, yet considered its servants since the conquest. But for our interference, these villagers, who had waded through the water and quicksands, would have been dismissed empty-handed at night. The bounty of the Maharajah enabled us daily to entertain sumptuously, with flour and ghee, 300 hungry villagers; and the Mihmandar further assured me that due remission would be made for the destruction of the fields in our progress. While we ourselves advanced by water, the elephants, camels, and escort seconded our motions on shore; and we always found them drawn up in parade array on the ground fixed for our night's encampment; we always slept on shore. Before dusk we rode out on elephants to the neighbouring villages, and conversed with the people. They are lamentably ignorant; and consisted chiefly of Juts, a tribe of Mahommedans engaged in agriculture. They are not allowed to pray aloud; but they stimulated each other when pressed in our service by loud shouts and invocations to Bhawul Huq, the revered saint of Mooltan.

Alexander.   As the sun set on the 23d, we moored below
the village of Fazil Shah, in the mouth of the
Ravee or Hydraotes, still called Iräotee by the
natives. This was the spot where Alexander of
Macedon met his anxious army after his severe
wound, and showed to his troops that his precious
life was yet preserved: but these are events which
live only in the historical works of Europe; they
are unknown to the natives of Asia. I must
mention, however, a circumstance corroborative
of the Greek historians, — the fields of beans
that I observed on the banks of this river. They
led Alexander, for some time, to mistake the
heads of the Indus for the Nile; and now
remain, in a distant age, as proofs of his journey,
and accuracy in the historians of his expedition.

Gifts from   The intelligence of our arrival in the country
Lahore.   of the Seiks soon reached Lahore; and a pair
of gold armlets, set with diamonds and emeralds,
arrived in due course as a gift from the Maharajah to our Mihmandar. The Lahore chief is
munificent in his distribution of presents among
his nobles, though less so than in former years.
Grants of land, and gifts of jewels and money,
are yet made. They attest the wealth of the
country, and the sound policy of the prince.

Enter the   On the 24th we quitted the Acesines, and
Ravee.   entered on the navigation of the Ravee. At the
point of union, the former river has a breadth of

three quarters of a mile, though the deep part
does not extend for 500 yards.

Lieut. Macartney makes mention of a report
which he had heard of the Chenab being fordable
in the cold season below this point; but the
natives assured me, that such an occurrence had
never happened in the memory of man, and I
found the soundings to exceed twelve feet. The
Chenab, indeed, is only inferior to the Indus ;
its current is more rapid than that river, and,
with its depressed banks, it yet preserves every
where a depth of two fathoms. The Ravee
throws itself into the Chenab by three mouths,
close to each other. This river is very small,
and resembles a canal, rarely exceeding 150 yards
in breadth in any part of its course. Its banks
are precipitous, so that it deepens before it expands.   Nothing can exceed the crookedness
of its course, which is a great impediment to
navigation, for we often found ourselves, after
half a day's sail, within two miles of the spot
from which we started. The water of the Ravee
is redder than that of the Chenab. It is fordable
in most places for eight months of the year. Its
banks are overgrown with reeds and tamarisk,
and for half the distance, from its estuary to the
capital, there is no cultivation. There are no
canals or cuts from this river below Lahore.
There is a very extensive one above that city,

which I shall have occasion to mention here-
after.

Tolumba.   On the 27th of June we reached the small
town of Tolumba, which is situated in a grove
of date trees, nearly three miles south of the
Ravee.   Sheriffo Deen, the historian of Timour,
informs us that that conqueror crossed the
Ravee at Tolumba on his route to Delhi, so
that we now found ourselves on the track of
another invader.

The Tartar is yet remembered by his offerings
at the shrines in this neighbourhood.   Below
the town, the Ravee assumes a straight course
for twelve miles, and presents a vista of beautiful scenery, as the banks are fringed with lofty
trees, that overhang the river.   The natives
attribute this peculiarity in the Ravce to divine
influence.   The clothes of a saint, when bathing,
were washed into the stream, and the eyes of
the holy man, when turned in search of them,
straightened the river !

Visit to the
Hydaspes.   The Hydaspes was now at hand, the spot
where it unites with the Acesines was only forty-
five miles distant : here the fleet of Alexander
encountered its disasters in the rapids, and the
hordes of Timour were terrified by the noise of
the waters.   Much to the surprise of our Seik
friends, who could not comprehend the motives
of our curiosity, we set out on a galloping ex-

pedition for the scene of these memorable events, and found ourselves on the second evening on the banks of the Hydaspes. Our anxiety to behold the " fabulous Hydaspes" was heightened by the belief, that this spot, so famous in its ancient history, had never been visited by an European since the days of the Greeks. The river joins the Acesines with a murmuring noise, but the velocity of the current is inconsiderable; and vessels pass it without danger, except in July and August. There are no eddies or rocks, nor is the channel confined, but the ancient character is supported by the noise of the confluence, which is greater than that of any of the other rivers.

The boatmen at the ferry said, that, during the swell of the river, they placed themselves under the protection of a saint, whose tomb stands at the fork of the two rivers. The superstitious reliance bespeaks danger. We stood on the verge of the river, talking with the people, till the sun set in the desert westward of us; our Seik companions in the mean time, bathing in the stream; for, if deprived of the enjoyment which we derived, they had a compensation in the belief of performing ablutions at a holy spot, the junction of one river with another.

The Hy-
daspes.

This river is named Behut or Bedusta, also Jelum, by the people on its banks, and falls into the
Acesines or Chenab in the latitude of 31° 11′ 30″,
forty-five miles north of the town of Tolumba,
on the Ravee.   The banks of the Hydaspes
coincide but faintly with the description of Arrian : they do not confine the river in a narrow
channel, nor are there rocks anywhere near to
mark the spot where the Greeks retired with
their dismantled fleet.   The name of Hydaspes
is yet discoverable in the modern appellation of
Bedusta.   The Hydaspes is less rapid, and altogether a smaller stream than the Acesines, being
about 500 yards in breadth at the point of conflux ; when joined, these rivers roll on for a
short distance in a channel full a mile in breadth,
and about twelve feet deep.

Boats of
the Greeks.

The timber of which the boats of the Punjab
are constructed is chiefly floated down by the
Hydaspes from the Indian Caucasus, which most
satisfactorily explains the selection of its banks
as the site of a naval arsenal by Alexander in
preference to the other rivers, by any of which
he might have reached the Indus without a
retrograde movement.   There are but few boats
on this river : about fifty are used in the salt
trade at Pind Dadun Khan, some of which
carry 500 maunds of salt, and exceed 100 feet

in length, being built like the " Zohruq,"
rounded at both ends. They do not hoist a
sail, and often pass the conflux in safety. We
are informed that the war-ships of the Greeks
encountered the greatest difficulties in the navigation of this river, and are naturally led to
attribute the calamities of some of them to the
build, since the provision boats, which are described as of " a round form ; " and, I presume,
like the " Zohruq," escaped uninjured. That
Alexander built the greatest part of his own
fleet, is certain, for he commenced his voyage
on the Hydaspes with 800 vessels ; and when
he first reached that stream he was entirely
destitute of them ; so that he ordered the boats
by which he passed the Indus to be broken up
and brought by land across the Doab. We
hear likewise of triremes and biremes, that in no
way correspond with the present description of
boats on the Indus ; from which it is probable
that the round boats which escaped uninjured
were country vessels.

The Hydaspes and Acesines have been forded Passage of
the Hydas-
in the cold season ; but when joined they have pes.
never been passed but by boats. Timour, in
his expedition to Delhi, threw a bridge across
the conflux at Trimo ferry. Runjeet Singh
swam the Hydaspes at Sahewal with a large

body of horse ; but that enterprising chief has crossed the Indus itself above Attok in the same manner. The merchants from Khorasan travel to India at all seasons, taking the route by Dera Ismael Khan, Mankere, and the Sandy Desert, crossing at Trimo, on the road to Toolumba. The country between these last two places differs from the right bank of the Hydaspes : destitute of sand hills, it is almost as barren and desert. A sheet of hard clay, with clumps of tamarisk, *khair, lan, kejra,* and such other shrubs as are to be found in the Thurr, or Desert of India, extends from the Chenab to the Ravee. There is not a blade of grass but on the banks of the rivers. Water is procurable from wells about thirty feet deep, but is scarce, and always fetid and noxious, though rarely salt.

Cathæi of
Arrian.

The population chiefly consists of the pastoral tribe of Kattia, or Jun, who are so called from their living an erratic life, " Jun" having that signification : few of them are found at any distance from the rivers but in the rainy season. They have immense herds of buffaloes and camels, from the milk of which they derive sustenance ; hardly cultivating the soil, though some tolerable fields of tobacco, raised by irrigation, may be seen near their habitations. They are a tall and handsome race ; which may be attributed to a rule among them, prohibiting marriages before their females attain the age of twenty years: they believe that the children of an early union, so common among every other Indian tribe, are puny and unhealthy. These Kattia are a predatory and warlike race: few of them are free from scars and wounds. They extend from the banks of the Hydaspes across the deserts to Delhi, and are the aborigines of this country, in whom, I think, we recognise the Cathæi of Arrian; as he calls them " a stout people, well skilled in military " affairs." I am aware that these people have been supposed to be the Kuttrees or Rajpoots; but their country is further to the south, and did not occupy this part of India on the Greek invasion.

In the space which intervenes between the Hydaspes and Ravee, and about equidistant from either river, stand the ruins of Shorkote, near a small town of that name. They occupy a considerable space, being much larger than Sehwun, and of the same description; viz., a mound of earth, surrounded by a brick wall, and so high as to be seen for a circuit of six or eight miles. The traditions of the people state that a Hindoo Rajah of the name of Shor ruled in this city, and was attacked by a king from " Wulayut," or the countries westward, about

Ruins of Shorkote.

K 2

1300 years ago, and overcome through supernatural . means.   Shorkote is mentioned by
Timour's historian; and its locality leads me to
fix on it as the place where Alexander received
his wound, for he crossed to the west bank of
the Hydraotes in pursuit of the Malli, who had
retired to " a fortified city not far off," the
walls of which were of brick.   The story of
the King of the West is, to say the least of it,
a very probable tradition of Alexander of Macedon.   The construction of the place throws
some light on the fortresses which were captured
by Alexander.   Ancient cities on the Indus
appear to have been mounds of earth surrounded by brick walls.   At Shorcote I had
the good fortune to procure a variety of coins,
which I long believed to be Hindoo; but my
surmise regarding the antiquity of the spot
received a strong and satisfactory confirmation
through the intelligence of the able secretary
to the Asiatic Society of Bengal, — Mr. James
Prinsep.   That gentlemen discovered it to be a
Bactrian coin, resembling that of an Appolodotus,
and shaped like a Menander, — two coins of the
Bactrian monarchs, found by Colonel J. Tod,
and engraved in the transactions of the Royal
Asiatic Society.   The Greek word Bazileos
mav be read; and I had, therefore, to congratulate myself on having, in my journey to

the Hydaspes, found the first Grecian relic in the Punjab.

We retraced our steps from this famous river, and saw much of the Kattia, or Jun tribe. They were greatly surprised by our visit, and approached in crowds to see us. They live in scattered villages, and move their houses from place to place. Both men and women were tall and stout, with sun-burnt complexions. The men allow their hair to grow in loose tresses over their shoulders: the women have ear-rings of an enormous size; but the stout and sturdy dames appeared not the least incumbered from their weight.

· We returned to Toolumba on the 1st of July, jaded from the excessive heat, but highly gratified with our journey. We immediately embarked, and prosecuted our voyage. During our absence the river had risen two feet, from a fall of rain in the mountains; but it did not appear much wider. We saw more aquatic birds in the Ravee than in our whole voyage; they consisted of cranes, storks, pelicans, ducks, teal, &c. Among the inhabitants of the river itself, a creature called " holun" was the most remarkable. We saw several of them in the mouth of the Ravee, which were of a black colour, and rolled like the porpoise. The natives class this fish with the alligator, and say it has four small

Return to the Ravee.

Birds and reptiles of the Ravee.

K 3

paws, and a long snout like a pig. Its habits
do not lead it on shore, and it lives on small
fish. The large alligator is unknown here; but
the long-nosed reptile called "ghuryal" abounds.
There is said to be a singular creature, called
" thundwa," in this river, which is described as
of the turtle species, and to have a string in its
mouth, by which it can entangle a man, or even
an elephant. It is mentioned in the Shasters
as having seized the elephant of a god. I have
not seen the " thundwa," nor do I believe the
story of it.

Table
supplies.

Though we had journeyed thus far in the
country of the Seiks, we had not passed a village
inhabited by them, or seen any others of the
tribe than were attached to our suite. The
country is very poorly peopled, and without
tillage for many miles. The means taken to
supply our wants in the voyage often excited a
smile. Every villager in office had been addressed, and a list of articles which are edible
to the " Firingees " ordered to be collected.
Baskets of eggs, kept for weeks in expectation
of our arrival, were daily brought to us, sometimes to the number of 400 or 500; but they
were better adapted for the punishment of a
malefactor in the pillory than the table, and, in
a few, chickens were to be found in the shell!
Butchers were brought from Mooltan to supply

our wants : loads of saltpetre were daily sent
to cool the wine and water, and the necessaries
and luxuries of life were supplied without
bounds.

The heat now became oppressive, and gave Heat.
indication of the monsoon, according to the
natives.   In the afternoon of the 3d of July we
had the thermometer so high as 110° at 4 P. M.;
and at sunset a storm set in from the north-west,
which was really sublime.   Clouds appeared to
approach us for about half an hour, gradually
rising from the horizon, and looking more like
mountains in motion.   When it came upon us,
we found it to be one of those tornadoes that
we experienced near Mooltan, and unaccom-
panied by rain.   The wind was hot and sultry,
and bore clouds of fine dust along with it.   It
passed over in an hour, and was succeeded by
vivid flashes of lightning from the same quarter.
Six days after the phenomenon the rain set in
with great violence; and till then we had a continuance of the dust every evening.

Our Mihmandar waited on us at the village Arrival of
of Cheechawutnee with an enormous elephant, an elephant.
and said that he had been instructed by the
Maharaja to place it at our disposal, as he feared
the native houda did not suit our taste : he was
right in his conjectures, and we appreciated the
civility.   The animal was richly caparisoned,

and bore a large chair, ornamented with silver
and enamel work, lined with red velvet.   He
was accompanied by six of the Maharaja's own
Orderlies, in dresses of scarlet faced with yellow,
which had a good appearance.   The Seiks, in
all the various military costumes that they have
adopted, never lay aside the small turban of
their tribe ; which, I must say, becomes them.

It was a source of no small amusement to
watch the love of gossip among the natives of
our suite.   We had a reporter sent purposely
from the Court, who daily despatched an account
of our employment and rides : the news-writer
of Mooltan followed us from that city, and every
day transmitted a Gazette; I had also letters from
the news-writer at Lahore, giving me a *précis* of
local news, and asking for a *morceau* in return.
Our Dewan corresponded with the Chevaliers
Ventura and Allard; and I was somewhat sur-
prized to receive answers to many of my enquiries regarding the country from the former
gentleman, to whom their subject had been communicated without my knowledge.   Nothing,
however, could exceed the politeness of all the
people towards us ; and the ready and happy
manner they acceded to our wishes made us
careful to wish for any thing.   As may be supposed, there were no bounds to their flattery ;
and we were daily informed that we were the

" second Alexander," the " Sikunder sanee,"
for having achieved so dangerous a voyage as the
Indus.   The polite natives of this quarter view
with dread the barbarity and customs of Sindees
and Beloochees.

About fifty miles eastward of Toolumba, I Ruins of
passed inland for four miles to examine the Harapa.
ruins of an ancient city, called Harapa.   The
remains are extensive, and the place, which
has been built of brick, is about three miles in
circumference.   There is a ruined citadel on the
river side of the town ; but otherwise Harapa is
a perfect chaos, and has not an entire building :
the bricks have been removed to build a small
place of the old name hard by.   Tradition fixes
the fall of Harapa at the same period as Shorkote
(1300 years ago), and the people ascribe its ruin
to the vengeance of God on Harapa, its governor, who claimed certain privileges on the
marriage of every couple in his city, and in
the course of his sensualities, was guilty of in-
cest.   At a later period, Harapa became a Mahommedan town ; and there is a tomb of a Saint
of the " faithful," eighteen feet in length, the
assigned, but fabulous, stature of the deceased.
A large stone of annular form, and a huge black
slab of an oval shape, which lie near the grave,
are said to represent the ring and its gem of this
departed giant, and to have been converted from

more valuable to their present base materials.
Where such fables are believed, we must cease
to hope for even reasonable fiction. I found
some coins in these ruins, both Persian and
Hindoo, but I cannot fix its era from any of
them.

The in-
habitants.

As we ascended the Ravee, and cleared the
country of the Kattias, the population increased,
and their hamlets, though small, were numerous.
Crowds of people flocked to the banks of the
river as we approached, and evinced the most
intense curiosity to see us.   One man would
call out that he was a Syud, another that he
was a Zemindar, a third that he was a Peer, or
Saint, and a fourth, that he was a Seik ; while
the ladies themselves were not backward in expressing their anxiety for a sight of us.   On such
occasions we always moved out of our cabin, or
bungalow ; but this ready exhibition only attracted another concourse of spectators.   The
notions which they entertained of us were most
extravagant : we were believed to be under the
guardian care of two pigeons, who shaded us
from the sun and rain.   One individual asked
us seriously to impart to him the secret of con-
verting shreds of onions into gold ducats, which
he had understood we had been practising !

A tiger
hunt.

The bravery of our Seik friends had been
already exhibited to us by their attacking the

wild hog with a sword, on foot; but a nobler
specimen of their courage was displayed in the
death of a tiger. We disturbed the animal in a
thicket of tamarisk close to our boats ; and the
Mihmandar immediately invited us to see the
sport. Mr. Leckie accompanied the party ; but
our elephant was not at hand, and I did not go.
The party was entirely composed of horsemen.
The monster was speedily wounded by some one,
and several riders were unhorsed from the fright
of their steeds. The Seiks then advanced on
foot, sword in hand, to attack the tiger : he
sprang at one man most furiously ; and, as he
fixed on his left shoulder, the poor fellow bravely
struck his head by a well-directed blow : the
contest was unequal, and the man fell, horribly
lacerated. His comrades instantly ran up, and,
with cuts and wounds, the tiger soon fell. He
was a huge animal, and measured ten feet :
his thigh was as large as that of a full-grown
man. The coolness and courage of the Seiks
surpass belief; they have great encouragement
from their chiefs. To all my enquiries regarding the unfortunate man that had been
wounded, they replied, with an ostentation of
indifference, that he was but a Seik, would
be well rewarded, and had already received a
horse, and his annual pay had been increased an
hundred rupees. The skin, head, and paws of

the tiger were immediately despatched to the Maharaja, whose bounty will be further extended to the wounded.   This encouragement makes these people the bravest of the Indians.

Strange treatment.

The faculty will be surprised at the Seik mode of curing a wound received from a tiger, at variance as it is with European practices. They entertain an opinion that, if a person who has been so wounded be allowed to sleep, he will see the tiger in his dreams, and thus lose his heart, and inevitably die. They therefore furnish the patient with the strongest stimulants, and set people to prevent his falling asleep for five or six days.   By that time the wounds assume a certain appearance; and they then permit the man to rest.   In the instance which I have mentioned, I can answer for the copious use of stimulants, as we supplied the brandy.

Intelligence of a Seik.

The intelligence of the Seik Sirdar Senu Sing, our Mihmandar, had, more than once, arrested my attention.   From a perusal of translations, he had acquired some knowledge of our astronomical system, and of the astrolabe, with several other such instruments.   He expressed his doubts on some parts of the theory; and asked me to explain the continuance of the pole star in one place when the earth was said to move so many miles daily in its orbit round the sun.   Among other information that I was enabled to impart to him, I showed him the thermometer, and explained the nature of the instrument. He immediately had the whole particulars committed to writing : and, where such avidity, and so laudable a thirst for know-ledge, were displayed, I could not withhold making him a present of the instrument. This Sirdar was equally expert in the martial exer-cises of his nation : he handled the bow with grace and dexterity ; he was an excellent horse-man, and could hit a mark at full speed ; and I have seen him touch the ground with both feet at the gallop, and regain his seat. I must mention that his curiosity did not always take a scientific turn ; for his wonder had been excited by our art in preserving meat, fish, &c. A ham, which I showed him, was calculated to satisfy his doubts ; and he was only contented when he had got a complete recipe for curing it. The Seiks are very fond of hog ; and ham bids fair to be a standing dish in the Punjab. By the 11th of July we had left the country of the Kattias, and reached Futtihpoor, where the land is cultivated. Our approach to Lahore seemed to facilitate every arrangement : a de-tachment of fifty lancers had been stationed in the intervening villages, to assemble the inhabit-ants, to drag the boats the moment we ap-proached. Our own suite was now increased to about 500 people; and to a drum and fife, which had always been with us, a bugle was added. Such dissonance as was now produced was never heard " at tattoo or reveille o;" and they played at both hours. We had also a Cashmere boat sent for our accommodation, called the " purinda" or bird. It was a complete skiff, about sixty feet long, and pointed at both ends, so that half of the boat did not even touch the water. I am informed that this style of build, not unlike the gondola of Venice, is general in the lake of Cashmere. The crew were natives of that country; and they impelled their vessel by small green-painted paddles, with which they struck the water in a peculiar manner. They were very handsome and athletic men, dressed in red jackets. The boat itself had a square bungalow in the centre, with a flat roof; where we sat during the cool of the evening. She was flat-bottomed; and had her planks clamped with iron. Her motion through the water was tremulous, and by no means agreeable; but the celerity with which vessels of this kind move is acknowledged.

On the 13th of July, a deputation from the Kardar of Kot Kamalia waited on us with presents of fruit, &c., and a sum of 1100 rupees. A letter was brought, at the same time, from the Maharaja, expressive of his great satisfaction

A Cashmere boat.

Letter from Lahore.

at our approach. The epistle was flowery to a
degree seldom met with even in the Persian
language; and filled with similes about gardens,
roses, zephyrs, and fountains. Every word of a
letter which I had addressed to his Highness
was declared to be a bud of everlasting friendship; and every letter of every word was a
blown rose! But the document would require
a translation, and that, perhaps, it does not
deserve.

Neither the congratulations nor munificence
of the Maharaja could keep our people well:
they were attacked with whitlow; and there
were no less than seven or eight of them laid up
at once with that painful complaint. They
themselves ascribed it to the water; but I was
rather disposed to attribute it to a want of it and
exercise; for they had had a voyage of longer
duration than a trip from India to England.
We now entered the country of the Seiks. All
these people are either soldiers or husbandmen,
like the Romans of old. They were very
communicative; and described with much ar- Religious
dour the campaigns in which they have fought, wars of the Seiks.
and their collision with the bigoted Euzoofzyes
across the Indus. I should hardly expect to
be credited if I recorded many of the circumstances that have been communicated to me,
and the number of people that have fallen.

in these religious wars. The Euzoofzyes entertain such hatred for the infidel Seiks, that they often declare themselves " ghazee," and devote their lives to their extinction; believing that the death of one of them is more meritorious than that of any other unbeliever.   As the Seik religion arose some hundred years after Mahommed, they are not certainly supported by their prophet.   To use an expression of the Seiks, the Euzoofzyes " laugh at death."   It has been justly remarked, that we know little and care less for the history of such transactions, when we have no connection with the parties concerned.

Deputa-
tion.

In the evening of the 15th we reached Changa, about twenty-five miles from Lahore, and were received by a deputation from the Maharaja, consisting of two Seik Sirdars, and Noorodeen Fakeer, of a Mahommedan family enjoying trust and influence at Court.   The meeting, as was requested, took place on elephants, five of which bore the magnates and ourselves.   Each individual delivered a purse of money in gold and silver, and, by his Highness' desire, asked for the health of the King of England, and the period that had elapsed since we left London : for the Maharaja, it seemed, believed us to have been deputed from the royal foostool.   I replied as circumstances required.   The principal Seik, by name Sham Sing, presented a bow.

The party also produced a letter from the Maharaja, mentioning that they had been instructed to congratulate us on our arrival, and use every expression which could be pleasing to the sense; and a tissue of flattery ensued, which I confess my inability to describe.

" The seasons," said the Fakeer, " have " been changed to aid your safe arrival; and " when it should have rained, the sun shines; but " it is the sun of England.   You must now con- " sider yourselves at home, and in a garden, of " which you are the roses; that such a friend- " ship had now grown up between the British " and the Seiks, that the inhabitants of Iran and " Room would hear it proclaimed in their distant " dominions; that light had succeeded darkness " when we merged from the barbarians of Sinde, " and that its genial influence had changed the " bud into the rose."   I should exhaust a vocabulary if I recorded all his expressions.   I replied as well as I could in the same style, asking after the Maharaja's health; and assured the deputation of our satisfaction at the kindness and attention which we had received in the Seik dominions.   Before taking leave, I showed the party the horses, with which they were delighted.

The Sirdars brought an escort of lancers and Escort. Seik cavalry: the latter party were entirely dressed in yellow, and had just returned with

Sham Sing from the campaign against Syud Ahmed, who had long carried on a fanatical war in this country, and had been lately killed.

Among the party, a boy was pointed out, who had been nominated to the command held by his fallen father, — a Seik rule admirably calculated to feed the military spirit of their nation. We rode among them, evidently much to their delight, and to our own amusement. The chiefs wore many valuable jewels ; but these ornaments did not become the wrists and brows of such warriors.

Seik ladies.   We had now an opportunity of seeing the Seik ladies, who are not less peculiar in their appearance than their husbands. They knot the hair at the crown, and throw a white robe over it, which entirely envelopes the body, and gives a conical shape to the head. They pull up the hair so tight to form this knot, that the skin of the forehead is drawn with it, and the eyebrows are considerably removed from the visual organ. As may be imagined, this fashion does not improve their personal appearance, yet it is general among all classes of the females. The Seik ladies are not so handsome as their husbands ; their features are sharp and regular. They are not confined to their houses as strictly as the Mahommedan women ; for the Seiks, in matrimony as well as religion, differ widely from the followers of the Prophet.

In the evening of the 16th, we had a second visit from the deputation of yesterday, who brought us a sum of 700 rupees, with an announcement from the Maharaja that that amount had been fixed on as our daily allowance during our further stay in the Punjab. I accepted the sum, but did not consider it proper to allow of such wasteful munificence being in future continued.

At noon, on the 17th of July, we came in sight of the lofty minarets of the King's mosque at Lahore, and might have reached the ancient capital of the Moghul empire, and the termination of our protracted voyage; but the ceremonial of our *entrée* required arrangement, and we halted three or four miles from the city, at the earnest request of our conductors. As the sun set, I saw, for the first time, the massy mountains which encircle Cashmere, clothed in a mantle of white snow. I felt a nervous sensation of joy as I first gazed on the Himalaya, and almost forgot the duties I owed to our conductors, in contemplating these mighty works of nature.

CHAP. VI.

LAHORE.

ON the morning of the 18th of June we made
our public entrance into Lahore. The Maharaja's minister, Uzeez-o-Deen, and Raja Ghoolab
Sing, with the principal men of the state, met
us at a distance of three miles from the city,
escorted by a guard of cavalry and a regiment
of infantry. We were introduced to these personages by Captain Wade, the political agent of
government at Lodiana, who had been deputed
to Lahore on the occasion, and was accompanied
by Dr. A. Murray. The sight of these gentlemen, after our long absence from European society, excited the most pleasurable feelings. Our
reception was also most gratifying, heightened,
as it was, by the reflection that our undertaking had been this day brought to a safe and
successful issue. We alighted at a garden about
a mile from Lahore, the residence of M. Chevalier Allard, whose manners and address were
engaging and gentlemanlike. We here parted
with the deputation, after receiving a large sum
of money and a profusion of sweetmeats in the
name of the Maharaja.

The Chevalier then conducted us to an upper room, where we sat down to a *déjeûné à la fourchette* of the richest cookery.

Another French gentleman, M. Court, was of our party. The scene was novel to us : the walls and roof of the apartment were entirely inlaid with small pieces of mirror. Champagne usurped the place of tea and coffee. M. Allard is the Maharaja's General of cavalry ; and we had the trumpets of his division in attendance during breakfast. We continued with our worthy host during the following day, which passed in preparations for our introduction at Court, which had been fixed for the 20th instant.

About 9 A. M., when the Maharaja had reached the ancient palace that stands within the walls of Lahore, he sent a deputation of his nobles to conduct us to Court. All the Sirdars and officers who had been from time to time sent to us were previously in attendance, besides a numerous escort; and the pageant was further swelled by a detachment of Bengal sepoys which Captain Wade had brought from Lodiana. The coach, which was a handsome vehicle, headed the procession ; and in rear of the dray-horses we ourselves followed on elephants, with the officers of the Maharaja. We passed close under the walls of the city, between them and the ditch, and entered Lahore by the palace gate. The streets were lined with cavalry, artillery,

Presentation at Court.

and infantry, all of which saluted as we passed. The concourse of people was immense; they had principally seated themselves on the balconies of the houses, and preserved a most respectful silence. On entering the first court of the palace, we were received by Raja Dihan Sing, a fine soldierlike looking person, dressed in armour, by whom we were conducted to the door of the palace. While stooping to remove my shoes at the threshold, I suddenly found myself in the arms and tight embrace of a diminutive old-looking man,—the great Maharaja Runjeet Sing. He was accompanied by two of his sons, who likewise embraced Mr. Leckie and myself; when the Maharaja conducted me by the hand to the interior of his court; our reception was of the most distinguished nature, and he had advanced that distance to do us honour. We found Captain Wade and Dr. Murray in the Durbar, and all of us were seated on silver chairs, in front of his Highness. The Maharaja made various complimentary remarks; asked particularly after the health of his Majesty the King of Great Britain; and, as we had come from Bombay, enquired for Sir John Malcolm. When we had been seated a short time, I informed his Highness that I had brought along with me in safety to Lahore five horses, which his most gracious Majesty the King of England had conferred upon him, in consideration of the relations of amity and concord subsisting between the states; as also a carriage from the Right Honourable the Governor-general of India, in token of his Lordship's esteem.   I then added, that the horses were accompanied by a most friendly letter from his Majesty's minister for the affairs of India, which I held in my hand in a bag of cloth of gold, sealed with the arms of England.   On this the Maharaja and his Court, as well as ourselves, rose up, and his Highness received the letter, and touched his forehead with the seal.   The letter was then handed to his minister, Uzeez-o-Deen, who read a Persian translation of it in the presence of the whole Court.   The envoys from the surrounding states were present.   The following is a copy of the communication with which his Majesty had honoured the ruler of Lahore : —

COPY OF A LETTER FROM HIS MAJESTY'S MINIS- Letter from
TER FOR THE AFFAIRS OF INDIA TO MAHARAJA   the King.
RUNJEET SING, DELIVERED TO HIS HIGHNESS
AT LAHORE, ON THE 20TH OF JULY, 1831.

To His Highness Maharaja Runjeet Sing, Chief
of the Seik Nation, and Lord of Cashmere.

MAHARAJA,
The King, my most gracious master, has commanded me to express to your Highness

his Majesty's acknowledgments of your Highness's attention in transmitting to his Majesty, by the esteemed and excellent Lord, Earl, Amherst, the splendid manufacture of your Highness's subjects of Cashmere.

The King, knowing that your Highness is in possession of the most beautiful horses of the most celebrated breeds of Asia, has thought that it might be agreeable to your Highness to possess some horses of the most remarkable breed of Europe ; and, in the wish to gratify your Highness in this matter, has commanded me to select for your Highness some horses of the gigantic breed which is peculiar to England.

These horses, selected with care requiring much time, I now send to your Highness ; and as their great weight makes it inexpedient that they should undergo the fatigue of a long march in a hot climate, I have directed that they shall be conveyed to your Highness by the Indus, and such river of the Punjab as may be most easy of navigation.

The King has given me his most special commands to intimate to your Highness the sincere satisfaction with which his Majesty has witnessed the good understanding which has for so many years subsisted, and which may God ever preserve, between the British Government and your Highness.

His Majesty relies with confidence on the

continuance of a state of peace, so beneficial to the subjects of both powers; and his Majesty earnestly desires that your Highness may live long in health and honour, extending the blessings of beneficent government to the nations under your Highness's rule.

By the King's command.

(Signed)   ELLENBOROUGH.

As the contents of the document were unfolded, the Maharaja gave evident symptoms of his satisfaction; and when the letter was half read, he said that he would greet its arrival by a salute; and a peal of artillery from sixty guns, each firing twenty-one times, announced to the citizens of Lahore the joy of their King. His Highness then expressed his intention of viewing the presents; and we accompanied him. The sight of the horses excited his utmost surprise and wonder, their size and colour pleased him: he said they were little elephants; and, as they passed singly before him, he called out to his different Sirdars and officers, who joined in his admiration. Nothing could exceed the affability of the Maharaja: he kept up an uninterrupted conversation for the hour and a half which the interview lasted: he enquired particularly about the depth of water in the Indus, and the possibility of navigating it; and put

various questions regarding the people who occupy its banks, and their political and military
importance.   I alluded to the riches of Sinde,
which seemed to excite his utmost cupidity.
He introduced us to all the representatives of
the neighbouring states, and concluded by ask-
Runjeet   ing if we should like to see his own stud.   About
Sing's stud.
thirty horses were immediately brought, and
passed in review order before us.   They were
caparisoned in the richest and most superb manner ; and some of them were adorned with very
valuable ljewels : he named each horse, and
described his pedigree and points, as he was
brought up.   They were of all countries ; and
from their necks being tightly reined up, certainly looked well ; but they were not the stud
which one would have expected at Lahore — all
the horses appeared to be under-limbed.   The
exertion which his Highness underwent seemed
to exhaust him, and we withdrew.   Nature
has, indeed, been sparing in her gifts to this
personage ; and there must be a mighty contrast between his mind and body.   He has
lost an eye, is pitted by the small pox, and his
stature does not certainly exceed five feet three
inches.   He is entirely free from pomp and
show, yet the studied respect of his Court is
remarkable ; not an individual spoke without a
sign, though the throng was more like a bazar

than the Court of the first native Prince in these times.

The hall of audience, in which the interview Hall of audience. took place, was built entirely of marble, and is the work of the Moghul Emperors; part of the roof was gorgeously decorated by a pavilion of silken cloth studded with jewels. The Maharaja himself wore a necklace, armlets, and bracelets of emeralds, some of which were very large. His sword was mounted with the most precious stones. The nobles were likewise dressed for the occasion with jewels; and all the Court appeared in yellow, the favourite colour of the nation, which has a gaudy but striking effect.

On the following morning, the Maharaja in- Military spectacle. timated his wish for our presence at a military review in honour of passing events. We found his Highness on the parade ground, seated on a terrace, a short distance from the walls of Lahore. Five regiments of regular infantry were drawn up in line, three deep. Runjeet requested we would pass down the line and inspect them. They were dressed in white, with black cross belts, and bore muskets, the manufacture of Cashmere or Lahore : there was a mixture of Hindoostanees and Seiks in every corps. After the inspection, the brigade manœuvred under a native general officer, and went through its

evolutions with an exactness and precision fully
equal to our Indian troops : the words of command were given in French.

Convers-
ations.

During the spectacle, his Highness conversed
with great fluency, and asked our opinions on
his army and their equipments. His muskets,
he said, cost him seventeen rupees each. He
was particularly desirous to know if a column of
British troops could advance against artillery.
From these subjects he passed to that of the
revenue of Cashmere ; he had just got thirty-
six lacs of rupees, he said, from it this year,
which was an increase of six lacs. " All the
" people I send to Cashmere," continued he,
" turn out rascals (haramzada); there is too
" much pleasure and enjoyment in that coun-
" try;" and when he considered the importance of the place, he believed he must send
one of his sons, or go himself. This is the
style of Runjeet Sing's conversation ; but his
inquisitive disposition, and pertinent questions,
mark the strength of his character. He found
out, among our establishment, a native of India,
who had been in England, whom he first in-
terrogated in our presence, and afterwards sent
for privately, to know if the wealth and power
of the British nation were as great as had been
represented. We left his Highness, on observing

preparations for breakfast, — a meal which he usually takes in the open air, and in presence of his troops, and even sometimes on horseback. His passion for riding and performing distant journeys is great ; and, on such occasions, he will take his meal on the saddle rather than dismount.

We took up our abode in the garden-house of French officers. M. Chevalier Ventura, another French General, who was absent on the Indus with his legion. The building had been constructed in the European style ; but the Chevalier has added a terrace, with ninety fountains, to cool the surrounding atmosphere. Our intercourse with the French officers was on the most friendly footing ; and it continued so during our residence at Lahore. Among these gentlemen, M. Court struck me as an acute and well informed person ; he is both a geographer and an antiquarian. M. Court, as well as his brother officers, was formerly in the service of one of the Persian Princes, and travelled to India as a native, which gave him an opportunity of acquiring the best information regarding the intervening countries. He showed me the route from Kermenshah, by Herat, Candahar, Ghuzni, and Cabool, to Attok, constructed topographically with great care ; and he informed me, at

the same time, that he had been less anxious to
obtain a complete map of that part of Asia, than
to ascertain one good route, with its détours,
and the military and statistical resources of the
country. The French have much better information of these countries than ourselves ; and
M. Court, in explaining his map to me, pointed
out the best routes for infantry and cavalry.
This gentleman has likewise employed a residence of four years in the Punjab to illustrate
its geography ; he has encountered jealousy
from Runjeet Sing, but still managed to complete a broad belt of survey from Attok to the
neighbourhood of our own frontier. I doubt
not but the antiquities as well as the geography
of the Punjab will be illustrated by this intelligent gentleman ; who, to his honour be it said,
adds to a zeal in the pursuit, the strongest desire
to disseminate his own knowledge and stimulate
others. The fruit of M. Court's labours, I believe, will, ere long, be given to the public by the
Geographical Society of Paris, or some other of
the learned bodies in that capital.

City of
Lahore.

In our evening rambles at Lahore, we had
many opportunities of viewing this city. The
ancient capital extended from east to west for a
distance of five miles; and had an average
breadth of three, as may be yet traced by the

ruins. The mosques and tombs, which have been more stably built than the houses, remain in the midst of fields and cultivation as caravansaries for the traveller. The modern city occupies the western angle of the ancient capital, and is encircled by a strong wall. The houses are very lofty; and the streets, which are narrow, offensively filthy, from a gutter that passes through the centre. The bazars of Lahore do not exhibit much appearance of wealth; but the commercial influence of the Punjab is to be found at Umritsir, the modern capital. There are some public buildings within the city that deserve mention. The King's mosque is a capacious building of red sandstone, which had been brought by Aurungzebe from near Delhi. Its four lofty minarets still stand, but the temple itself has been converted into a powder magazine. There are two other mosques, with minarets, to proclaim the falling greatness of the Mahommedan empire; where the " faithful," as every where else in the Punjab, must offer up their prayers in silence.

But the stranger must cross the Ravee to behold the finest ornament of Lahore, — the " Shah Dura," or tomb of the Emperor Juhangeer, which is a monument of great beauty. It is a quadrangular building, with a minaret at

Tomb of
Juhangeer.

each corner, rising to the height of seventy feet. It is built chiefly of marble and red stone, which are alternately interlaid in all parts of the building. The sepulchre is of most chaste workmanship, with its inscriptions and ornaments arranged in beautiful mosaic; the shading of some roses and other flowers is even preserved by the different colours of the stone. Two lines of black letters, on a ground of white marble, announce the name and title of the " Conqueror of the World," Juhangeer; and about a hundred different words in Arabic and Persian, with the single signification of God, are distributed on different parts of the sepulchre. The floor of the building is also mosaic. The tomb was formerly covered by a dome; but Bahadoor Shah threw it down, that the dew and rain of heaven might fall on the tomb of his grandfather Juhangeer. It is probable that this beautiful monument will soon be washed into the river Ravce, which is capricious in its course near Lahore, and has lately overwhelmed a portion of the garden wall that environs the tomb.

Shalimar.   The next, though by no means the least, object of interest at Lahore is the garden of Shah Jehan; the Shalimar or " house of joy." It is a magnificent remnant of Moghul grandeur, about half a mile in length, with three successive terraces, each above the level of the other.   A canal, which is brought from a great distance, intersects this beautiful garden, and throws up its water in 450 fountains to cool the atmosphere. The marble couch of the Emperor yet remains; but the garden suffered much injury before Runjeet Sing obtained his present ascendancy. The Maharaja himself has removed some of the marble houses; but he has had the good taste to replace them, though it be by more ignoble stone.

As we were proceeding one morning to examine the tomb of Juhangeer, we found Runjeet Sing seated on the plain, and surrounded by his troops.   He sent one of his officers to call us; and we passed about half an hour with him. He gave us an account of the inroads of the Afghans into the Punjab, and told us that we now sat on their ground of encampment. Zuman Shah, the blind king at Lodiana, he said, had thrice sacked the city of Lahore; he also talked of his designs on India, and the vicissitudes to which kings are subject.   The Maharaja was the plainest dressed man at his Durbar; his clothes were shabby and worn.   On the evening of the 25th, his Highness gave us a private audience, in which we saw him to great advantage; for he directed his Court to withdraw. On our arrival, we found him seated on a chair, with a party of thirty or forty dancing girls, dressed uniformly in boys' clothes. They were mostly natives of Cashmere or the adjacent mountains, on whom grace and beauty had not been sparingly bestowed. Their figures and features were small; and their Don Giovanni costume of flowing silk most becoming, improved as it was by a small bow and quiver in the hand of each. The " eyes of Cash- " mere " are celebrated in the poetry of the East, of which these Dianas now furnished brilliant specimens, in gems black and bright; disfigured, however, by a kind of sparkling gold dust glued round each organ. " This," said Runjeet Sing, " is one of my regiments (pultuns), but " they tell me it is one I cannot discipline ; " a remark which amused us, and mightily pleased the fair. He pointed out two of the ladies, whom he called the " Commandants " of this arm of his service, to whom he had given villages, and an allowance of five and ten rupees a day. He shortly afterwards called for four or five elephants to take these, his *undisciplined* troops, home. Runjeet then commenced on more important subjects; and ran over, among other things, the whole history of his connexion with the British Government. It had at first, he said, excited great suspicion and discontent among the Seik Sirdars; but he himself was satisfied of its advantage from the outset. Sir John Malcolm, he continued, had first stood his friend in 1805; and Sir Charles Metcalfe had completed his happiness. Sir David Ochterlony had further cemented the bonds of friendship; and the letter which I had now delivered to him from the minister of the King of England partook more of the nature of a treaty than a common epistle, and had gratified him beyond his powers of expression. He here recurred to the riches of Sinde, expressing an earnest desire to appropriate them to his own use; and put the most pointed questions to me regarding the feelings of Government on such a subject. Runjeet is very fond of comparing the relative strength of the European nations; and, on this occasion, he asked whether France or England were the greater power. I assured him they were both great; but he had only to remember our power in India to be satisfied of the military character of Britain. " Well, then," added he, " what do you think of my French offi-" cers?" After this, he wished to know if I had heard of his campaigns across the Indus against the " Ghazees," or fanatics of the Mahommedan religion; and said that he owed all his successes to the bravery of his nation, who were very free from prejudice, would carry eight days' provision on their backs, dig a well if water were scarce, and build a fort if circumstances required it; a kind of service which he could not prevail on the natives of Hindostan to perform. " The " bravery of my troops, as you are aware, con- " quered Cashmere for me; and how do you " think," said he, " I dispose of the shawls and " productions of that country in the present glut " of trade ?   I pay my officers and troops with " them; and as I give a Chief, who may be en- " titled to a balance of 300 rupees, shawls to the " value of 500, he is well pleased, and the state " is benefited."   From the shawls of Cashmere, Runjeet passed to the praises of wine and strong drinks, of which he is immoderately fond: he beg- ged to know if I had drank the supply which he had sent me, which, as a recommendation, he as- sured us was mixed with pearls and precious gems. This, I should mention, is a common beverage in the East; a fashion which probably had its origin in the giver desiring to make the grounds as well as the contents of the bottle acceptable : pearls would form a good glass for the butler. We continued, till it was late, conversing with Runjeet in this desultory manner; when he pro- duced a splendid bow and quiver, as also a horse richly caparisoned, with a shawl cloth thrown over his body, a necklace of agate, and a heron's plume stuck on his head, saying, " This is one of " my riding horses, which I beg you will accept."

He also gave a similar present to Mr. Leckie; and while we were looking at the animals, one of the dray horses was brought forward, dressed out in cloth of gold, and bearing an elephant's saddle on his back! I could not suppress a smile at the exhibition. Runjeet then sprinkled sandal oil and rose water over us with his own hands, which completed the ceremony. As we were moving, he called us back to beg that we would attend him early next morning, and he would order a review of his horse artillery for our amusement.

We met his Highness at an appointed hour on the parade ground, with a train of fifty-one pieces of artillery which he had assembled on the occasion. They were brass 6-pounders, each drawn by six horses. The command was taken by a native officer, who put them through the movements of horse artillery, and formed line and column in every direction. The evolutions were not rapidly performed; but the celerity was considerable; and no accident in overturning or firing occurred throughout the morning. There were no waggons in the field, and the horses and equipments were inferior. The guns, however, were well cast, and the carriages in good repair: they had been made at Làhore, and had cost him 1000 rupees each. As the troops were passing in review order,

Horse ar-
tillery.

M 3

he asked for our candid opinion regarding the
display. " Every gun which you now see costs
" me 5000 rupees annually, in the pay of the
" officers and men, and in keeping up the horses.
" I have 100 pieces of field artillery, exclusive
" of battering guns and mortars, and my French
" officers tell me I have too many. I can re-
" duce their number," added he, " but it is a
" difficult matter to increase it." We had not
sat much longer with him, when he said, " You
" must breakfast with me;" an honour with which
we would have rather dispensed, but there was
no retreating. The chairs were removed, and a
velvet cushion was placed for each of us in front
of the Maharaja, and the simple fare of this potentate produced. It consisted of various kinds
of rice, with milk, sugar, and some preserved
mangoes; all of which were served up in leaves
sewed together. Runjeet selected the choicest
parts, and handed them to us himself; politeness compelled us to keep him company. The
thumb and fingers are certainly a poor substitute
for the knife and fork. When breakfast was
finished, Runjeet asked if we would accept a
dinner from him; and immediately gave instructions for its preparation, and we had it sent
to us in the evening. It was much the same
as the breakfast, and served up in a similar
manner.

Runjeet Sing is, in every respect, an extraordinary character.   I have heard his French officers observe that he has no equal from Constantinople to India ; and all of them have seen the intermediate powers.

We continued at Lahore as the guests of the Maharaja till the 16th of August, and had many opportunities of meeting him; but I do not think I can add any thing to the history of his rise, drawn up by the late Captain William Murray, Political agent at Ambala.   The most creditable trait in Runjeet's character is his humanity; he has never been known to punish a criminal with death since his accession to power; he does not hesitate to mutilate a malefactor, but usually banishes him to the hills.   Cunning and conciliation have been the two great weapons of his diplomacy.   It is too probable, that the career of this chief is nearly at an end ; his chest is contracted, his back is bent, his limbs withered, and it is not likely that he can long bear up against a nightly dose of spirits more ardent than the strongest brandy. *Character of Runjeet Sing.*

On the 16th of August we had our audience of leave with Runjeet Sing, but my fellow traveller was unable to attend from indisposition.   Captain Wade accompanied me.   He received us in an eccentric manner, under an open gateway *Audience of leave. Precious stones.*

leading to the palace. A piece of white cloth
was spread under our chairs instead of a carpet,
and there were but few of his Court in attendance. In compliance with a wish that I had
expressed, he produced the " Koh-i-noor " or
mountain of light, one of the largest diamonds
in the world, which he had extorted from Shah
Shooja, the ex-King of Cabool.   Nothing can be
imagined more superb than this stone ; it is of
the finest water, and about half the size of an
egg.   Its weight amounts to $3\frac{1}{2}$ rupees, and if
such a jewel is to be valued, I am informed it is
worth $3\frac{1}{2}$ millions of money, but this is a gross
exaggeration.   The " Koh-i-noor " is set as an
armlet, with a diamond on each side about the
size of a sparrow's egg.

Runjeet seemed anxious to display his jewels
before we left him ; and with the diamond was
brought a large ruby, weighing 14 rupees.   It
had the names of several kings engraven on it,
among which were those of Aurungzebe and
Ahmed Shah.   There was also a topaz of great
size, weighing 11 rupees, and as large as half
a billiard ball: Runjeet had purchased it for
20,000 rupees.

Presents.   His Highness, after assuring us of his satisfaction at a communication having been opened
with so remote a quarter of India as Bombay, as it

cemented his friendship with the British Government, then invested me with a string of pearls : he placed a diamond ring on one hand, and an emerald one on the other, and handed me four other jewels of emeralds and pearls. He then girt round my waist a superb sword, adorned with a knot of pearls. A horse was next brought, richly dressed out with cloth of gold, and golden ornaments on the bridle and saddle. A " khi-" lut," or robe of honour, composed of a shawl dress, and many other manufactures of Cashmere were then delivered to me, as well as presents of a similar nature for Mr. Leckie. Three of our attendants were likewise favoured by his Highness ; and in his munificence, he sent a sum of 2000 rupees for distribution among the remainder of the suite. Maharaja Runjeet then produced a letter in reply to the one which I had brought from his Majesty's minister, which he requested I would deliver. It was put up in a silken bag, and two small pearls were suspended from the strings that fastened it. It occupied a roll from four to five feet long. The following is a verbal translation of the letter ; nor will it escape observation, that, with much which is flowery and in bad taste to a European, there is some display of sterling sense and judgment. The titles which I had the honour to

receive from his Highness will not pass without
a smile.

*Copy of a Letter from Maharaja Runjeet Sing,
to the address of his Majesty's Minister for the
Affairs of India. Delivered on the audience
of Leave.*

" At a happy moment, when the balmy zephyrs
" of spring were blowing from the garden of
" friendship, and wafting to my senses the grate-
" ful perfume of its flowers, your Excellency's
" epistle, every letter of which is a new-blown
" rose on the branch of regard, and every word
" a blooming fruit on the tree of esteem, was
" delivered to me by Mr. Burnes and Mr.
" John Leckie, who were appointed to convey
" to me some horses of superior quality, of
" singular beauty, of alpine form, and ele-
" phantine stature, admirable even in their own
" country, which had been sent as a present to
" me by his Majesty the King of Great Britain,
" together with a large and elegant carriage.
" These presents, owing to the care of the above
" gentlemen, have arrived by way of the river
" Sinde in perfect safety, and have been de-
" livered to me, together with your Excellency's
" letter, which breathes the spirit of friendship,
" by that *nightingale of the garden of eloquence,*

" *that bird of the winged words of sweet dis-*
" *course, Mr. Burnes ;* and the receipt of them
" has caused a thousand emotions of pleasure and
" delight to arise in my breast.

" The information communicated in your Ex-
" cellency's letter, that his gracious Majesty
" the King of England had been much pleased
" with the shawl tent of Cashmere manufacture,
" which I had the honour to forward as a
" present, has given me the highest satisfaction ;
" but my heart is so overflowing with feelings
" of pleasure and gratitude for all these marks
" of kindness and attention on the part of his
" Majesty, that I find it impossible to give them
" vent in adequate expressions.

" By the favour of Sri Akal Poorukh Jee *,
" there are in my stables valuable and high-bred
" horses from the different districts of Hindoo-
" stan, from Turkistan, and Persia ; but none of
" them will bear comparison with those presented
" to me by the King through your Excellency ;
" for these animals, in beauty, stature, and dis-
" position, surpass the horses of every city and
" every country in the world.   On behold-
" ing their shoes, *the new moon turned pale*
" *with envy, and nearly disappeared from the*
" *sky.* Such horses, the eye of the sun has
" never before beheld in his course through the

* God.

" universe. Unable to bestow upon them in
" writing the praises that they merit, I am com-
" pelled to throw the reins on the neck of
" the steed of description, and relinquish the
" pursuit.

" Your Excellency has stated, that you were
" directed by his Majesty to communicate to me
" his earnest desire for the permanence of the
" friendship which has so long existed between
" the two states, and which has been so con-
" ducive to the comfort and happiness of the
" subjects of both. Your Excellency has further
" observed, that his Majesty hopes that I may
" live long in health and honour to rule and pro-
" teet the people of this country. I beg that
" you will assure his Majesty, that such senti-
" ments correspond entirely with those which I
" entertain, both with respect to our existing
" relations, and to the happiness and prosperity
" of his Majesty and his subjects.

" The foundations of friendship were first
" established between the two states through
" the instrumentality of Sir C. T. Metcalfe, a
" gentleman endowed with every excellence of
" character ; and after that period, in conse-
" quence of the long residence of Sir C. T. Met-
" calfe in Hindostan, the edifice of mutual amity
" and good understanding was strengthened and
" completed by his attention and exertions.

" When the Right Honourable the Earl of
" Amherst came on a visit to Hindoostan and
" the Simla Hills, the ceremonials and practices
" of reciprocal friendship were so well observed,
" that the fame of it was diffused throughout the
" whole country.

" Captain Wade, since his appointment at
" Lodiana, has ever been solicitous to omit
" nothing which was calculated to augment and
" strengthen the feeling of unanimity between
" the two powers.

" The Right Honourable Lord William Ben-
" tinck, the present Governor-general, having
" arrived some time since at Simla, I took the
" opportunity of deputing respectable and con-
" fidential officers, in company with Captain
" Wade, on a complimentary mission to his
" Lordship, with a letter enquiring after his
" health.   These officers, after having had the
" honour of an interview, were dismissed by his
" Lordship with marks of great distinction and
" honour.   On their return, they related to me
" the particulars of the gracious reception they
" had met with, the excellent qualities of his
" Lordship, and also the sentiments of friendship
" and regard which he had expressed towards
" this state.   These circumstances were very
" gratifying to my feelings.   Through the fa-
" vour of the Almighty, the present Governor-

" general is, in every respect, disposed, like the
" Earl of Amherst, to elevate and maintain the
" standard of harmony and concord subsisting
" between the two Governments ; nay, from his
" excellent qualities, I am disposed to cherish
" the hope that he will be even more attentive
" to this subject than his predecessor.   Mr.
" Burnes and Mr. John Leckie, before men-
" tioned as the bearers of the presents from his
" Majesty, have extremely gratified me with
" their friendly and agreeable conversation.   The
" mark of kindness and attention on the part of
" the British Government, evinced by the de-
" putation of these officers, has increased my
" friendship and regard for it a hundredfold ; a
" circumstance which, having become known
" throughout the country, has occasioned great
" satisfaction and pleasure to the friends and
" wellwishers of both states, and a proportionate
" regret in the hearts of their enemies.   All
" these particulars I hope you will bring to the
" notice of his gracious Majesty.

    " I am confident, that, through the favour of
" God, our friendship and attachment, which
" are evident as the noonday sun, will always
" continue firm, and be daily increased under
" the auspices of his Majesty.

    " I have dismissed Mr. Burnes and Mr.
" John Leckie with this friendly letter in

" reply to your Excellency's, and hope that
" these officers will, after their safe arrival at
" their destination, fully communicate to you
" the sentiments of regard and esteem which I
" entertain for your Excellency. In conclusion,
" I trust that, knowing me always to be anxious
" to receive the happy intelligence of the health
" and prosperity of his Majesty, and also of your
" own, your Excellency will continue to gratify
" me by the transmission of letters, both from
" the King and from yourself."

(*True translation.*)

(Signed)   E. RAVENSHAW,

Depy. Pol. Secretary.

On presenting this letter his Highness em- Departure
from La-
hore.
braced me; and begged I would convey his high
sentiments of regard to the Governor-general
of India, I then took leave of Maharaja Runjeet
Sing, and quitted his capital of Lahore the same
evening in prosecution of my journey to Simla,
on the Himalaya Mountains, where I had been
summoned to give an account of my mission to
Lord William Bentinck, then residing in that
part of India.

We reached Umritsir, the holy city of the Umritsir;
its temple.
Seiks, on the following morning, — a distance of
thirty miles. The intervening country, called
Manja, is richly cultivated. The great canal, or

" nuhr," which was cut from the Ravee by one of the Emperors of Hindostan, and brings the water for a distance of eighty miles, passes by Umritsir, and runs parallel with the Lahore road. It is very shallow, and sometimes does not exceed a width of eight feet : small boats still navigate it. We halted a day at Umritsir, to view the rites of Seik holiness ; and our curiosity was amply gratified. In the evening we were conducted by the chief men of the city to the national temple. It stands in the centre of a lake, and is a handsome building covered with burnished gold. After making the circuit of it, we entered, and made an offering to the " Grinth Sahib," or holy book, which lay open before a priest, who fanned it with the tail of a Tibet cow, to keep away impurity, and to add to its consequence. When we were seated, a Seik arose and addressed the assembled multitude ; he invoked Gooroo Govind Sing, and every one joined hands ; — he went on to say, that all which the Seiks enjoyed on earth was from the Gooroo's bounty ; and that the strangers now present had come from a great distance, and brought presents from the King of England, to cement friendship, and now appeared in this temple with an offering of 250 rupees. The money was then placed on the Grinth, and a universal shout of " Wagroojee ka futtih !" closed the oration. We were then clad in Cashmere shawls ; and, before departing, I begged the orator to declare our desire for a continuance of friendship with the Seik nation, which brought a second shout of " Wagroojee ka futtih ! " " Khal- " sajee ka futtih ! "   May the Seik religion prosper !   From the great temple, we were taken to the Acali boonga, or house of the Immortals, and made a similar offering.   We were not allowed to enter this spot, for the Acalis or Nihungs are a wrong-headed set of fanatics, not to be trusted.   In reply to the offering, the priest sent us some sugar.   The Acalis are clothed in turbans of blue cloth, which run into a peak : on this they carry several round pieces of iron, weapons of defence, which are used like the quoit.   These bigots are constantly molesting the community by abuse and insult, or even vio-lence ; a week does not pass in the Punjab with-out a life being lost : but Runjeet suppresses their excesses with a firm and determined hand, though they form a portion of the establishment in a religion of which he himself is a strict observer.   He has attached some of the greatest offenders to his battalions, and banished others. Our conductor, Desa Sing Majeetia, father of our Mihmandar, a Seik of the confederacy, and a kind old man, was very solicitous about our safety, and led us by the hand, which he

grasped firmly, through the assembled crowd.
From the temple we made the tour of Umritsir,
which is a larger city than Lahore.   This place
is the great emporium of commerce between
India and Cabool.   The traders are chiefly
Hindoos, before whose door one wonders at
the utility of large blocks of red rock salt being
placed, till informed that they are for the use
of the sacred city cows, who lick and relish
them.   In our way home we visited the Ram-
bagh, the favourite residence of the Maharaja
when at Umritsir.   His passion for military works
also shows itself here, and he has surrounded a
pleasure garden by a massy mound of mud, which
he is now strengthening by a ditch.

Beas or
Hyphasis.

At a distance of twenty-three miles from Umritsir, we came on the Beas or Hyphasis of
Alexander.   The country is varied by trees, but
not rich, and the soil is gravelly.   On the 21st
we crossed the Beas, at Julalabad, where it was
swollen to a mile in width from rain.   Its current
exceeded in rapidity five miles an hour; we
were nearly two hours in crossing, and landed
about two miles below the point from which we
started.   The greatest depth was eighteen feet.
The boats used in this river are mere rafts with a
prow; they bend frightfully, and are very unsafe;
yet elephants, horses, cattle, and guns are conveyed across on them.   We passed in safety, but

an accident, which might have proved serious, befel us in one of the small channels of this river.   It was about thirty yards wide, and eighteen feet deep, and we attempted the passage on an elephant.   No sooner had the animal got out of his depth, than he rolled over, and precipitated Mr. Leckie and myself head-foremost into the water, wheeling round at the same time to gain the bank he had quitted ; Dr. Murray alone retained his seat : but we were not long in regaining terra firma, without any other inconvenience than a ducking.   We did not again attempt the passage on an elephant, but crossed on inflated buffalo skins supporting a framework.

Our halting place was at Kuppertulla, ten miles from the Beas, the estate of Futtih Sing Aloowala, one of the Seik chiefs, who was present with Lord Lake's army in 1805, when encamped in this vicinity.   He is yet a young man.   He received us with great respect and kindness, and sent his two sons to meet us as we approached. He came himself in the evening on a visit, and on the following day, when we returned it, he gave us a grand fête in his garden house, which was illuminated.   The display of fireworks was varied, and we viewed it with advantage from a terrace.   Futtih Sing is the person whom Sir John Malcolm describes in his " Sketch of the

Kuppertulla. Seik Chief.

Fête.

Seiks " as requiring his dram, and years have
not diminished his taste for liquor.   Immediately
we were seated he produced his bottle, drank
freely himself, and pressed it much upon us;
it was too potent for an Englishman, but he
assured us, that whatever quantity we drank,
it would never occasion thirst.   We filled a
bumper to the health of the Sirdar and his
family, and were about to withdraw, when he
produced most expensive presents, which could
not in any way be refused; he gave me a string
of pearls, and some other jewels, with a sword,
a horse, and several shawls.   Futtih Sing is an
uncouth looking person, but he has the manners
of a soldier.   His income amounts to about four
lacs of rupees annually, and he lives up to it,
having a strong passion for house building.   Besides a board of works in two of his gardens, he
was now constructing a house in the English
style, but has sensibly added a suite of rooms
under ground for the hot season.   When we left
Futtih Sing, he urgently requested that we would
deliver his sincere sentiments of regard to his old
friend Sir John Malcolm.

Doab of
the Sutlege.

We made three marches from Kuppertulla to
Fulour, on the banks of the Sutlege, a distance of
thirty-six miles, passing the towns of Jullinder
and Jumsheer.   The former place is large, and
was at one time inhabited by Afghans.   It is

surrounded by a brick wall, and the streets are paved with the same material. Jullinder gives its name to the " Doab," or country between the Beas and Sutlege, while the other Doabs are named by compound words, formed by contracting the names of the rivers. Between the Chenab and Behut, we have the Chenut; between the Ravee and Chenab, the Reechna; and between the Beas and Ravee, the Barree. From Jullinder to the banks of the Sutlege, the country is highly cultivated and well peopled. All the villages are surrounded by mud walls, and many of them have ditches to bespeak the once unsettled state of this land. The houses are constructed of wood, with flat roofs covered over by mud, and have a hovel-like appearance.

The town of Fulour, on the banks of the Sut-lege, is the frontier post of the Lahore Chief, and here we left our escort and Seik friends, who had accompanied us from Mooltan. We distributed cloths to the commissioned and non-commissioned officers, and a sum of 1000 rupees among the men, which gratified all parties. The Maharaja continued his munificence to the last, and, before crossing the Sutlege, he had sent us no less than 24,000 rupees in cash, though we had declined to receive the sum of 700 rupees, which had been fixed for our daily allowance after reaching Lahore.

N 3

Before I finally quit the Punjab, I must
not omit a few particulars regarding its antiquities, which must ever attract attention. It
seems certain, that Alexander the Great visited
Lahore, and to this day the remains of a city
answering to Singala, with a lake in the vicinity,
are to be seen S. E. of the capital. The tope
of Manikyala, first described by Mr. Elphinstone, and lately examined by M. Ventura, has
excited considerable interest in the East. The
French gentlemen were of opinion, that these remains are of an older date than the expedition
of Alexander, for the coins have a figure not
unlike Neptune's trident, which is to be seen on
the stones at Persepolis. In my progress through
the Punjab, I was not successful in procuring
a coin of Alexander, nor any other than the
Bactrian one which I have described; nor have
any of the French gentlemen, with all their opportunities, been so fortunate. I am happy, however, in being able to state the existence of two
other buildings like the " Tope" of Manikyala,
which have been lately discovered among the
mountains, westward of the Indus, in the country
of the Eusoofzyes. The opening of these may
throw light on the interesting subject of Punjab
antiquities. * By the natives of this country,
the most ancient place is considered to be Seeal-

* My journey to Bokhara made me better acquainted with
these topes, as has already appeared in Vol. I.

cote, which lies upwards of forty miles north of
Lahore.   It is said to be mentioned in the Persian Sikunder Namu.

At noon, on the 26th of August, we left Cross t ie
Sutlegd.
Fulour and marched to Lodiana, crossing the
river Sutlege, or Hesudrus of antiquity.   It is
yet called Shittoodur or the Hundred Rivers by
the natives, from the number of channels in
which it divides itself.   Where we passed, its
breadth did not exceed 700 yards, though it had
been swollen two days before our arrival.   The
greatest depth of soundings was eighteen feet,
but the average was twelve.   It is a less rapid
river than the Beas.   The waters of the Sutlege
are colder than those of any of the Punjab
rivers, probably from its great length of course,
and running so far among snowy mountains.
This river is variable in its channel, and often
deserts one bank for the other.   The country
between it and the British Cantonment of Lodiana, is intersected by nullas, one of which,
that runs past the camp, formed the bed of the
Sutlege fifty years ago.   This river is generally
fordable after November.   Lord Lake's army
crossed it in 1805, two miles above Lodiana;
but the fords vary, and the watermen look
for them annually before people attempt to
cross, as there are many quicksands.   When the
Beas falls into the Sutlege, the united stream,

N 4

called Garra, is no longer fordable.   The boats
of the Sutlege are of the same description as
those on the Beas : there are seventeen of them
at the Fulour ferry.   The country between the
Sutlege and Lodiana is very low, which I observed
to be a characteristic of the left bank of this
river, till it meets the mountains.   One would
expect to find this depressed tract of ground
alluvial, but it is sandy.

Exiled   At Lodiana, we met two individuals, who
Kings of
Cabool.   have exercised an influence on the Eastern
world, now pensioners of the British, the ex-
Kings of Cabool, Shah Zuman, and Shah Shooja-
ool-Moolk.   The ceremonial of our introduction
to Shah Shooja corresponded nearly with that
described by Mr. Elphinstone ; for, in his exile,
this fallen monarch has not relinquished the
forms of royalty.   The officers of his court still
appear in the same fanciful caps, and on a signal
given in Turkish, (*ghachan*, begone,) the guards
run out of the presence, making a noise with
their high-heeled boots.   The person of the Shah
himself has been so correctly described, that I
have little to say on that subject.   In his misfortunes, he retains the same dignity and pre-
possessing demeanour as when king.   We found
him seated on a chair in a shady part of his
garden, and stood during the interview.   He
has become somewhat corpulent, and his ex-

pression is melancholy ; but he talked much, and
with great affability.   He made many enquiries
regarding Sinde, and the countries on the Indus,
and said, that " he had rebuked the Ameers for
" their suspicion and jealousy of our intentions in
" coming to Lahore.   Had I but my kingdom,"
continued he, " how glad should I be to see an
" Englishman at Cabool, and to open the road
" between Europe and India."   The Shah then
touched upon his own affairs, and spoke with
ardent expectations of being soon able to retrieve
his fortunes.   In reply to one of his questions,
I informed him that he had many well-wishers in
Sinde   " Ah !" said he, " these sort of people
" are as bad as enemies ; they profess strong
" friendship and allegiance, but they render me
" no assistance.   They forget that I have a
" claim on them for two crores of rupees, the
" arrears of tribute."

Shah Shooja was plainly dressed in a tunic of Reflec-
tions.
pink gauze, with a green velvet cap, something
like a coronet, from which a few emeralds were
suspended.   There is much room for reflection
on the vicissitudes of human life while visiting
such a person.   From what I learn, I do not
believe the Shah possesses sufficient energy to
seat himself on the throne of Cabool ; and that
if he did regain it, he has not the tact to discharge the duties of so difficult a situation.

The brother of Shah Shooja, Shah Zuman, is
an object of great compassion, from his age, appearance, and want of sight. We also visited
him, and found him seated in a hall with but one
attendant, who announced our being present,
when the Shah looked up and bade us " Wel-
" come." He is stone blind, and cannot dis-
tinguish day from night; he was as talkative as
his brother, and lamented that he could not pass
the remainder of his days in his native land,
where the heat was less oppressive.

Shah Zuman has lately sunk into a zealot: he
passes the greater part of his time in listening
to the Koran and its commentaries. Poor man,
he is fortunate in deriving consolation from
any source. When taking leave, Shah Zuman
begged I would visit him before quitting Lodiana, as he was pleased at meeting a stranger.
I did not fail to comply with his wishes, and saw
him alone. I had thought that his age and misfortunes made him indifferent to all objects of
political interest; but he asked me, in a most
piteous manner, if I could not intercede with
the Governor-general in behalf of his brother,
and rescue him from his present exile. I assured him of the sympathy of our government,
and said, that his brother should look to Sinde
and the other provinces of the Dooranee empire for support; but he shook his head, and

said the case was hopeless.   After a short
silence, the Shah told me that he had inflam-
mation in the eyes, and begged I would look at
them.   He has suffered from this ever since his
brother caused him to be blinded with a lancet.
As he has advanced in years, the organ seems to
have undergone a great change, and the black
part of the eye has almost disappeared.   It is
impossible to look upon Shah Zuman without
feelings of the purest pity; and, while in his
presence, it is difficult to believe we behold that
king, whose name, in the end of last century,
shook Central Asia, and carried dread and terror
along with it throughout our Indian possessions.
Infirm, blind, and exiled, he now lives on the
bounty of the British Government.

After a ten days' recreation at Lodiana, where Journey to
we mingled once more with our countrymen, we the Himalaya.
prosecuted our journey to Simla, on the Himalaya
mountains, a distance of about 100 miles, which
we reached in the course of a few days.   We here
beheld a scene of natural sublimity and beauty,
that far surpassed the glittering court which we
had lately left: — but my narrative must here
terminate.   At Simla we had the honour of
meeting the Right Honourable Lord William
Bentinck, the Governor-general of India; and
his Lordship evinced his satisfaction at the result
of our mission, by entering at once into negoti-

ations for laying open the navigation of the Indus
to the commerce of Britain, a measure of enlightened policy, considered both commercially
and politically.   I had the honour of receiving
the following acknowledgment of my endeavours
to elucidate the geography of that river, and the
condition of the princes and people who occupy
its banks.

Conclu-
sion.   " Delhi, 6 December, 1831.
        " Political Department.

            " TO LIEUT. ALEXANDER BURNES,
                        &c. &c. &c.
        " Sir,
        " I am directed by the Right Honourable the
    " Governor-general to acknowledge the receipt
    " of your several letters, forwarding a memoir
    " on the Indus, and a narrative of your journey
    " to Lahore.
        " 2. The first copy of your map of the Indus
    " has also just reached his Lordship, which com-
    " pletes the information collected during your
    " mission to Lahore, in charge of the presents
    " from the late King of England to Maharaja
    " Runjeet Sing.
        " 3. The Governor-general, having perused
    " and attentively considered all these documents,
    " desires me to convey to you his high appro-
    " bation of the manner in which you have ac-

" quitted yourself of the important duty assigned
" to you, and his acknowledgments for the full
" and satisfactory details furnished on all the
" points in which it was the desire of government
" to obtain information.

" 4. Your intercourse with the chiefs of Sinde,
" and the other Sirdars and persons with whom
" you were brought into contact in the course
" of the voyage up the Indus, appears to the
" Governor-general to have been conducted with
" extreme prudence and discretion, so as to
" have left a favourable impression on all classes,
" and to have advanced every possible object,
" immediate, as connected with your mission,
" as well as prospective; for, while your com-
" munications with them were calculated to
" elicit full information as to their hopes and
" wishes, you most judiciously avoided the as-
" sumption of any political character that might
" lead to the encouragement of false and ex-
" travagant expectations, or involve you in any
" of the passing intrigues. The whole of your
" conduct and correspondence with the chiefs
" of the countries you passed through in your
" journey, has the Governor-general's entire
" and unqualified approbation.

" 5. In like manner, his Lordship considers
" you to be entitled to commendation for the
" extent of geographical and general information

" collected in the voyage, and for the caution
" used in procuring it, no less than for the per-
" spicuous and complete form in which the re-
" sults have been submitted for record and con-
" sideration.   The map prepared by you forms
" an addition to the geography of India of the
" first utility and importance, and cannot fail to
" procure for your labours a high place in this
" department of science.

" 6. The result of your voyage in the dif-
" ferent reports, memoirs, and maps above ac-
" knowledged, will be brought without delay to
" the notice of the authorities in England, under
" whose orders the mission was, as you are aware,
" undertaken.   His Lordship doubts not that
" they will unite with him in commending the
" zeal, diligence, and intelligence displayed by
" you in the execution of this service, and will
" express their satisfaction at the manner in which
" their views have been accomplished, and the
" objects contemplated in the mission to Lahore
" fully and completely attained.

" I have the honour to be, &c.

(Signed)   " H. T. Prinsep,

" Secretary to the Governor-general."

A

MEMOIR ON THE INDUS,

AND

ITS TRIBUTARY RIVERS

IN

THE PUNJAB.

NOTICE

REGARDING

THE MAP OF THE INDUS.

A NEW map of the Indus and Punjab Rivers from the sea to Lahore seems to require some notice explanatory of its construction, and I have to offer the following observations on that subject : —

The River Indus, from the southern direction in which it flows in its progress to the ocean, presents few difficulties to the surveyor, since an observation of latitude serves to fix the daily progress in the voyage, and its comparatively straight course admits of easy delineation. The map rests on a series of observations by the stars. I should have preferred altitudes of the sun; but, with a people so suspicious as we encountered, it was impossible to use an instrument in daylight, and I should have required to halt the fleet twice to procure equal altitudes, since the sun was south of the equator during the voyage. Many of the large places, such as Tatta, Sehwun, Ooch, Mooltan, &c., where we necessarily halted, have been laid down from a mean of eight or ten stellar observations.

The longitude and general delineations in the curvature of the river rest on a minute protraction of its turnings, observed with care every half hour, and some-

times oftener, with the approved compass by Schmal-
calder. The attention given to this important portion
of the undertaking may be imagined, when I state
that my field books exhibit, on an average, twenty
bearings each day from sunrise to sunset. I was
early enabled to rate the progress of the boats through
the water, by timing them on a measured line along the
bank, and apportioned the distance to the hours and
minutes accordingly. We could advance, I found, by
tracking, or being pulled by men, at one mile and a half
an hour; by gentle and favourable breezes at two miles,
and by violent winds at three miles an hour; while any
great excess or deficiency was pointed out by the latitude
of the halting place.

The base on which the work rests, is the towns of
Mandivee and Curachee: the one a seaport in Cutch,
and the point from which the mission started; the other
a harbour in sight of the western mouth of the Indus,
which we saw before entering the river. Mandivee
stands in the latitude of $22° 50'$, and Curachee in $24° 56'$
north; while their longitudes are respectively in $69° 34'$,
and $67° 19'$ east, as fixed, in 1809, from the chronometers
of the Sinde mission by Captain Maxfield.

Assuming these points as correct, the line of coast
intermediate to them has been laid down from my own
surveys in Cutch; while that of Sinde rests on observations of the sun's altitude at noon and the boats' daily
progress, determined by heaving the log hourly. We
sailed only during the day, and at all times along shore,
often in a small boat, and were attended by six or eight
pilots, who had passed their lives in the navigation of
these parts.

The great difference in the topography of the mouths
of the Indus, from what is shown in all other maps,

will no doubt arrest attention; but it is to be re-marked, that I call in question no former survey, since the river has been hitherto laid down in this part of its course from *native information;* and I can bear testimony to the correctness of such portions of the Indus as were actually traversed by the mission of 1809. From the jealousy of the Government of Sinde, we had to pass up and down the coast no less than five times, which gave ample opportunities to observe it; and I have a strong fact to adduce in verification of the chart as it now exists. On the third voyage we ran down so low as the latitude of 20° 30′ N., and were out of sight of land for six days. At noon, on the last day (17th of March), while standing on a due northerly course, I found our latitude to be 23° 50′, or a few miles below that mouth of the river which I had resolved to enter. I immediately desired the pilots to steer a north-easterly course for the land. We closed with it at sunset, a couple of miles above Hujamree, the very mouth of the Indus I wished to make. At daylight we had had no soundings in fifty fathoms, at seven A.M. we had bottom at forty-two fathoms, and at eleven in thirty-four. By two in the afternoon we were in twenty-one fathoms, and at dusk anchored in twelve feet of water, off Reechel, having sighted the land at half past four.

In delineating the Delta of the Indus below Tatta, I have not only had the advantage of sailing by a branch to that city, but approached it on land by one route, and returned by another. I also ascended the Pittee, or western mouth of the Indus, for thirty miles. The opposition experienced from the Sinde Government gave rise to these variations of route: they long tried to im-pede our progress; but the result of their vacillation

has happily added to our knowledge of their country, in
a degree which the most sanguine could not have anticipated.   In addition to my own track, I have added
that of the Sinde mission, from Curachee to Hydrabad,
and thence to Lueput in Cutch.   My own surveys in
Cutch, which extend high up the Koree, or eastern
branch of the Indus, together with every information,
compel me to place the Goonee or Phurraun River
(which is the name for the Koree above Ali bunder),
in a more westerly longitude than in the maps hitherto
published.   Sindree and Ali bunder lie north of Nurra
in Cutch, so that the river cannot extend so far into the
desert as has been represented.

From Hydrabad upwards, and, I may add, in all parts
of the map, the different towns rest on the latitudes as determined by the sextant.   Most of them are in a higher
parallel than in the maps, but it was satisfactory to find,
on reaching Ooch, that the longitude of that place, as
taken from my own protraction, coincides pretty well with
that which has been assigned to it by Mr. Elphinstone's
surveyors, who must have fixed it from Bhawulpoor.
This was not the case with Bukkur ; but, as the latitude
of that place was twenty-two minutes below the true
parallel, I have reason to be satisfied with the result
above stated.   I likewise found that the Indus receives
the Punjab rivers at Mittun, in the latitude of 28° 55′,
instead of 28° 20′ north, as given in the map of the
Cabool mission : but no one can examine that document
without acknowledging the unwearied zeal of its con-
structor, and wondering that he erred so little when he
visited few of the places, and had his information from
such sources.

The Punjab rivers have been laid down on the same
principle as the Indus.   The Chenab (Acesines), which

has been erroneously styled Punjnud, after it has gathered the other rivers, is very direct in its course; but the Ravce (Hydräotes), on the other hand, is most tortuous, and appears in its present shape after incredible labour for twenty days spent in its navigation. The latitude of its junction with the Chenab, and that of the city of Lahore, which stands in 31° 35′ 30″ north, and in 70° 20′ east longitude, have materially assisted me in the task. I have also placed the confluence of the Jelum, or Behut (Hydaspes), with the Chenab, twelve miles above the latitude in which it has hitherto stood. The survey eastward terminates on the left bank of the Sutledge (Hesudrus), with the British cantonment of Lodiana, which I find stands in 30° 55′ 30″ north latitude. I have used the longitude of the latest and best map, and placed it in 75° 54′ east.

With the Indus and Punjab Rivers, I have embodied a survey of the Jaysulmeer country, which was finished in the year 1830, when I visited Southern Rajpootana with Lieut. James Holland. The province of Cutch, with the configuration of the Run, rests on my own surveys made in the years 1825, 1826, 1827, and 1828.*

* Instead of giving separate maps of the Indus and Central Asia, I have now combined the whole of the geographical matter in one map, as has already been explained.

MEMOIR OF THE INDUS.

CHAPTER I.

A GENERAL VIEW OF THE INDUS.

THERE is an uninterrupted navigation from the Inland navigation to Lahore.
sea to Lahore. The distance, by the course of the river, amounts to about a thousand British miles : the following papers detail its practicability with minuteness, but not more so, I trust, than the great importance of the subject deserves. They also describe the state of the countries and people.

The Indus, when joined by the Punjab rivers, Depth of water.
never shallows, in the dry season, to less than fifteen feet, and seldom preserves so great a breadth as half a mile. The Chenab, or Acesines, has a medium depth of twelve feet, and the Ravee; or Hydräotes, is about half the size of that river. These are the minima of soundings on the voyage ; but the usual depth of the three rivers cannot be rated at less than four, three, and two fathoms. The soundings of each day's voyage are shown by the figures on the map.*

* These have been necessarily omitted in the reduced map.

Boats.

This extensive inland navigation, open as I have stated it to be, can *only* be considered traversable to the boats of the country, which are flat bottomed, and do not draw more than four feet of water, when heavily laden. The largest of these carry about seventy-five tons English : science and capital might improve the build of these vessels; but in extending our commerce, or in setting on foot a flotilla, the present model would ever be found most convenient. Vessels of a sharp build are liable to upset when they run aground on the sand-banks. Steamboats could ply, if constructed after the manner of the country, but no vessel with a keel could be safely navigated.

Period of a voyage to Lahore.

The voyage from the sea to Lahore occupied exactly sixty days; but the season was most favourable, as the south-westerly winds had set in, while the stronger inundations of the periodical swell had not commenced. We reached Mooltan on the fortieth day, and the remaining time was expended in navigating the Ravee, which is a most crooked river. The boats sailed from sunrise to sunset, and, when the wind was unfavourable, were dragged by ropes through the water.

Steam most available for the Indus.

There are no rocks or rapids to obstruct the ascent, and the current does not exceed two miles and a half an hour. Our daily progress

sometimes averaged twenty miles, by the course
of the river; for a vessel can be haled against the
current at the rate of one mile and a half an
hour.   With light breezes we advanced two
miles an hour, and in strong gales we could
stem the river at the rate of three miles. Steam
would obviate the inconveniences of this slow
and tedious navigation ; and I do not doubt but
Mooltan might be reached in ten, instead of
forty days.   From that city a commercial communication could best be opened with the
neighbouring countries.

A boat may drop down from Lahore to the Return
sea in fifteen days, as follows: — to Mooltan in voyage.
six, to Bukkur in four, to Hydrabad in three,
and to the sea-ports in two. This is, of course,
the very quickest period of descent ; and I may
add, that it has never been of late tried, for
there is no trade between Sinde and the Punjab
by water.

There are political obstacles to using the Political
Indus as a channel of commerce. The people trading on
and princes are ignorant and barbarous : the
former plunder the trader, and the latter over-
tax the merchant, so that goods are sent by land,
and by circuitous routes : this absence of trade
arises from no physical obstacles, and is to be
chiefly traced to the erroneous policy of the
Sinde government.   The are about 700 boats

between the sea and Lahore ; and this number
suffices for ferrying, and all other purposes.

Military
importance
of the
Indus.

The defence of the Indus, the grand boundary
of British India on the West, is nowise affected
by these trifling impediments, and we can command its navigation without obstruction from
both Cutch and the Sutledge. The military
advantages of the Indus are great : it is navigable for a fleet from Attok to the sea. The
insulated fortress of Bukkur is a most important position.

CHAP. II.

A COMPARISON OF THE INDUS AND GANGES.

I HAVE recorded with care and attention the information which I have collected regarding the Indus and its tributaries; yet the magnitude of that river must be decided by a comparison with the other great rivers of the world. An European, in the East, may appropriately narrow his field, and confine such a comparison to its great twin river, the Ganges, which, with the Indus, folds, as it were, in the embrace our mighty empire of British India. At this time, too, in a publication which has appeared at Calcutta, by Mr. G. A. Prinsep, regarding the introduction of steam navigation into India, we have late and valuable matter, both of an interesting and scientific nature, regarding the peculiarities of the Ganges; which, with the previous papers of Rennell and Colebrooke, afford very precise information regarding that river. I have ventured, therefore, however incompetent, to lay down the observations that have occurred to me regarding the

Indus, that the requisite comparison might be instituted.

The Ganges and Indus, rising in the same mountains, traverse, with an unequal length of course, the same latitudes : both rivers, though nearly excluded from the tropics, are yet subject to be annually flooded at a stated and the same period. The quantity of water, therefore, which these rivers respectively discharge, will determine their relative size ; and we shall afterwards consider the slope or fall by which they descend to the ocean. Sicriguli, on the Ganges, and Tatta, on the Indus, seem to be the preferable sites for drawing a comparison, since both places are situated at a point *before* the rivers have subdivided to form a delta, and *after* they have each received the whole of their tributary streams. The Indus certainly throws off two branches above 'Tatta, the Fulailee and Pinyaree ; but they are only considerable rivers in the rainy season.

It appears, then, from Mr. G. A. Prinsep's essay, that in the month of April the Ganges discharges, at Sicriguli, about 21,500 cubic feet of water in a second. The average breadth of the river at that place is given at 5000 feet, which is also the velocity in a second of time ; while its average depth does not exceed three feet. That in this result we form a pretty correct estimate of the magnitude of the Ganges, is

further proved by the state of the river at Be-
nares in the same month (April), where, though
contracted to a breadth of 1400 feet, the depth
exceeds thirty-four feet, and the discharge
amounts to 20,000 cubic feet per second, which
differs in but a trifling degree from that at Sicriguli.

In the middle of April, I found the Indus at
Tatta to have a breadth of 670 yards, and to be
running with a velocity of two miles and a half
an hour. It happens that the banks are steep
on both sides of the river in this part of its
course; so that the soundings, which amount to
fifteen feet, are regular from shore to shore, if
we except a few yards on either side, where the
water is still. This data would give a discharge
of 110,500 cubic feet per second; but by Buat's
equations for the diminished velocity of the
stream near the bed, compared with that of the
surface, it would be decreased to 93,465 cubic
feet. Some further deduction should be made
for the diminished depth towards the shores;
and 80,000 cubic feet per second may be taken
as a fair rate of discharge of the Indus in the
month of April.* It is a source of regret to me

* In this part of my subject, I have to express my fullest
acknowledgments to Mr. James Prinsep, Secretary to the
Asiatic Society of Calcutta, who has kindly afforded me his
valuable assistance.

that I am unable to extend my observations to
the river during the rainy season ; but I had not
an opportunity of seeing it at that period, and
do not desire to place opinion in opposition to
fact.   I may mention, however, that at Sehwun,
where the Indus is 500 yards wide, and thirty-
six feet deep, and sweeping with great velocity
the base of a rocky buttress that juts in upon
the stream, there is a mark on the precipice
which indicates a rise of twelve feet during the
inundation. This gives a depth of eight fathoms
to this part of the Indus in the rainy season.
If I could add the increase of width on as
sound data as I have given the perpendicular
rise or depth of water, we should be able to
determine the ratio between its discharge at the
opposite seasons ; but I have only the vague
testimony of the natives to guide me, and dis-
miss the subject.

From what has been above stated, it will be
seen that the Indus, in discharging the enormous volume. of 80,000 cubic feet of water in a
second, exceeds by *four times* the size of the
Ganges in the dry season, and nearly equals the
great American river, the Mississippi.   The
much greater length of course in the Indus and
its tributaries, among towering and snowy mountains near its source, that must always contribute
vast quantities of water, might have prepared us

for the result; and it is not extraordinary, when
we reflect on the wide area embraced by some
of these minor rivers, and the lofty and elevated
position from which they take their rise: the
Sutledge, in particular, flows from the sacred
Lake of Mansurour, in Tibet, 17,000 feet above
the sea.   The Indus traverses, too, a comparatively barren and deserted country, thinly
peopled and poorly cultivated; while the Ganges
expends its waters in irrigation, and blesses the
inhabitants of its banks with rich and exuberant
crops.   The Indus, even in the season of inundation, is confined to its bed by steeper and more
consistent banks than the other river; and, as I
have stated, seldom exceeds half a mile in width:
the Ganges, on the other hand, is described as an
inland sea in some parts of its course; so that,
at times, the one bank is scarcely visible from
the other, — a circumstance which must greatly
increase the evaporation.   The arid and sandy
nature of the countries that border the Indus
soon swallow up the overflowing waters, and
make the river more speedily retire to its bed.
Moreover, the Ganges and its subsidiary rivers
derive their supply from the southern face of
the great Himalaya; while the Indus receives
the torrents of either side of that massy chain,
and is further swollen by the showers of Cabool
and the rains and snow of Chinese Tartary.   Its

waters are augmented long before the rainy season has arrived ; and, when we look at the distant source of the river, to what cause can we
attribute this early inundation but to melting
snow and ice ?

The slope on which the Indus descends to
the ocean would appear to be gentle, like that
of most great rivers. The average rate of its
current does not exceed two miles and a half an
hour; while the whole of the Punjab rivers,
which we navigated on the voyage at Lahore,
were found to be one full mile in excess of the
Indus. We readily account for this increased
velocity by their proximity to the mountains ;
and it will serve as a guide in estimating the
fall of the river. The city of Lahore stands at
a distance of about 1000 British miles from the
sea, by the course of the river ; and I am indebted to Dr. J. G. Gerard, for a series of ba-
rometrical observations, made some years ago
at Umritsir, a city about thirty miles eastward
of Lahore.

The mean of eighteen of these observ-
    ations gives us the height of the
    barometer at   -   -   -   - 28,861·3
The corresponding observations at Cal-
    cutta give   -   -   -   - 29,711·5

       Making a difference of   -   850·2

I am informed that the height of the instrument registered in Calcutta may be twenty-five feet above the level of the sea ; and as the city of Umritsir is about the same level as Lahore (since both stand on the plains of the Punjab), it must have an elevation of about 900 feet from the sea.

Having now stated the sum of our knowledge regarding this subject, it remains to be considered in what, and how great a proportion, the slope is to be distributed among the rivers from Lahore downwards. By a comparison with the Ganges in Rennell's work, and the late treatise to which I have alluded, and assisted by the same scientific gentleman, to whom I have before expressed my obligations, we cannot give a greater fall downwards from Mittun, where the Indus receives the Punjab rivers, than six, or perhaps five, inches per mile : nor can we allow more than one fourth of 900 feet as the height of that place above the level of the sea ; for the river has not increased here in velocity of current, though we have neared the mountains. Mittun is half way to Lahore, about 500 miles from the sea, and nearly 220 feet above it. The remaining 680 feet we may fairly apportion to the Punjab rivers, from their greater rapidity of course; which would give them a fall of twelve inches per mile.

VOL. III.   P

In these facts, we have additional proof of
the greater bulk of the Indus, as compared with
the Ganges; when at the lowest, it retains a
velocity of two and a half miles, with a medial
depth of fifteen feet, and though running on as
great, if not a greater slope than that river, never
empties itself in an equal degree, though much
more straight in its course. The Indus has
none of those ledges, which have been lately
discovered as a peculiarity of the Ganges, and
which are described in Mr. Prinsep's work as
" making the bed of that river consist of a series
" of pools, separated by shallows or sand-bars, at
" the crossing of every reach." Were the Indus
as scantily supplied with water as the Ganges,
we should, doubtless, find a similar state of
things; and, though the bed of the one river
would appear to far exceed in magnitude that
of the other, we find the Ganges partaking much
of the nature of a hill-torrent, overflowing at
one season, insignificant at another; while the
Indus rolls on throughout the year, in one
majestic body, to the Ocean.

Before bringing these remarks on the Indus
to a close, I wish to add a few words regarding
the effect of the tide on the two rivers. In the
Ganges it runs considerably above Calcutta,
while no impression of it is perceptible in the
Indus twenty-five miles below Tatta, or about

seventy-five miles from the sea.   We are either
to attribute this occurrence to the greater co-
lumu of water resisting the approach of the
sea, " whose vanquished tide, recoiling from the
" shock, yields to the liquid weight;" or to the
descent of the delta of the one river being
greater than that of the other.   The tide in the
Indus certainly runs off with incredible velocity,
which increases as we near the sea.   It would
appear that the greatest mean rise of tide in
the Ganges is twelve feet: I found that of the
Indus to be only nine feet at full moon; but
I had, of course, no opportunity of determin-
ing the *mean* rise of the tide as in the Ganges.
The tides of Western India are known to ex-
cecd those in the Bay of Bengal, as the construction of docks in Bombay testifies; and I
should be disposed to consider the rise at the
mouths of the Indus and Ganges to be much
the same.   Both rivers, from the direction they
fall into the ocean, must be alike subject to an
extraordinary rise of tide from gales and winds;
and, with respect to the whole coast of Sinde,
the south-west monsoon blows so violently, even
in March, as to break the water at a depth of
three or four fathoms from the land, and long
before its depressed shore is visible to the
navigator.

CHAP. III.

ON SINDE.

Sinde; its extent.

THE first territory which we meet in ascending the Indus is Sinde. The subversion of the Cabool monarchy has greatly raised the political importance of this country; and, while it has freed the rulers of it from the payment of a yearly tribute, has enabled them to extend widely the limits of their once circumscribed dominion. The principality is at present in the zenith of its power, and comprises no less than 100,000 square miles, extending from the longitude of 69° to 71° east, and from the latitude of 23° to 29° north. The Indian Ocean washes it on the south, and a diagonal line of 400 miles is terminated a short distance below the junction of the waters of the Punjab with the Indus. The eastern portion of this fine territory is sterile and unproductive; but the Indus fertilises its banks by the periodical swell, and the waters are conducted by canals far beyond the limits of inundation.

Its chiefs and re-venue.

The territory is divided among three different branches of the Belooche tribe of Talpoor, who are nearly independent of one another. The principal family resides at Hydrabad, at the head of which is Meer Moorad Ali Khan, and, since the death of his three elder brothers, its sole representative.* The next family of importance consists of the descendants of Meer Sohrab Khan of Khyrpoor, whose son, Meer Roostum Khan, is the reigning Ameer, and holds the fortress of Bukkur, with the northern portion of Sinde. The third family, descended of Meer Thara Khan, at the head of which is Ali Morad, resides at Meerpoor, and possesses the country south-east of the capital. These three chiefs are, properly speaking, the "Ameers of Sinde," a name which has been sometimes applied to the members of the Hydrabad family. The relative importance of the Ameers is pointed out in their revenues : fifteen, ten, and five lacs of rupees are the receipts of the different chiefs ; and their aggregate amount, thirty lacs of rupees, shows the annual revenue of Sinde. The treasure, it is said, amounts to about twenty millions sterling, thirteen of which are in money, and the remainder in jewels. The greater portion of this cash lies deposited in the fort of Hydrabad, and is divided between Moorad Ali and the wives of his late brother, Kurm Ali.

* As this work is passing through the press, intelligence has reached England of the death of this Ameer, which has been followed by a civil war.

Its power
and con-
quests.

If we except the Seiks, the Ameers are more powerful than any of the native princes to whose dominions the territories of Sinde adjoin; for on every side they have seized and maintained by force the lands of their neighbours. To the westward they hold Curachee as a conquest from the chief of Lus, and are at present meditating an extension of their boundary towards Sonmeeanee, that they may keep the trade to Candahar entirely within their own dominions. To the north-west they seized the fort of Bukkur, and the fertile territory of Shikarpoor, from the Afghans; and, though it latterly belonged to the powerful family of Barakzye (who now hold Cabool, Candahar, and Peshawur), they have hitherto engaged in annual but fruitless attempts to retake it. A force of 6000 men were encamped at Sewee, in the plains of Cutch Gundava, when we passed Shikarpoor; but they were unable to meet the Sindians in the field. On the north-east the Ameers hold Subzulcote and a large portion of the Daoodpootra country. To the eastward, they captured the fortress of Omercote, in 1813, from the Joodpoor Raja, and have since pushed their troops far into that Prince's territories. If we exclude a portion of that country which belongs to Jaysulmeer, they now possess the whole country south of that capital to the Runn of Cutch, Parkur included.

On the side of Cutch alone their progress has
been arrested by the British Government.

The value of these conquests is greatly en- Its military
strength.
hanced by the trifling increase of expense which
they have entailed on the government; for, except in the forts of the Desert, neither garrisons
nor troops are kept in pay to protect them,
while every attack endangering their security
has been hitherto successfully resisted. The
conduct of the Sindian in the field is brave;
and if we are to judge by results, he is superior
to his neighbours. They parried off an inroad
of one formidable army from Cabool by a retreat to the Desert; and they defeated a second
with great slaughter in the vicinity of Shikarpoor. Destitute as they are of discipline, and
unable, assuredly, to cope with regular troops,
we must admit that they excel in the art of war
as practised by themselves and the adjacent
nations. The Sindians, unlike other Asiatics,
pride themselves on being foot soldiers, and
they prefer the sword to the matchlock: their
artillery, formidable in number, is contemptible
in strength; their cavalry does not deserve the
name: horses are scarce, and of a very diminutive breed. Various surmises have been made
regarding the strength of their army, but they
seem to me vague and indefinite; for every
native who has attained the years of manhood,

the mercantile classes alone excepted, becomes a soldier by the constitution of the government; and he derives his food and support in time of peace from being pledged to give his services in war. The host to be encountered is therefore a rabble, and, as infantry, their swords would avail them but little in modern warfare with an European nation. On an attack from the British Government, it is probable that the rulers of Sinde, after a feeble resistance, would betake themselves, with their riches, as of yore, to the Desert, a retreat which would cost them, in this instance, their country. They might foment for a while conspiracy and rebellion, but the misfortunes of the house of Talpoor would excite compassion nowhere; for their government is unpopular with their subjects, and dreaded, if not hated, by the neighbouring nations.

In the decline of other Mahommedan states, the prosperity of Sinde has exalted it in the eyes of foreigners.

Its external policy.   Of the princes bordering on Sinde, the Ameers have most intercourse with Mehrab Khan, the Brahooee chief of Kelat and Gundava, who, like themselves, was formerly a tributary of Cabool. By this alliance they have skilfully interposed a courageous people together, with a strong country between their territories and that kingdom. The Afghans have endea-

voured by bribes and promises to bring over the
Kelat chief to their interests, but he has not
been hitherto persuaded, and professes himself,
on all occasions, ready to assist the Ameers in
the protection of that part of their frontier adjoining his dominions.   He is related by marriage to the Hydrabad Ameer; and the Brahooees
and Beloochees, considering themselves to be
originally descended from one stock, may be
therefore supposed to have one common interest.
With the Seiks at Lahore there is no cordiality,
and but little intercourse : they dread, and with
reason, Runjeet Sing's power, and they are likewise anxious to avoid giving offence to any of
the Cabool family by a show of friendship.
They owe the Maharaja no allegiance, nor has he
hitherto exacted any; but it has not escaped
their observation, that, of all the countries which
adjoin the Sindian dominions, there are none
from which an invasion can be so easily made
as from the Punjab, and it is very doubtful if
they could withstand an attack conducted by
the Seiks from that quarter.   With the Rajpoot
chiefs on their eastern frontier their intercourse
is confined to the exchange of presents.

The internal resources of Sinde are considerable; nor must we look to the confined revenues
of her rulers for an index to that wealth, as in
their struggle for supremacy, the Ameers re-

Its in-
ternal state.

ceived many favours from their Belooch brethren, which have been repaid by large and numerous grants of land. By deteriorating the value of what remained as their own share, they hope to allay the cupidity of their neighbours. Trade and agriculture languish in this land. The duties exacted on goods forwarded by the Indus are so exorbitant that there is no merchandise transported by that river, and yet some of the manufactures of Europe were to be purchased as cheap at Shikarpoor as in Bombay. We are informed in the Periplus of the Erythrean sea, that the traffic of Sinde, when ruled by a powerful prince in the second century of the Christian era, was most extensive, and it is even said to have been considerable so late as the reign of Aurungzebe. The present rulers, possessing as they do such unlimited authority over so wide a space, might raise up a wealthy and commercial kingdom; but the river Indus is badly situated for the trader, and has no mouth like the Ganges accessible to large ships: it is separated, too, from India by an inhospitable tract; and a very vigorous and energetic government could alone protect commerce from being plundered by the Boordees, Moozarees, and other hill tribes to the westward. The Indus can only become a channel for commerce when the chiefs possessing it shall entertain more enlightened notions.

At present much of the fertile banks of this river, so admirably adapted for agriculture, are only used for pasture. Flocks and herds may be driven from the invader; but the productions of the soil can only be reaped in due season, after care and attention. I now proceed to describe the state of parties at present existing in Sinde.

The Hydrabad family, from having been visited by several British missions, is better known than any of the others. It includes the southern portion, or what is called " Lower Sinde." Since its first establishment, in 1786, it has undergone great change; and the reins of government, from being wielded by four brothers, have been left without bloodshed in the hands of the last survivor. But the struggle for dominion, so long warded off, has been bequeathed to a numerous progeny; and on the death of Moorad Ali Khan, who has attained his sixtieth year, the evil consequences of the founder of the family, raising his brothers to an equality with himself, will be felt in a disputed succession, and perhaps in civil war.* One Ameer died without issue; two of them left sons who have now attained to manhood, and the remaining Ameer has a family of five chil-

---

* The death of the last Ameer has amply verified such a supposition.

dren, two of whom, Noor Mahommed and Nusseer Khan, have for years past sat in durbar on
an equality with their cousins, Sobdar and Mahommed.   The different parties of these four
young princes form so many separate factions
in the court of Sinde, and each uses that influence and policy which seems best suited to
advance its ends.   Three of them, as the eldest
descendants of Ameers, might claim a right of
sharing as their fathers ; but the second son of
Moorad Ali Khan has greater weight than any
of them, and the government of the Ameers of
Sinde could never, as it first stood, be considered
an hereditary one.

Meer Nus-
seer Khan,
and Meer
Mahom-
med.

Meer Nusseer Khan, to whose influence I have
just alluded, has been brought forward by his
father in the intercourse with the British, and
though fourth in rank below the Ameer himself:
he is the only person who, with his father,
addresses, on all occasions, and is addressed by,
the British Government.   He openly professes
his attachment to the English, and informed me
by letters, and in two public durbars, that he
had been the means of procuring a passage for
the mission by the Indus to Lahore.   Strange
as it may appear, it is said that his parent, otherwise so jealous of the British, had strenuously
advised this line of procedure in his son ; nor
was it disguised from me by many who had

opportunities of knowing, that the Prince acted under the hope of assistance from our Government when the hour of difficulty arrived. Nusseer Khan maintains likewise a friendly intercourse with several members of the fallen monarchy of Cabool; and while we were at Hydrabad he was despatching presents to Kamran at Herat. This prince is a mild and engaging man, much attached to the sports of the field. He has more liberality than talent, and less prudence than becomes one in the difficult part which he will shortly have to perform. His success will depend on the possession of his father's wealth, for money is the sinew of war; and the good will of a venal people like the Sindians is not to be retained by one who has spent his inheritance. Noor Mahommed, the eldest brother of Nusseer Khan, cultivates a closer friendship with the Seiks than any other of the Talpoor family, but he has neither partisans nor ability to achieve an enterprise. He is, besides, addicted to the grossest debauchery and the most odious vices; but it is always to be remembered that he is the eldest son of the reigning chief.

Meer Mahommed seems to hope, and not without cause, that the services of his father, Gholam Ali, will secure to him his rights. He sent a messenger to me privately with an offer to enter into a secret treaty with the British Go-

Mahommed and Sobdar.

vernment, which I declined for obvious reasons.
Sobdar is the rightful heir of Moorad Ali, being
the eldest son of the founder of the house.   He
is no favourite with the Ameers; but, besides a
treasure of three millions sterling, and lands
which yield him three lacs of rupees annually, he
has many chiefs and partisans, who cling to him
from a remembrance of his father's virtues.   He
is, too, the ablest " scion of the stock," and by
one rebellion has already asserted his rights.   The
contest will probably lie between Sobdar and Nusseer Khan ; and if these two choose to govern as
those who preceded them, they may revive the
title and retain the power of the Ameers of
Sinde.   At present, Meer Sobdar conceals his
plans and intentions from dread of his uncle;
and I may mention, as a specimen of Sindian
jealousy, that because I asked several times after
his health (according to the formality of this
court), seeing him seated on the right hand
of the Ameer, he was displaced at our second
interview to make room for Meer Nusseer Khan.
Should Moorad Ali attain " a good old age "
these opinions may prove fallacious, as the stage
will then be occupied by other competitors, who
are at present in their childhood, and from
among whom some one, more daring than his
relations, may meet with success and power.

The Khyr-
poor family.   The Khyrpoor chief, Meer Roostum Khan,

succeeded to his father, who was killed in 1830 by a fall from a balcony. He is about fifty years of age, and has five sons and two brothers. This family is so numerous that there are at present forty male members of it alive, descended in a right line from Meer Sohrab Khan. The chief maintains greater state than the Hydrabad family. The territory is extensive and productive, extending on the east bank from a short distance above Sehwun to the latitude of 28° 30′ north, and on the west bank from Shikarpoor to within fifteen miles of Mittun, on the verge of the Punjab, skirting to the westward the mountain of Gendaree and the plains of Cutch Gundava. There is little cordiality existing between the Khyrpoor and Hy-drabad Ameers; and the breach has been lately increased by some disputes relative to the duties on opium, of which the former have hitherto, and in vain, claimed a share. The whole family expressed themselves cordially attached to the British Government; and evinced, by a continual succession of kindness, and even munificence towards our party, that they were sincere in their sentiments : none of them had ever before seen an European. The treasure, which amounts to three millions of money, is held by Ali Moorad, the youngest brother of Meer Roostum Khan, who having access to it, as the favourite son, seized it on Sohrab's death, and still retains it. With this exception, the family are united, and have no subject of dissension.

The influence of the chief of Khyrpoor in the affairs of Sinde is considerable. No undertaking which has reference to the well-being of the country is planned without his being consulted; and hitherto no operations have been carried on without his sanction. The refusal of Meer Sohrab to enter into a war to protect the Daoodpootras, and prevent encroachment by the Seiks, defeated the plans of the Ameers; for though the families are independent of one another, they will only act when united. Meer Roostum Khan is on much better terms with his neighbours than the Hydrabad family: he has agents from the Jaysulmeer and Beecaneer Rajas, and from the Daoodpootras, resident at his court, and has more intercourse with the Seiks at Lahore. Meer Roostum is prepared, however, on all occasions with his troops to protect from invasion the boundaries of Sinde as they at present exist; and has readily furnished his quota of troops when the Afghans have endeavoured to retake Shikarpoor from the Hydrabad chief.

Meerpoor family.

The Meerpoor family, at the head of which is Ali Moorad, has the least influence of the Sinde Ameers. His immediate vicinity to Hydrabad, and his less fertile and more circumscribed boundary, have kept it more under the subjection of the principal Ameer. The territory, however, is exactly situated on the line of invasion for an army from Cutch; and this Ameer might render material service to any expedition. The family is allied to Sobdar; and will, in all probability, follow that prince's fortunes on a change of government.

With reference to the condition of the people in these different chiefships, much has been said by various writers; and I would have willingly passed it unnoticed, did not the means of observation, which I enjoyed for so many months, lead me to dissent from some of their opinions. The Sindians are passionate and proud; and all of them would be considered deceitful, in so far as they praise and promise without sincerity. Their passion proceeds from their savage ignorance, and their pride from jealousy: their deceit does not deceive each other, and, cousequently, ought not to deceive a stranger. I found those in my employ most honest and faithful servants, and passed from one extremity of Sinde to another without any other guard than the natives of the country, and without losing a trifle, though our boats were boarded by crowds daily. The Sindians are governed by their princes, after the spirit of the country; and if

Condition of the people.

they could discern how much the advantages of
civil life, and the encouragement of industry
and art, rise superior to despotic barbarism, we
might look upon Sinde and her people in a different light : but these rulers, who seized it by
the sword, must be excused for so maintaining
it.   Where the principles of honour are not understood (as has ever been too much the case in
Asiatic governments), men must be ruled by
fear ; and it is only as the subject gets liberal
and civilised, that he can appreciate the advantages of free institutions, and deserves such or
any share in the government of his country.
The inhabitants of Sinde are miserably poor,
both in the towns and villages ; for when we
except a few Belooche chiefs, and some religious
families, who are attached to the court, there is
no distributed wealth in the land but among a
few Hindoo merchants.   The people of that
tribe share no greater evils than their Mahommedan brethren, and enjoy as much toleration
and happiness as in other Moslem governments.
If they were formerly treated with rigour, the
age of fanaticism has passed; and the Hindoo De-
wans of Sinde now transact the entire pecuniary
concerns of the state, while the Shroffs and Banians, who are also Hindoos, pursue their vo-
cations without interruption, marry off their
children, when they attain the prescribed age,

to inherit, after their demise, the substance
which had been realised by commerce.

It is difficult to fix the population of Sinde, *Its extent*
and I bear in mind that I have seen the fairest *of popula-*
tion.
portion of the country in my progress through
it by the Indus.   The large towns are neither
numerous nor extensive : Hydrabad, the capital,'
has about 20,000 people, but it is exceeded by
Shikarpoor : Tatta, Currachee, and Khyrpoor
have 15,000 each ; Meerpoor, Hala, Sehwun,
Larkhana, and Roree (with Sukkur), have each
about 10,000 ; Muttaree, Ulyartando, and Subzul, with five or six others, have 5000 each ;
which gives a population of nearly 200,000
souls.   The number of people in the delta
does not exceed 30,000 ; and the parts away
from the river, both to the east and west, are
thinly peopled, for pastoral countries are not
populous.   The villages within reach of the
inundation are, however, large and numerous;
and, including the whole face of the country,
there cannot be less than a million of human
beings.   One fourth of this number may be
Hindoos ; and the greater portion of the Mahommedans are descended from converts to that
religion.

CHAP. IV.

ON THE MOUTHS OF THE INDUS.

The Indus. THE Indus, like the Nile and the Ganges, reaches the ocean by many mouths, which, diverging from the parent stream, form a delta of rich alluvium. At a distance of sixty miles from the sea, and about five miles below the city of Tatta, this river divides into two branches. The right arm is named Buggaur, and the left Sata. This separation is as ancient as the days of the Greeks, and mentioned by the historians of Alexander the Great.

Two great branches forming its delta. Of these two branches, the left one, or Sata, pursues nearly a southern course to the ocean, following the direction of the great river from which it is supplied; while the right, or Buggaur, deviates at once from the general track of the Indus, and reaches the sea, by a westerly course, almost at right angles to its twin river.

The Sata. The eastern branch, or Sata, is the larger of the two, and below the point of division is one thousand yards wide : it now affords egress to the principal body of the water ; and though it divides and subdivides itself into numerous channels, and precipitates its water into the sea by no less than seven mouths within the space of thirty-five miles, yet such is the violence of the stream, that it throws up sand banks or bars, and only one of this many-mouthed arm is ever entered by vessels of fifty tons.   The water sent out to sea from them during the swell of the river is fresh for four miles; and the Gora, or largest mouth, has cast up a dangerous sand bank, which projects directly from the land for fifteen miles.

The western arm, which is called Buggaur, on the other hand, flows into one stream past Peer Putta, Bohaur, and Darajee, to within five or six miles of the sea, when it divides into two navigable branches, the Pittee and Pieteanee, which fall into the ocean about twenty-five miles apart from each other.   These are considered the two great mouths of the Indus, and were frequented till lately by the largest native boats. They are yet accessible, but for three years past the channel of the Buggaur has been deserted by the river; and though it contains two fathoms of water as high as Darajee, it shallows above that town.   In the dry season it is in some places but knee-deep, and its bed, which continues nearly half a mile broad, has at that time but a breadth of 100 yards.   The name of Buggaur signifies " destroy."   While

The Buggaur.

Q 3

this alteration has diverted the trade from Darajee to the banks of the Sata, the country near
the Buggaur is as rich as it was previously;
and though the branch itself is not navigated,
yet there are frequently two fathoms in its bed,
and every where a sufficiency of water for flat-
bottomed boats. During the swell it is a fine
river, and will in all probability shortly regain
its former pre-eminence

Delta; its
size.

The land embraced by both these arms of the
delta extends, at the junction of the rivers with
the sea, to about seventy British miles; and so
much, correctly speaking, is the existing delta
of this river. The direction of the sea-coast
along this line of rivers is north-north-west.

Delta may
be con-
sidered
longer.

But the Indus covers with its waters a wider
space than that now described, and has two
other mouths still further to the eastward than
those thrown out by the Sata, the Seer, and
Koree, the latter the boundary line which divides
Cutch from Sinde, though the rulers of that
country have diverted the waters of both these
branches by canals for irrigation, so that none
of them reach the sea. With the addition
of these forsaken branches, the Indus presents
a face of about 125 British miles to the sea,
which it may be said to enter by eleven
mouths. The latitude of the most western
embouchure is about 24° 40′ N., that of the

eastern below 23° 30′, so that in actual latitude there is an extent of about eighty statute miles.*

The inconstancy of the Indus through the delta is proverbial, and there is here both diffi- culty and danger in its navigation.   It has in these days, among the people of Sinde, as bad a character as has been left to it by the Greek historians.   The water is cast with such im- petuosity from one bank to another, that the soil is constantly falling in upon the river ; and huge masses of clay hourly tumble into the stream, often with a tremendous crash. In some places the water, when resisted by a firm bank, forms eddies and gulfs of great depth, which contain a kind of whirlpool, in which the vessels heel round, and require every care to prevent accident.   The current in such places is really terrific, and in a high wind the

Dangers of navigating the delta.

* This limited extent of the delta of the Indus is quite inconsistent with the dimensions assigned to it by the Greeks. Arrian informs us that the two great branches below Pattala are about 1800 stadia distant from each other, " and so much " is the extent of the island Pattala along the sea coast." The distance of 125 British miles, the face of the modern delta, does not amount to 1125 stadia, or little more than one half the assigned distance of Arrian.   On this point the Greeks had not personal observation to guide them, since Nearchus sailed out of the western branch of the Indus, and Alexander made but a three days' journey between the two branches of the river, and could not have entered Cutch, as has been surmised by Dr. Vincent.

waves dash as in the ocean. To avoid these eddies, and the rotten parts of the bank, seemed the chief objects of care in the boatmen.

Peculiari-
ties of
navigation.
It is a fact worthy of record, that those mouths of the Indus, which are least favoured by the fresh water, are most accessible to large vessels from the sea ; for they are more free from sand banks, which the river water, rushing with violence, never fails to raise. Thus the Buggaur, which I have just represented as full of shallows, has a deep and clear stream below Darajee to the sea. The Hoogly branch of the Ganges is, I believe, navigable from a similar cause.

Individual
mouths.
I shall now proceed to describe the several mouths with their harbours, depth of water, together with such other facts as have fallen under notice.

The Pittee.
Beginning from the westward, we have the Pittee mouth, an embouchure of the Buggaur, that falls into what may be called the bay of Curachee. It has no bar ; but a large sand bank, together with an island outside, prevent a direct passage into it from the sea, and narrow the channel to about half a mile at its mouth. At low water its width is even less than 500 yards : proceeding upwards, it contracts to 160, but the general width is 300. At the shallowest part of the Pittee there was a depth of nine feet at low water, and the tide

rose nine feet more at full moon. At high water there is every where a depth of two fathoms to Darajee, and more frequently five and six, sometimes seven and eight. Where two branches meet, the water is invariably deep. At a distance of six miles up the Pittee there is a rock stretching across the river: it has nine feet of water on it at low tide. The general course of the Pittee for the last thirty miles is W.N.W., but it enters the sea by a channel due south. The Pittee is exceedingly crooked, and consists of a succession of short turnings, in the most opposite directions; even from south to north the water from one angle is thrust upon another, which leaves this river alternately deep on both sides. Where the banks are steep, there will the channel be found; and, again, where they gradually meet the water, shallows invariably exist. This, however, may be remarked of all rivers which flow over a flat country. There is no fresh water in the Pittee nearer than thirty miles from the sea: the brushwood on its banks is very dense, and for fifteen miles up presses close in upon the river. We navigated this branch to that extent, and crossed it in two places higher up, at Darajee and Bohaur, where it had two fathoms' water.

The Pieteeanee quits the Pittee about twenty   Pieteeanee.

miles from the sea, which it enters below the
latitude of 24° 20'.   It is narrower than the
Pittee, and in every respect an inferior branch ;
for there are sand banks in its mouth, which
overlap each other, and render the navigation
intricate and dangerous.   We found it to have
a depth of six feet on its bar at low tide, and
fifteen at full ; but when once in its channel,
there were three fathoms' water.   At its mouth
it is but 300 yards wide, and higher up it contracts even to fifty ; but it has the same depth
of water every where till it joins the Pittee.
The Pieteeanee runs north-easterly into the
land, and from its shorter course the tide makes
sooner than in the Pittee, which presented the
singular circumstance of one branch running
up, and the other down, at the same time.

Inferior
creeks.

Connected with these two mouths of the
Indus, there are three inferior creeks, called
Koodee, Khow, and Dubboo.   The two first join
the Pittee ; and the Koodee was in former years
one of the great entrances to Darajee, but its
place has been usurped by the Pieteeanee, and
it is now choked.   Dubboo is only another
entrance to the Pieteeanee.

Indus na-
vigated by
flat-bot-
tomed
boats.

However accessible these two branches have
been found, neither of them are navigated by
any other than flat-bottomed boats, which carry
the entire cargo to and from the mouth of the

river, inside which the sea vessels anchor. It was an unheard-of occurrence for boats like the four that conveyed us (none of them twenty-five tons in burden) to ascend so high up the Pittee as we did, a distance of thirty miles; but assuredly we encountered no obstacles.

Of the seven mouths that give egress to the waters of the Sata, or eastern branch, below Tatta, the Jooa, Reechel, and Hujamree, lie within ten miles of each other. One of these mouths has been at all times more or less navigable; and while they are the estuaries of the waters of the Sata, still a portion of those thrown off by the Buggaur, or other grand arm, reach them by inferior creeks during the swell, forming an admirable inland navigation through all parts of the delta. The mouths of the Jooa and Reechel are choked; but the latter was at a late period the most frequented of all the branches of the Indus. It was formerly marked by a minaret, which has, I suppose, fallen down, as this fact is particularly mentioned by our early navigators. There is yet a village, near its mouth, called Moonara, or minaret. The Hujamree is now accessible to boats of fifty tons. Its port is Vikkur, twenty-five miles from the sea, which, with Shah-bunder (still further eastward), seems alternately to share the trade of the delta. This

Jooa, Reechel, and Hujamree.

season Shah-bunder is scarcely to be approached, and the next season Vikkur will perhaps be deserted. We entered the Indus by the Hujamree mouth, and disembarked at Vikkur. At the bar we had fifteen feet of water at high tide, and a depth of four fathoms all the way to Vikkur, even when the tide was out.

Khedy-
waree.

The Khedywaree is the next mouth eastward of Hujamree, with which it is connected by small creeks; it is shallow, and not much frequented by boats but to cut firewood.

Gora, or
Wanyanee.

Of the remaining mouths of the left arm, the next is Gora, the largest of all the mouths. It derives its supply of water direct from the Sata, which near the sea feeds numerous small creeks, and is named Wanyanee. From the Hujamree we passed by a narrow creek into this mouth of the Indus. The Gora (or, as it is also called towards the sea, Wanyanee,) has every where a depth of four fathoms. It is not more than 500 yards wide, and runs with great velocity. Its course is somewhat crooked, but it pursues a southerly line to the sea, and passes by a fine village on the left bank called Kelaun. Though the Gora possesses such facilities for navigation, yet it is not to be entered from the sea by the smallest boats, from a dangerous sand bank, to which I have before alluded. It is clear that such sand

banks are thrown up by the impetuosity of the
stream, for the Reechel, till it was deserted by
the great body of the Indus, had as large a bar
as is now opposite Gora, which has entirely disappeared with the absence of the fresh water.
This branch of the Indus in the last century was
open to large boats; and a square-rigged vessel
of 70 tons now lies near it on dry land, where it
has been left by the caprice of the river.

Below the Gora we have the Khaeer and Mull, Khaeer and
Mull.
mouths communicating with it.   All three dis-
embogue within twelve miles of each other.
The Khaeer, like the Gora, is unnavigable.   The
Mull is safe for boats of 25 tons; and being
the only entrance now open to Shah-bunder, is
therefore frequented.   The boats anchor in an
artificial creek four miles up it, called Lipta,
and await the flat-bottomed craft from the port,
distant about twenty miles north-east.

About five-and-twenty miles below Mull we The Seer.
meet the Seer mouth of the Indus, but have
salt instead of fresh water.   There are several
minor creeks that intervene, but they do not
form any communication.   The Seer is one of
the destroyed branches of the Indus.   A dam
has been thrown across it below Mughribee, fifty
miles from its mouth; and though it ceases to
be a running stream on that account, the super-
fluity of fresh water from above forces for itself

a passage by small creeks till it regains the Seer,
which thus contains fresh water twenty miles
from its mouth, though it is but a creek of the
sea.   The river immediately below Mughribee
is named Goongra; higher up it is called
Pinyaree, and leaves the parent stream between
Hydrabad and Tatta.   The Seer is accessible
to boats of 150 candies (38 tons) to a place
called Gunda, where they load from the flat-
bottomed boats of Mughribee.   With some extra
labour, these same boats could reach the dam
of Mughribee; and from that town the inland
navigation for flat-bottomed boats is uninterrupted to the main Indus, though it becomes
more difficult in the dry season.   The dam of
Mughribee is forty feet broad.   The Seer at
its mouth is about two miles wide, but it gets
very narrow in ascending; within, it has a depth
of four and six fathoms, but below Gunda there
is a sand bank with but one fathom water on it.
There is a considerable trade carried on from
this branch of the Indus with the neighbouring
countries of Cutch and Kattywar; for rice, the
staple of Sinde, is to be had in abundance at
Mughribee.

The Koree,
or eastern
mouth.

The Koree, or eastern branch of the Indus,
completes the eleven mouths of the river.   It
once discharged a portion of the waters of the
Fulailee that passes Hydrabad, as also of a branch

that quits the Indus near Bukkur, and traverses
the desert *during the swell;* but it has been
closed against both these since the year 1762,
when the Sindians threw up bunds, or dams, to
inflict injury on their rivals, the inhabitants of
Cutch.* Of all the mouths of the Indus the
Koree gives the grandest notion of a mighty
river. A little below Lucput it opens like a
funnel, and at Cotasir is about seven miles wide;
and continues to increase till the coasts of Cutch
and Sinde are not visible from one another.
When the water here was fresh it must have
been a noble stream. The depth of this arm
of the sea (for it can be called by no other
name) is considerable. We had twenty feet of
water as high as Cotasir, and it continues equally
deep to Busta, which is but eight miles from
Lucput. A Company's cruiser once ascended
as high as Cotasir; but it is considered dangerous, for there is an extensive sand bank at
the mouth called Adheearee, on which the water
at low tide is only knee deep. There are also
several sand banks between it and Cotasir, and
a large one opposite that place. The Koree

* See "A Memoir" regarding this mouth, at the end of
the volume, which contains an account of some singular
alterations in physical geography, as well as a notice of the
Run of Cutch.

does not communicate with the Seer or any other mouth of the Indus, but it sends off a back water to Cutch, and affords a safe inland navigation to small craft from Lucput to Juckow on the Indian Ocean, at the mouth of the gulf of Cutch.

Advantages of these to Sinde.

The Sindians, it will therefore appear, have choked both eastern branches.   There being no communication by the Indus and the Koree, the trade of Sinde is not exported by it.   It finds a vent by the Seer; but this has not given rise to any new town being built on its banks.   Such, indeed, is the humidity, that this country is only tenable for a part of the year.

The sea outside the Indus; its dangers.

We here complete the enumeration and description of the mouths of the Indus.   Out from them the sea is shallow; but the soundings are regular, and a vessel will have from twelve to fifteen feet of water a mile and a half off shore.   The Gora bank presents the only difficulty to the navigation of these coasts, from Mandivee, in Cutch, to Curachee.   Breakers are to be traced along it for twelve miles.   The sailors clear it by stretching at once out of sight of land, and keeping in twelve fathoms' water till the danger is over: they even state that a vessel of twenty-five tons would be wrecked on a course where the depth is ten fathoms.   This bank is much resorted to by fishermen; and it may generally be distinguished by their boats and nets.

The coast of Sinde, from its entire exposure to the Indian ocean, is so little protected against storms, that the navigation is much sooner suspended than in the neighbouring countries. Few vessels approach it after March; for the south-west monsoon, which then partially commenees, so raises the sea that the waves break in three and four fathoms water, while the coast is not discernible from its lowness till close upon it, and there is a great risk of missing the port, and no shelter at hand, in such an event.

Coast of Sinde exposed.

The tides rise in the mouths of the Indus about nine feet at full moon : they flow and ebb with great violence, particularly near the sea, where they flood and abandon the banks with equal and incredible velocity. It is dangerous to drop the anchor but at low water, as the channel is frequently obscured, and the vessel may be left dry. The tides in the Indus are only perceptible seventy-five miles from the sea, that is, about twenty-five miles below Tatta.

Tides of the Indus.

There is not a more miserable country in the world than the low tract at the mouths of the Indus. The tide overflows their banks, and recedes to leave a desert dreary waste, overgrown with shrubs, but without a single tree.

Country at the mouths of the Indus.

VOL. III.   R

If a vessel be unfortunately cast on this coast, she is buried in two tides; and the greatest despatch can hardly save a cargo. We had proof of this in an unfortunate boat which stranded near us; and, to add to the miseries of this land, the rulers of it, by a barbarous law, demand every thing which is cast on shore, and confiscate any vessel which, from stress of weather, may enter their ports.

Curachee, why preferred to the Indus.

The principal sea-port of Sinde is Curachee, which appears remarkable, when its rulers are in possession of all the mouths of the Indus; but it is easily explained. Curachee is only fourteen miles from the Pittee, or western mouth of the Indus; and there is less labour in shipping and unshipping goods at it, than to carry them by the river from Darajee or Shahbunder in flat-bottomed boats. Curachee can also throw its imports into the peopled part of Sinde without difficulty, by following a frequented and good level road to Tatta. The unshipment, too, at that port, supersedes the necessity of shifting the cargo into flat-bottomed boats; and the actual distance between Curachee and Tatta (about sixty miles) is half exceeded by following the windings of the stream to any of the harbours in the Delta. As the ports in the river and Curachee are both subject to Sinde, it is conclusive that that sea-port has advantages over

those of the river, which have led to their being
forsaken by the navigator.   In former years,
before Curachee was seized by the Sindians, the
exports from the Delta were more considerable ;
since then all articles of value are brought to
Curachee by land, and there shipped.   The
opium from Marwar is never put into a boat
but to cross the Indus on its way to Curachee.

The boats of the Indus claim attention.   Including Curachee and all the ports of the
country, there are not, perhaps, a hundred
dingees, or sea vessels, belonging to the dominions of the Ameer.   These boats are of a
peculiar construction — of a sharp build, with a
very lofty poop; the large ones never ascend
the rivers, and are principally used at the port
of Curachee, and sail from thence to Muscat,
Bombay, and the Malabar coast : they carry no
guns.   A smaller dingee is used at the mouths
of the Indus, chiefly for fishing : they are good
sea-boats, and sail very quickly.   The fisheries
in the mouths of the Indus being extensive,
and forming a source of commerce, these craft
abound.

The traffic on the Indus, commencing from
its very mouth, is carried on in flat-bottomed
boats, called doondees.   They are large and
unwieldy, and never exceed 100 kurwars (fifty
tons) in burthen, and, when laden, draw only

The sea boats of Sinde.

Flat-bottomed boats.

four feet of water. They have two masts, the
larger in front; they hoist their sails behind
them, to prevent accident, by giving less play
to the canvass. The foresail is of a lateen
shape; that aft is square, and very large. With
these set, they can stem the current, in a good
wind, at the rate of three miles an hour. We
came from the sea to Hydrabad in five days.
When the wind fails, these boats are dragged,
or pushed up by spars against the stream. With
ropes, they can be pulled a mile and a half in
the hour; and they attach these to the mast-
head, to have a better purchase. The helm is
shaped like the letter P, and in the larger vessels
is managed by ropes from each side; at a distance, it seems quite detached from the doondee.
These vessels are also furnished with a long
supple oar astern, which they work backwards
and forwards, the steersman moving with it on
an elevated frame. It is possible to impel the
doondee with this oar alone, and nothing else is
used in crossing the different ferries. When
coming down with the stream, this oar, too, is
again in requisition, they work it to and fro,
to keep the broadside of the vessel to the current. In descending the river, the masts are
invariably struck, and the helm even is stowed
away. I can compare these boats to nothing so
correctly as the drawing of Chinese junks; the

largest are about eighty feet long and eighteen broad, shaped something like a ship high astern and low in front, with the hull slanted off at both ends, so as to present less resistance to the water. They are floating houses; for the people who navigate them take their families, and even their herds and fowls, along with them. All the boats on the river, large and small, are of the above description. In navigating the doondees, the boatmen always choose the shallow water, and avoid the rapids of the river.

From the account of the River Indus at its mouths, which is above given, it will appear that it would be accessible to steam-boats of a certain size and build; but I am thoroughly satisfied that no boat *with a keel* could ever navigate this river with any hopes of safety. The flat-bottomed boats are constantly grounding, but they sustain no injury; while boats differently constructed would be at once upset by the violence of the stream, and destroyed. It is not to be doubted, however, that steam-vessels could be adapted to this navigation as well as the existing boats on the river; and had not coal been found both at the head and mouth of the Indus, fuel could be supplied from the great abundance of wood which the banks of this

river every where furnish.   The Americans use
wood for this purpose ; and the supply of brushwood on the Lower Indus is abundant.

I make allusion to the navigation of this river
by steam, because I am aware it is an object of interest; but, in conducting any expedition against Sinde, I feel satisfied, from
what I have seen, that there would be little
advantage, in a military point of view, derived
from the river Indus below Tatta.   It would
be impracticable to march a force through the
Delta, from the number of rivers; and it would
be equally impossible to embark it in flat-
bottomed boats, for there are not 100 of them
below Hydrabad ; few are of burthen, and the
very largest would not contain a company of
infantry.   The vulnerable point of Sinde is Curachee, and a landing might be effected on either
side of the town without difficulty.   The Creek
of Gisry, to the south-east, has been pointed
out * as a favourable place, and I can add my
concurrence in the opinion ; but a force would
easily effect its disembarkation anywhere in
that neighbourhood.   For a land expedition,
the route from Cutch to Ballyaree, by the
Thurr, seems to me the most feasible.   While I
represent the mouths of the Indus as unfavour-

* By Mr. Crow.

able for conducting an attack from India on Sinde, I do not wish to be understood as hazarding at this time any opinion on like obstacles presenting themselves in an attack from its banks on India.

With regard to the supplies which an army is to expect in the lower parts of Sinde, my report will be more favourable.   Grain, that is, rice and bajree, will be found in great abundance. Horned cattle and sheep are numerous.   The pasturage is not good, but near the sea abundant.   Almost all the villages are mere hamlets; for Darajee, Lahory, and Shahbunder, which figure on the map as places of importance, have none of them a population of 2000 souls.   The two first, indeed, have not that between them; and there are not ten other places that have a hundred souls below Tatta.   Camels would be found in great abundance, as also horses: these are of a small and diminutive breed, but the camels are very superior.   From the number of buffaloes, milk and ghee are to be had in great abundance, and all the rivers abound in fish.   The country is peopled to the sea-shore; but the inhabitants are thinly scattered over its surface in temporary villages; and near many of the mouths experience great inconvenience from the want of fresh water, which they bring from a distance for themselves and cattle: the banks of the

Supplies of the Delta.

Gora form the only exception. The people consist chiefly of erratic and pastoral tribes; for though the Indus presents such facilities to the cultivator, there is not a fourth of the cultivable land below Tatta brought under tillage; it lies neglected and overgrown with tamarisk.

CHAP. V.

ON THE DELTA OF THE INDUS.

HERODOTUS said of Egypt, that it was the Delta of the Indus. " gift of the Nile;" the same may be said of the country at the mouths of the Indus. A section of the banks of the river shows a continued succession of earth, clay and sand in layers, parallel to one another; and deposited, without doubt, at different periods. It would be perhaps hazarding too much to state, that the whole of the Delta has been gradually acquired from the sea; but it is clear that the land must have greatly encroached on the ocean. Nothing is more corroborative of this fact than the shallowness of the sea out from the mouths of the Indus, and the clayey bottom and tinge of the water.

The country from Tatta, which stands at the Inundation. head of the Delta, to the sea downwards, is in most parts influenced by the periodical swell of the Indus: the great branches of this river are of themselves so numerous, and throw off such an incredible number of arms, that the inundation is general; and in those places which are

denied this advantage by fortuitous circumstances, artificial drains, about four feet wide
and three deep, conduct the waters through the
fields. The swell commences in the latter end
of April, and continues to increase till July, dis-
appearing altogether in September : a northerly
wind is supposed to accelerate it. It begins
with the melting of the snow in the Himalaya
mountains, before the rainy season. At other
times the land is irrigated with the Persian
wheel, which is turned by a camel or bullock,
and in general use every where. One eighth of
the Delta may be occupied by beds of rivers and
inferior streams. Ten miles from the sea, the
country is so thickly covered with furze and
bushes, that it is incapable of being brought
under tillage. Close upon the sea coast, however, there is abundance of green forage, which
furnishes pasture to large herds of buffaloes.
These animals reward the herdsmen with an
abundant supply of ghee ; but his labour is in-
cessant, for he must bring fresh water from the
interior for himself and his herd.

Towns.   In a tract peopled by a pastoral race, there
are few permanent towns or villages. When we
except Darajee, Vikkur, Shahbunder, Mughribee, and one or two others, the inhabitants
reside in temporary villages called " raj," which
they remove at pleasure ; their huts are con-

structed of reeds and mats made from rice straw; each house is surrounded by a grass "tatty" or fence, to exclude the cold wind and humid vapours which prevail in this low country, and are considered noxious. These are the houses of which Nearchus speaks, and are, I believe, peculiar to the river Indus. They very much resemble the huts of tumblers in India.

It becomes a difficult matter to form any cor- Population. rect opinion as to the number of inhabitants in such a country, where the body of the people are wanderers, and not confined to narrow limits: huts are, however, to be seen every where, and, excluding the city of Tatta, the population of the Delta cannot be rated at less than 30,000 souls; of this estimate, one third may be composed of those who reside in the fixed towns. This census gives seven and a half to the square mile.

The erratic tribe, in the Delta of the Indus, Tribes. is called Jut; these people are the aborigines of the country; they are a superstitious race of Mahommedans, and exceedingly ignorant. The different banks of the rivers are peopled by watermen of the tribe of Mooana; they are emigrants from the Punjab, and are employed in navigating the boats, or fishing in the sea or river. There is also another tribe from the same country, called Seik Lobana, whose occupation it is to make reeds and mats. They also kill wild animals and game, but are held in no estimation by the rest of the people. Jookeas or Jukreeas, an aboriginal race from the mountains over Curachee, are to be found, but they are not numerous. Some of their chiefs have land assigned to them. There are also a few Beloochees. On the fixed population there is little to remark; it is chiefly composed of Hindoos, of the mercantile caste, who carry on the foreign and internal commerce of Sinde. They do not differ from their brethren in India.

Jokeea tribe.

The only tribe which calls for further comment, is that of Jokeea. These people are the descendants of the Suma Rajpoots, who governed Sinde in former years. They became converts to the Mahommedan faith when the Hindoo dynasty was subverted, and still retain the Hindoo name of their tribe, and claim consanguinity with the Jhareja Rajpoots of Cutch. They are mountaineers from the west bank of the Indus, not very numerous, and little favoured by the government. They can bring 2000 men into the field.

Fisheries.

The fisheries in the river, and out from its different mouths, are extensive. They are chiefly carried on by hooks, and some of the fish caught are of enormous dimensions. One species called " Kujjooree " is killed for its sound, which, with

the fins of small sharks that abound near the
Indus, form an article of export to China.   The
river fish are likewise abundant; of these, the
most remarkable is the " Pulla," a kind of carp,
delicious in flavour, and only found in the four
months that precede the swell of the river.
Another species, called the " Singalee," and
about the size of a small haddock, likewise
abounds.   On the approach of the tide, they
make a noise under the ship, louder than a bull
frog.   They have a large head, and are very
bony.   They exist in all the rivers of Western
India, and are not peculiar to the Indus

I am not aware that there are any animals pe-   Animals.
culiar to the Delta of the Indus.   Otters abound;
camels are numerous, and superior; buffaloes
are reared in great numbers; horned cattle and
sheep are plentiful.   The dog, too, is here
elevated to his proper situation, and is an attendant on man.   They watch the flocks, and
are of a ferocious description, and will not allow
a stranger to approach a " raj" or village; they
swim the rivers with great dexterity.

The staple production of the Delta of the   Produc-
Indus is rice : it is to be had of many different   tions.
kinds, but its value seems to depend chiefly on
its preparation for the market.   Bajree and all
other Indian grains are raised.   From extensive
plantations of cane, " goor," a coarse kind of

sugar, is produced; which, with wheat, barley, and moong, are reared by irrigating the fields from cuts to the river, some months before the periodical swell, and form what may be called a second crop. Saltpetre is found in the Delta, but it is not exported, though formerly an object of commerce to the East India Company.

Climate.   The climate of Lower Sinde is sultry and disagreeable. The thermometer ranges as high as 90° in March, and though the soil is a rich alluvium, the dust blows incessantly. The dews are very heavy and dangerous. It is in every respect a trying country to the human constitution, and this was observable in the premature old age of the inhabitants. I could not hear of their being subject to any marsh fever, or other evil effect from the inundation; they confined their complaints to the inconvenience and annoyance which they suffered from insects and musquitoes generated in the mud.

CHAP. VI.

THE INDUS FROM TATTA TO HYDRABAD.

F<small>ROM</small> the city of Tatta, which stands at a dis- Indus from
Tatta to
Hydrabad.
tance of three miles from the river, we cease to
have the Indus separated into many channels.
On the right bank it is confined by low rocky
hillocks of limestone formation; and on the left
there is but one narrow branch, the Pinyaree,
which is accessible to boats from the town of
Mughribee, when the superfluous water of the
floods follows its course to the sea. Yet the
general width of the channel is less than half a
mile; at Hydrabad it is but 830 yards, at Tatta
less than 700, and below the village Hilaya,
fifteen miles from that town, it does not indeed
exceed 600. The greatest depth of water lies
opposite the capital, and is five fathoms; the
least at Tatta, where it is but fifteen feet; generally, there is a depth of twenty feet.

The Delta of the Indus is free from sand- Its sand-
banks.
banks; from Tatta to Hydrabad, they occur
every where, and, as the sides of the river are
here more frequently shelving than steep, it is
difficult to discover the deep channel, which

perplexes the navigator. Many of these sand-
banks are but knee deep in the water, and are
constantly shifting their position ; the current
being less rapid than near the sea, they are not
easily swept away. In several places they have
become islands, and divide the stream into two
channels, one of which will *always* be found
navigable. This subdivision of the river has
occasioned many of these branches being given
as separate rivers in our maps, but, as I have
before stated, none such exist, excepting the
Pinyaree. In the floods there is a narrow channel above Triccul, communicating with the
Fulailee branch, which insulates Hydrabad at
that season.

Course and
extent.

The distance by land from Tatta to Hydrabad
is less than fifty miles, nor do the windings of
the stream increase it, even by water, to sixty-
five. Its course is south-west by south, and
rather direct, with one decided turn, below
Jurruk, where it throws off the river leading to
Mughribee. We made the voyage against the
stream in two days.

Towns, &c.

There are not a dozen places between Tatta
and the capital ; the only one of note is Jurruk,
situated near some low rocky hillocks, nor does
it boast a population of 1500 souls : none of
them are fortified.

Country.

This country, which might be one of the

richest and most productive in the world, is devoted to sterility.   Hunting preserves, or, as they are called, "shikargahs," follow one another in such succession, as to leave no land for tillage ; and the fences which confine the game approach within a few yards of the Indus.   The interior of these preserves forms a dense thicket, composed of tamarisk, saline shrubs, and other underwood, with stunted trees of bramble, which are not allowed to be pruned or cut; so that the banks of the Indus, if in the hands of a formidable enemy, afford cover from which an expedition conducted by water might be constantly and grievously harassed.   The roads through this tract are equally close and strong.

Neglected as is this portion of Sinde, it is not destitute of supply ; grain is cheap and plentiful everywhere.   Tatta and Hydrabad are the ancient and modern capitals of the country.

The productions of the soil in the gardens of Tatta exhibit the fertility of this land : the vine is successfully reared, as also the fig and the pomegranate.   There are apple-trees in abundance, and though the fruit is small, it increases in size about Hydrabad.   In the few patches of cultivation may be seen indigo, tobacco, sugar-cane, with wheat, barley, and all the other Indian grains ; but it is the policy of the rulers of Sinde to keep every thing in a state of nature,

Productions.

that their territories may not excite the cupidity
of surrounding states.   Agriculture and commerce are alike depressed.

Trade.   With regard to the trade of this country, it
may be said there is little or none anywhere
but at Curachee.   The Indus is as if it existed
not ; and, though grain is sent by it to the delta,
no advantage is taken of the river to convey
goods to Hydrabad.   The imports are landed at
Curachee, and the most valuable export, which
is Malwa opium, is shipped from the same port.
The merchants, in prosecuting their journey to
Candahar, and the upper provinces of the Indus,
quit the Sindian territories with all dispatch.
The only encouragement which the chiefs give
to trade is in opium, yet they levy the exorbitant duty of 250 rupees for a camel-load.
The revenue from this article alone amounted last
year it is said to seven lacs of rupees ; a sum equal
to the land revenue of the Hydrabad Ameer.

Means of   Nor do there exist any hopes of improving or
improving increasing commercial intercourse by this river,
it.
till the rulers of it have more just notions of
policy, and some one of them, more enlightened
than the rest, discovers that the true riches
of a country are to be found by encouraging
the people in industry and art.   At present
there is no wealth in Sinde but what is possessed by its rulers ; and had the people the in-

clination, they have not the means of purchasing the manufactures of Europe. The case was otherwise in the beginning of this century, when the East India Company traded at Tatta by a factory, and the rulers, intimidated by their lord paramount in Cabool, did not object to the transit of goods to that and other countries. Sinde must follow the fate of that portion of Asia; and, if any of the Dooranee tribes be yet able to seize the crown of Cabool, we may expect a change for the better in the dependent provinces at the mouths of the Indus.

At present there are not vessels sufficient for any considerable trade : between the capital and Tatta they do not exceed fifty, many of them small and used for fishing, others old and worn out, that cross the stream in certain places as ferry-boats. Encouragement would soon re-medy what may be considered a defect in a military, as well as a commercial point of view. Sinde has no wood for ship building, that which is used being imported from Malabar.

Boats, de-ficiency thereof.

CHAP. VII.

FROM HYDRABAD TO SEHWUN.

Sehwun, its position.

THE town of Sehwun stands at a distance of two miles from the west bank of the Indus, and is exactly 1° of latitude north of Hydrabad, for it is crossed by the parallel of 26° 22'. The voyage is performed in eight days, against the stream, and the distance is 105 miles.

Indus, its course and depth.

The river, in this part of its course, is named "Lar," which, in the Belooch language, means south : it flows about S. S. E., being resisted at Sehwun by rocky mountains, which change the direction of the stream. Its banks are very low, and the country bordering on them frequently overflowed, particularly on the eastern side : the western bank is more firm, but seldom exceeds eight feet in height. This expansion of the river diminishes its general depth to eighteen feet : during the swell the increase is twelve feet additional ; the width is frequently 1000 yards and upwards. About six miles above Hydrabad, the Indus divides into two channels, one of which is fordable, and the other but 400 yards wide, which points to this as the place for crossing

an army.   At Sehwun the rocky buttress of the
Lukkee hills hems the waters into a channel of
500 yards; but the depth is nearly forty feet,
and the current rapid.

The river throws off no branches, in this Fulailee
part of its course, save the Fulailee, which leaves River.
the Indus twelve miles above Hydrabad, and
passes eastward of that city : it is only a stream
during the swell.   It was dry at Hydrabad when
we were at that city, and but a 100 yards wide,
and knee-deep where it separated from the
Indus ; yet it is a very considerable river in the
wet season, and fertilises a vast portion of Sinde
by its water, which it may be said to exhaust
between Hydrabad and Cutch.   The maps give
most erroneous ideas of the Indus, for the
numerous branches which appear to leave the
river are only watercourses for the periodical
swell, many of them artificial, dug for the purposes of irrigation.   The river for nine months
runs in one trunk to Tatta.

The current never exceeds three miles an Current,
hour in this part of the Indus, unless at some and effects
places where it is confined, when its rapidity of it.
undermines its banks, and carries villages along
with it.   The towns of Majindu and Amree, on
the right bank, have both been swept away, the
former no less than eight or ten times within
the last twelve years ; but the people retire a

few hundred yards, and again erect their habitations. Hala, on the eastern side, has shared a like fate; but the channel of the river lies to the westward, where the banks are more steep, and the left bank of the river, though consisting of a flat field of sand, is only inundated in the swell. At that period, for eight miles eastward of the Indus, it is not possible to travel from the number of shoots the river casts off. The Indus itself is here pretty constant in its course; and, though the country eastward would, as I have observed, favour the escape of the water in that direction, it clings for some time to the Lukkee mountains.

Its military importance.

This section of the river is of great importance: about two miles below Sehwun these mountains run in upon the Indus, leaving two practicable passes over them. The one leads across a depressed part of the range, called Buggotora, westward of the village of Lukkee (which signifies a pass), and might be obstinately defended: it is not a gun-road. The other passes between the river and the mountains, and is a cart-road, running in a valley among the lower rocks, at the base of the Lukkee mountains. The ground is very strong for about two miles.

Crossing the Indus.

I have before mentioned that the river near Sehwun is confined to a narrow bed. The right bank is very remarkable, consisting of a natural buttress of solid rock, about fifty feet high, which extends for 400 yards along the river, and, slanting upwards, is barely accessible to a foot passenger. The Indus passes with such a sweep under the base of this rampart, that, though but 500 yards wide, I question if a bridge could be thrown across it. There is a more favourable place immediately north of this precipice, where the breadth is but 100 yards greater, and the water more still. Thirty or forty flat-bottomed boats would always be found at Sehwun : they lie on the left bank, which is flat and sandy. There are good roads from Sehwun to Hydrabad on both sides of the Indus; and there is a footpath along the base of the mountains to Curachee.

The river can only be navigated by dragging the boat against the stream, for there is very little wind in the upper parts of Sinde : the progress by this method is sure, and averages from fifteen to twenty miles a day. It would be impossible, without steam, to conduct any military expedition against the stream of the Indus, for the labour of dragging the boats would be great, from constant accidents, by ropes breaking, and the vessels being hurried into the stream. The case would be very different in an army descending the Indus. Trading vessels,

Navigation of the Indus.

s 4

however, would not be liable to any such impediments.   We only counted 180 boats in our progress from Hydrabad to Sehwun.

Towns, country.

Of the country and towns which intervene between Sehwun and the capital, a few words will suffice.   There are none of any size but Sehwun itself: Muttaree, sixteen miles from Hydrabad, contains 4000 people; and Hala, Beyan, Majindu, and Sen about 2000 each. The other places are few, and thinly peopled: three or four of them have frequently one name. The country is much neglected, the banks of the river are, in most places, covered with tamarisk, towards the hills it is open.   Cotton, indigo, wheat, barley, sugar, tobacco, &c. are produced by irrigation in the dry season; but the limited extent of the cultivation may be discovered, by their being but 194 wells, or cuts, from the river on one side of the Indus, between Hydrabad and Sehwun, a distance of 100 miles, where the greater part of the soil is rich and cultivable.   In a few places the land is salt and sterile.   Rice is only produced during the swell, and yet provisions are dearer here than in the neighbouring and less favoured country of Marwar.   The people live chiefly on fish and milk.

Sehwun.

The town of Sehwun bears alone the marks of opulence in this portion of Sinde; and it is indebted for its prosperity to the shrine of a holy saint from Khorasan, by name Lal Shah baz, whose tomb is a place of pilgrimage from afar to Hindoo and Mussulman.   A branch of the Indus, called Arrul, runs immediately past the town, in its course from Larkhana; but this will be described in the next chapter.   Four years since, the Indus passed close under Sehwun; but it has retired, and left a swamp on all sides of the town.   About Sehwun the country is rich and productive, and the bazar is well supplied. Looking north, the eye rests on a verdant plain, highly cultivated, which extends to the base of the mountains : mulberries, apples, melons, and cucumbers grow here; the grain crops are luxuriant, and, for the first time, we saw gram. The melons are tasteless, I presume from the richness of the soil : cucumbers grow in Sinde only at Sehwun.   The climate is sultry, oppressive, and disagreeable.

The Lukkee mountains run in upon the Indus at Sehwun, extending from near the seaport of Curachee, and gradually encroaching upon the river, till they meet in a bold buttress.   The elevation of this range does not, I think, exceed 2000 feet; their formation is limestone; the summits are flat and rounded, never conical : they are bare of vegetation, and much furrowed by watercourses, all of which present a concave turn towards the Indus.   There is a hot spring

Lukkee mountains. Runna.

near Sehwun, at the village of Lukkee, situated
at the base of these mountains, adjoining one of
a cold description : the hot spring is a place of
Hindoo pilgrimage, and considered salutary in
cutaneous disorders. There is a spring of the
same kind in the neighbourhood of Curachee, at
the other extremity of the same range, so that
similar springs would probably be found in the
intervening parts. On this range, and about
sixteen miles westward of Majindu, on the
Indus, stands the fortified hill of Runna, a place
of strength in by-gone years, but, till lately, neglected. The Ameer of Sinde has repaired it
at considerable expense ; but, from what I could
learn, Runna owes its chief strength to the
absence of water from the bleak mountains
which surround it, and the copious supply within
its walls.

CHAP. VIII.

THE INDUS, FROM SEHWUN TO BUKKUR.

THE insulated fortress of Bukkur is situated on Bukkur, it a rock in the Indus, between the towns of position. Roree and Sukkur. It is a degree and twenty minutes north of Sehwun, being in latitude 27° 42′; and in longitude it is 56 miles eastward of that town. The distance by the river amounts to 160 miles, and we voyaged it in nine days.

Between these points the Indus flows in a Indus. zigzag course, nearly south-west, till it is impeded by the Lukkee mountains, below Sehwun. The intervening country is richly watered by its meanderings, and, from the lowness of the banks, the tract is disputed by the river and its ramifications, and formed into numerous islets of the richest pasture. On the least approach of the swell, both banks are inundated and irrigated : the superfluous water often forces for itself a passage into the desert by Omercote, and joins the eastern mouth of the Indus or Koree, which passes Cutch. The channel of this watercourse commences above Bukkur, and passes four miles eastward of that place, the ancient city of Alore.

Fertility of
the country. About twenty-five miles below Bukkur, the Indus sends to the westward a branch called Nara, that washes the base of the Hala, or mountains of Beloochistan, and, after pursuing a parallel course of many miles, rejoins the river at Sehwun. Its waters are courted, and distributed by canals, which add to the blessings bestowed by nature on this flat and fertile land. The eastern bank, though less favoured than the opposite one, is highly cultivated, and most of the towns and villages stand on the verge of canals, which bounteously distribute the waters of the periodical swell, and attest the industry and assiduity of the inhabitants.

Current,
depth, &c. The river but rarely flows here in one undivided stream; with a width of three quarters of a mile, in some places, it preserves a depth of fifteen feet in its shallowest bed. There is nothing approaching to a ford in any part of its course : two hundred boats would be found at the various villages in this part of the river. The declivity on which the Indus runs to the ocean must be gentle, for above the delta it glides sluggishly along at less than two miles and a half in the hour. From Sehwun upwards, the Indus is called " Sira," which means north, in contradistinction to the southern portion, which is

called "Lar."   Mehran is a foreign term, with
which the natives of the country are not acquainted.

The immediate vicinity of the Indus is alike   Eastern
bank of the
destitute of beauty and inhabitants.   It is over-   Indus.
grown with tamarisk shrubs, and the villages are
purposely raised at the distance of two or three
miles, to avoid the calamities of inundation ; yet
there were an hundred wheels at work on the
verge of the river.   The eastern bank, from
Sehwun to Bukkur, is by far the best peopled
portion of Sinde ; but the inhabited places which
do occur are rather numerous and thriving than
large and wealthy : many of them have 500
houses.   This territory is subject to the chief
of Khyrpoor, and is enriched by a canal forty
feet broad, called "Meerwah," which conducts,
by a southerly course, the waters of the Indus
from the neighbourhood of Bukkur to a distance
of ninety miles, where they are lost in sands, or
deposited in the fields.   There are numerous
other canals beside the one which I have now
described; and, while their banks are fringed
with villages and agriculture, they likewise afford
the means of transporting, by boats, the pro-
duce of the soil.   In the fair season, when dry,
they.become the beaten footpaths of the people,
and are excellent cart-roads, preferred at all
times to the common pathway, which, from the

exuberance of vegetation in this country, is
generally impeded by bushes.

The western bank of the Indus, which is intersected by the Nara, is called Chandkoh, from
a Belooche tribe of that name, and yields the
greater portion of the land revenue of the Hydrabad Ameers.   This branch, which leaves the
Indus below Bukkur, in the latitude of Larkhana,
in its passage to the main stream, forms a small
lake, called Munchur, which abounds in fish.
Further down, it changes the name of Nara into
that of Arrul, before falling into the Indus ; it
is a narrow river, about 100 yards broad, and
only navigable during the inundation. Numerous
cuts, the chief of which is the Larkhana canal,
extend the cultivation beyond its banks ; and, in
addition to the swell of the Indus, this district
is watered by rills from the lofty mountains to
the westward.   The lake of Munchur is envi-
roned by fields of wheat in the dry season: its
waters then partially subside, and leave a rich
mould on which good crops are reared.

The fortress of Bukkur is constructed of
brick, on a low rocky island of flint, at a distance
of 400 yards from the left bank of the Indus,
and about fifty less from the eastern side of the
river.   Its walls are loop-holed, and flanked with
towers, that slope to the water's edge : they do
not exceed twenty feet in height.   There is a

gateway on each side of the fortification facing
Roree and Sukkur, and likewise two wickets.
The interior of the works is crowded with houses
and mosques, many of which, as well as parts of
the rock itself, appear above the wall.   In shape
it approaches to an oval, and is about 800 yards
long, and 300 in diameter.   At some places the
rock has been pared and scraped ; but Bukkur
has no strength in its works, and is formidable
only from its position.   The garrison consists
of 100 men of the Khyrpoor Ameer : there are
fifteen pieces of artillery, few of which are ser-
viceable.   The walls enclose the entire island,
with the exception of a small date grove on the
northern side, where a landing might be effected
without difficulty, from the right bank, and the
place would fall by escalade ; or it might be previously breached from the bank of the river.
There is a depth of four fathoms on both
sides of the island ; but the eastern channel
becomes shallow in the dry season, and is said
to have been once forded.   The navigation of
the Indus at Bukkur is dangerous, from eddies
formed under the fortress itself, and several
other rocky islets below it ; but the watermen
are considered the most experienced in Sinde,
and, as a boat never attempts to pass up or down
without a pilot, there are but few accidents.

Roree and
Sukkur.
The town of Roree, which faces Bukkur,
stands close on the bank of the Indus, on a
flinty precipice forty feet in height, over which
the houses tower.   A road cut in the rock, down
to the edge of the river, at a place where it does
not approach the precipice, is the point of em-
barkation for those passing to Bukkur; but a
landing would be difficult and dangerous when
the river is high.   The town of Roree has about
8000 inhabitants, chiefly Hindoos.   To the eastward of it, several detached hillocks of flint present a most bleak and barren appearance, but
add to the strength of the country; beyond
their limits a grove of date trees extends for
three or four miles to the southward of the
town, shading numerous orchards and gardens.
Sukkur, which stands opposite Roree, is about
half the size of that town : both have been considerable places in former years, and the ruins of
minarets and mosques remain.   The bank of the
river at Sukkur is not precipitous, and the town
runs in from it, instead of extending, like Roree,
along its banks.   These two towns doubtless owe
their position to Bukkur, which, as a protection in troubled times, added to the courage
and hopes of the inhabitants.

Khyrpoor
and Lark-
hana.
The only modern towns of note which require
remark, are Khyrpoor and Larkhana, on the left
and right banks of the river, nearly under the

same parallel of latitude, both distant from it about fourteen miles, and watered by canals from the Indus. Khyrpoor is a modern town, built by the Talpoor chief, Sohrab, who seized on the northern part of Sinde, after the subversion of the Caloras. It contains a population of about 15,000 souls, but is merely a collection of mud hovels heaped together in narrow lanes. It is destitute of fort or defence, unless a mud wall about a foot thick, which surrounds the house of the Ameer and his family, can be considered in that light. The country near it is flat and bushy, and a low dyke has been drawn round the town, to keep the inundations of the river at a distance. Larkhanu, which stands on the western bank, is the capital of the Pergunna of Chandkoh : it has about 10,000 people, and is the head quarters and rallying point of the Sinde Ameers on their N. W. frontier. It has a small mud fort ; and an inefficient train of artillery, about twenty in number, frightens the refractory in the neighbouring mountains, and maintains the peace of Sinde. It is governed by a Nuwab, the individual next in rank to the rulers of the land.

The productions of Sinde are very similar in different parts of the country, and the same kinds of grain are produced here as at Sehwun. There is a shrub very like the wall-flower called

Produc-tions.

" syar," that grows in this tract, and the juice of
which is considered a valuable medicine for the
diseases of children.   The wheat-fields are
invariably surrounded by a low dyke, like rice
ground : tobacco grows very luxuriantly near
Roree.   The greatest want in Sinde is grass,
which is choked by the tamarisk ; to which the
people set fire, and derive, by such means,
an abundant crop.   There are but few trees in
Sinde ; the babool*, even, does not attain any
considerable size ; the neem† and sirs, so abundant in India, are rarely seen, and the banian‡
tree is a stranger.   The shrubs of the thurr, the
kejra, khair, bair, akra (swallow-wort), and tamarisk, grow every where.   I have already alluded
to the date grove of Roree.

* Mimosa Arabica.   † Melia Azadarachta.
‡ Ficus religiosa.

CHAP. IX.

THE INDUS FROM BUKKUR, TILL JOINED BY THE PUNJAB RIVERS.

THE waters of the Punjab, united in one stream, The Indus. fall into the Indus at Mittun, in the latitude of 28° 55′ north. From this point to Bukkur, the river pursues a south-westerly course, is direct in its channel, but frequently divided by sand banks. Various narrow, crooked branches also diverge from the parent stream, retaining a depth from eight to fifteen feet of water, which are navigated by boats ascending the Indus, in preference to the great river itself. They extend throughout the whole intervening space which I have now under review.

The Indus is widely spread in many parts of Its breadth its course above Bukkur. It often exceeds a and depth. thousand yards in breadth, and at Mittun was found to be even double that width. The depth was not proportionally diminished: in some places it exceeded sixteen fathoms, and four fathoms were to be found every where; which, it is to be recollected, was at a season when the waters are lowest. There was no greater acceleration of

T 2

current than in the lower parts of the river, and the serpentine course of the narrows just mentioned proves the great flatness of this country.

Boats of the Indus.

From Bukkur the Indus is navigated by a different description of boat from the Doondee, called "zohruk," and admirably adapted to the transport of troops, both horse and foot, from being as roomy before as astern : they are not numerous, but we met ninety-five of them in our voyage to Mittun. We made the passage in these boats from Bukkur to Mittun in nine days, a distance of 170 miles by the river.

Country on its banks.

The country which this portion of the Indus traverses is of the richest nature, particularly on the eastern bank, where it is flooded from innumerable channels, which are generally cut in those parts of the river running east and west, that the water may be thrown south into the interior. On the right bank, about twenty-six miles above Bukkur, a navigable canal called the "Sinde," the work of the emperors, conducts a great body of water to Shikarpoor and Noushera, and joins that of Larkhanu. On that side of the river the cultivation is limited, as the districts of Boordgah, Ken, and Moozarka, which succeed each other, are peopled by wandering and unsettled Belooche tribes, who lead a pastoral and plundering life. The territory on

both sides chiefly belongs to Sinde, for the
boundary line stretches, on the right bank, to
within fifteen miles of Mittun, and adjoining
the dominions of the Seik; but it overlaps that
on the left, which terminates lower down in the
latitude of 28° 33', twenty-five miles above Subzul. This stripe of land on the left bank forms
a portion of the territories of the Daoodpootra
chief, Bhawul Khan; and the district immediately
below that chief's territory in Sinde is named
Oobaro, and inhabited by the Duhrs and Muhrs,
who are the aborigines of the country, and known
by the name of Sindees.

The town of Shikarpoor, which stands thirty-
two miles from Bukkur, is by far the largest in
this tract, indeed in Sinde, for in size it exceeds
the capital, Hydrabad. The country around it
is very productive, but in the change of masters,
from the Afghans to the Sindians, its revenue
has deteriorated to half a lac of rupees annually :
the government is oppressive. It still carries
on an extensive inland trade, for the greater
portion of its merchants and people are Hindoos,
and have agents in the surrounding countries.
Shikarpoor is surrounded by a mud wall, and
the governor of the place holds an important
post, and with it the title of Nuwab. This town
and district fell into the hands of the Sindians
about eight years ago, and is the only unsettled

Shikarpoor, Subzul, and other places.

T 3

portion of their country, the Afghan family to whom it belonged making frequent attempts to recover it.   The frontier town of Subzul on the left bank of the Indus, and twelve miles inland, is about one fifth the size of Shikarpoor: it contains a population of 5000 souls, and like it is surrounded by a mud wall.   There are no other places of note but these which I have mentioned.   Mittun, or, as it is sometimes called, Mittun Kote, has not a population of 1500 people, and its fort has been demolished.

Swell of the Indus.

It will be observed in this part of its course, as well as elsewhere, that there are no towns or places of size in the immediate vicinity of the Indus; which is owing to the annual swell of the river rendering it impossible to cultivate or raise a crop within its reach.   This leads to the waters being conducted inland by canals, the banks of which being frequently overflowed render the country untenable.   The neighbour-hood of Subzul Kote has been deserted on this account, and the great quantity of water forces for itself a channel from this direction upon the watercourse at Alore   The Indus is very variable in its rise in different years, and for these two by-gone seasons has not attained its usual height.

Cattle, animals,&c.

The number of horned cattle to be seen in this part of the Indus is exceedingly numerous.

Buffaloes are so plentiful as to be only a fourth the value of those lower down the river, and the very best may be purchased for ten rupees each. Deer, hog, and partridge abound, and the water-fowl above Bukkur are numerous, even in this season (May).

I have mentioned the districts lying westward of the Indus, and the predatory habits of the inhabitants.   The Boordees occupy all the plains north of Shikarpoor, to the borders of the Brahooee country, or Cutch Gundava.   They are emigrants from Kej and Mekran, and of the Belooche family of Rind.   They are a fair and handsome race of men, more like Afghans than Beloochees: they do not wear the costume of Sinde, but roll a cloth in folds loosely round their brows, and allow their hair in long tresses to hang suspended, which gives them a savage appearance.   They took the name of Boordee, from a noted individual in the tribe, according to the Belooche custom, for the various tribes are nothing more than descendants of some person of note.   The chief place of the Boordees is Duree, but they have no large towns. The whole " Oolooss," or tribe, is rated at 10,000 fighting men, and till their chiefs were taken into the service of the Ameers, they were constantly marauding : petty robberies are yet committed. Their language is a corrupted Persian : of the

T 4

other tribes, the Juttooees, Moozarees, Boogtees, and Kulphurs, with many more, they differ from the Boordees only in name.   The Juttooees are to be found in Boordgah : the Moozarees, whose chief town is Rozan, extend as far as Dera Ghazee Khan, but their power is now broken, though they plundered in former times the armies of Cabool.   The Kulphurs and Boogtees occupy the hills called Gendaree, which commence below the latitude of Mittun, and run parallel with the Indus.

CHAP. X.

THE INDUS FROM MITTUN TO ATTOK.

WHILE on our progress to Mooltan, by the Chenab or Acesines, I made various enquiries, and sent different people to acquire precise information, regarding the Indus above Mittun. The Cabool mission in 1809 came upon that river, at Oodoo da Kote, about 100 miles north of the point in question; and I was desirous of connecting my own surveys with that place, and thus complete our knowledge of the Indus from the sea to Attok. *The Indus above Mittun.*

The river runs, in this part of its course, nearly due south, and is free from danger and difficulty in navigation. It is here generally known by the name of Sinde or Attok, and traverses a country much the same as I have described near Mittun, being often widely spread from the lowness of its banks. Its breadth is considerably diminished; for at Kaheree, when Mr. Elphinstone crossed it in January, the soundings did not exceed twelve feet, with a breadth of 1000 yards, while the Indus, after it has received the Punjab rivers, rolls past Mittun *Description of it.*

with a width exactly twofold.   On the left
bank, too, the soundings were found to be four
fathoms deep.

Province
of Dera
Ghazee
Khan.

On the right bank of the river the province
of Dera Ghazee Khan occupies the country as
far as the mountains.   It is a fertile territory,
and the capital which bears its name is one of
the largest towns on the Indus.   It is surrounded
by gardens and date-groves, and stands in a
very rich country : it has been long numbered
among the conquests of the Seiks, who farmed
it, till lately, to the Khan of Bhawulpoor at an
annual rent of six lacs of rupees ; but as the
district originally produced but four, every
species of extortion was practised which led
to its late resumption.   The tract being remote
from Runjeet Sing's dominions, he is anxious
to hold it without requiring the services of his
troops ; and the Maharajah has given Dajil and
some portion of the territory to the Brahooees,
its former owners, on condition of military
service.

Commerce,
its line of
route.

The productions of Demaun, and the countries
westward of the Indus, are sometimes brought
by Dera Ghazee Khan, and crossed to Ooch;
but the more frequented route lies higher up,
and passing the ferry at Kaheree leads to Mooltan.   The river is not used in the transport of
any portion of the trade, for the hire of boats is

exorbitant, and it is sent on camels or bullocks. Madder (called munjoot) is an article of export from this part of the Indus, and used to dye the fabrics of Bhawulpoor.

It is a remarkable fact that the various ex- *Expedi-* peditions that have been conducted from the *tions, why* upper provinces of the Indus, to the countries *they avoid-* lower down, have taken the rivers of the Punjab, *Indus.* as far as they went, in preference to the Indus itself; but we are certainly not to infer there-from that the greater river is shut against navi-gation.   The conquests of Alexander led him beyond the neighbourhood of the Indus, and in the case of the emperors their capital was long fixed at Lahore, and several of their fleets against lower Sinde were fitted out at Mooltan, always a city of great importance in the empire, and on a river as accessible to the boats of the country as the Indus itself.

The Indus has been crossed at Attok, and an *Bridge of* account of it, and that fortress, will be found in *boats at* Mr. Elphinstone's work ; but the means which *Attok.* the ruler of Lahore has used of late years to transport his army to the right bank of the river, and which I heard from his officers, and after-wards had confirmed on the spot, deserve mention.   Runjeet Sing retains a fleet of thirty-seven boats, for the construction of a bridge at Attok, where the river is only 260 yards wide.

The boats are anchored in the stream, a short distance from one another, and the communication is completed by planks, and covered with mud : immediately below the fortress of Attok, twenty-four boats are only required, but at other places in the neighbourhood, so many as thirty-seven are used. Such a bridge can only be thrown across the Indus from November to April, on account of the velocity of the stream being comparatively diminished at that season, and even then the manner of fixing the boats seems incredible. Skeleton frame-works of wood, filled with stones, to the weight of 250 maunds (25,000 lbs.), and bound strongly by ropes, are let down from each boat, to the number of four or six, though the depth exceeds thirty fathoms, and these are constantly strengthened by others to prevent accident. Such a bridge has been completed in three days, but six is a more usual period. We are struck with the singular coincidence between this manner of throwing up a bridge, and that described by Arrian*, when Alexander crossed the Indus. He mentions his belief regarding Alexander's bridge at Attok, and except that the skeleton frame-works are described as " huge wicker-baskets," the modern and ancient manner of

* Vide lib. v. c. 7.

crossing the river appears to have been the same. The Afghans farmed the construction of a bridge at Attok for the sum of 14,000 rupees ; but the Seik has put a stop to the ruin of habitations and houses which it invariably caused, and keeps up an efficient supply of materials. ·An army which does not exceed 5000 men is crossed at Attok by the ferry boats with less labour than by a bridge.

CHAP. XI.

THE CHENAB OR ACESINES JOINED BY THE
SUTLEGE OR HESUDRUS.

Chenab or
Acesines.

THE Acesines of the Greeks, or the modern
Chenab, is lost in the Indus at Mittun, having
previously gathered the waters of the Punjab
rivers. The junction is formed without noise or
violence, for the banks are depressed on both
sides, and the river is expanded : an eddy is cast
to the eastern side, which sinks the water below
the usual level, but it does not occasion danger.
The Euphrates and Tigris, when joined, pass to
the ocean under the name of the " river of the
Arabs," and the appellation of Punjnud, or " the
five rivers," has been bestowed on this portion
of the Chenab ; but it is a designation unknown
to the people living on its banks, and adopted,
I conclude, for geographical convenience.

Joined by
the Sut-
lege.

Under the parallel of 29° 20′ north latitude,
and five miles above Ooch, the Chenab receives
the Garra, or joint stream of the Beas and Sutlege (Hyphasis and Hesudrus of antiquity).
This junction is also formed without violence,
and the low banks of both rivers lead to constant

alteration in the point of the union, which, but a year ago, was two miles higher up. .This circumstance renders it difficult to decide on the relative size of these rivers at their junction; both are about 500 yards wide, but the Chenab is more rapid. Immediately below the confluence, the united stream exceeds 800 yards; but in its course to the Indus, though it expands sometimes to a greater size, the Chenab rarely widens to 600 yards. In this part of its course it is likewise subject to change. The depth is greatest near its confluence with the Indus, exceeding twenty feet, but it decreases in ascending the river to about fifteen. The current is swifter than the Indus, running at the rate of three and a half miles an hour. The Chenab has some sand banks, but they do not interrupt its navigation by the " zohruks," or flat-bottomed boats, forty of which will be found between Ooch and Mittun, a distance of forty miles, and a five days' voyage.

The banks of the Chenab seldom rise three feet above the water's edge, and they are more open and free from thick tamarisk than the Indus. Near the river there are green reeds, not unlike sugar-cane, and a shrub called " wahun," with leaves like the beech-tree, but the country is highly cultivated, and intersected by various canals. The soil is slimy, and most

Banks of the Chenab.

productive : the crops are rich, and the cattle
large and abundant ; the villages are exceedingly numerous, and shaded by lofty trees. Some
of these are the temporary habitations of pastoral
tribes, who remove from one place to another,
but there are many of a permanent description
on both banks. Their safety is nowise affected
by the inundations of the river or those of the
Indus, for the expansion of these has been exaggerated, and it rarely extends two miles from
the banks of either river.

Ooch, its produc-
tions, &c.   The only place of note on the Chenab, below
its junction by the Garra, is Ooch. It stands
four miles westward of the river, and no doubt
owes its site to the junction of two navigable
streams in the vicinity. The country around it
is highly cultivated : the tobacco plant in particular grows most luxuriantly; and after the
season of inundation, the tract is one sheet of
green fields and verdure. The productions of
the gardens are various ; the fig, vine, apple, and
mulberry, with the " falsa," which produces an
acid berry, may be seen, also the "bedee mishk"
(odoriferous willow). Roses, balsams, and the
lily of the valley, excite a pleasing remembrance, and there are many plants foreign to
India. A sensitive shrub, called " shurmoo," or
" the modest," particularly struck me : its leaves,
when touched, close and fall down upon the

stalk, as if broken.   The mango does not attain perfection in this soil or climate, and seems to deteriorate as we advance north.   Indigo is reared successfully.   Wheat and other grains are cultivated in preference to rice, which does not form here, as in Sinde and the lower provinces of the Indus, the food of the people, though it may be had in great quantities.

CHAP. XII.

ON BHAWUL KHAN'S COUNTRY.

Its extent.   THE small territory eastward of the Indus, which lies between the confines of the chief of Lahore and the Ameers of Sinde, belongs to Bhawul Khan Daoodpootra. His frontier to the north may be loosely said to be bounded by the Sutlege, or Garra, but at Bhawulpoor it crosses that river, and, running westward to a place called Julalpoor, comprises a portion of the country between the Sutlege and Acesines, the Acesines and the Indus. The Rajpoot princi- pality of Beecaneer bounds it to the east. It has Jaysulmeer to the south, and, on that part where it approaches Sinde, a tract of four miles in either country is left without tillage, to pre- vent dispute on the marches.

Its nature.   The greater part of this country is a barren waste of sand-hills. In the vicinity of the rivers, the tract is rich and fertile, watered, like the other banks of the Indus, by the annual swell. The towns are few in number, and scantily distributed, but there are numerous hamlets on the Acesines. Bhawulpoor, which

stands on the left bank of the Sutlege, has a
population of about twenty thousand people, and
is the mercantile capital ; the walled town of
Ahmedpoor, further south, and about half the
size, is the residence of the chief, as it lies
closer to Durawul, an ancient fort in the desert
(without a town), and the only place of strength
in the country.   Durawul is mentioned in the
histories of Sinde as a fortress worthy of Alexander : it was taken by Mirza Shah Hoosein, in
the year of the Hejira 931 ; but an account of
the siege proves its position to have been more
formidable than its strength : it is built of brick.

The influence of the chief of Bhawulpoor is Power and import-ance.
as limited as his territory, his power having been
crushed by the Seiks, and only saved from
entire overthrow by a treaty, which prevents
Runjeet Sing from crossing the Sutlege.   The
revenues do not exceed ten lacs annually (excluding Dera Ghazee Khan, which, properly,
belongs to the Seik), three of which are demanded in tribute by the Lahore chief, for his
lands north of the Sutlege ; yet Bhawul Khan
maintains some state, and has about two thousand
regular troops (such as they are), with a train of
artillery, to second the efforts of his feudatories
in the field ; and his forces collected would
exceed twenty thousand men.   The present chief
inherited a large patrimony in treasure.

Daoodpoo-
tras, their
descent.

The Daoodpootras are a tribe of Mabom-
medans from the district of Shikarpoor, on the
right bank of the Indus, which they held in the
earlier part of Aurungzebe's reign. They crossed
the river, and achieved, by daring acts of bravery,
the conquest of the lands now held by them,
from the Duhrs, Muhrs, and other Sindee tribes,
and have been settled in Bhawulpoor for five
generations. As the name Daoodpootra implies,
they are descendants of one Daood or David; but
the chiefs claim a lineage from the holy line of
Abbas, the uncle of Mahommed.   The chiefs of
the tribe are named Peerjanee, and the common
people Kihranee. The community are not allowed to assert their right to the same holy
descent as their masters, which casts some doubt
on the lustre of their parentage. The whole
tribe does not exceed fifty thousand souls. They
are a fair and handsome race of people, but disfigured by long bushy tresses of hair, which they
allow to hang over their shoulders.

The reign-
ꞁ family.

Bhawulpoor was tributary to Cabool as long
as that kingdom lasted; and the chief had the
title of Nawab, but was nearly independent.
The three last rul ers have taken the name of
Bhawul Khan, from a saint of great repute in
Mooltan; and the designation of Nawab has
been changed to th at of Khan, by which title
he is familiarly kno wn to his subjects. The

present Bhawul Khan is about thirty years old, and much beloved by his people : he has a turn for mechanics, and gives great encouragement to trade and agriculture.   He succeeded, about five years ago, to the prèjudice of his elder brother, who now holds an office under him; his power is firmly fixed, and he has a family of three sons. The form of government is despotic, and there is no chief of any great importance in the country but the Khan himself; and the style and formality of his court keep even these humble, and at a respectful distance.

The manufactures of Bhawulpoor consist of loongees, which are celebrated for the fineness of their texture.   The weavers are Hindoos, a numerous class in this country, and who enjoy more toleration in their trade than their religion.   The merchants of Bhawulpoor deal extensively in goods of European manufacture, which they receive from Pallee, in Marwar, by way of Beecaneer and the desert, and send into the Dooranee country by the route of Mooltan and Leia, crossing the Indus at Kaheree.   The Hindoos of Bhawulpoor, and, indeed, of all this country, are a most enterprising race of men : they often travel to Balkh and Bokhara, and sometimes to Astracan, for purposes of commerce : they take the route of Peshawur, Cabool, and Bamean, and, crossing the Oxus, exchange

Trade of Bhawulpoor.

u 3

at Bokhara the productions of India, for that
quarter of Asia and Russia, which are annually
brought by the merchants of that country. They
spoke highly of the Uzbek King, and praised
Dost Mahommed, of Cabool, for the protection he
afforded to trade.   The Sutlege, or, rather, the
joint stream of it and the Beas, called Garra,
on which Bhawulpoor stands, is a navigable
river, though not used in the transport of its
merchandise.   It does not lie, however, on any
available line of route, except that of Sinde; from
which country, as I have before repeated, there
is no trade with the upper provinces of the Indus.
Of the name of this river, the Beas, I may add,
that it is a contraction of Bypasa, in which we
have nearly all the letters of Hyphasis, the designation of it found in the ancient authors.

CHAP. XIII.

THE PUNJAB.

THE territories of Maha Rajah Runjeet Sing stretch from the Sutlege to the Indus, from Cashmere to Mooltan, and comprise the whole of the countries watered by the Punjab, or five tributary rivers, eastward of the Indus. The power of the Maha Rajah over this tract of country is consolidated : he commands the fastnesses of the mountains, and its alluvial plains. So entirely has the Seik nation altered its constitution, under this chief, that, within a period of twenty years, it has passed from a pure republic to an absolute monarchy. The genius of one man has effected this change, though contending with powerful opposition, from a religion, that inculcates, above every other, democracy and the equality of all.

This change of habits has been general, and the fortunate prince who achieved it, is not more pre-eminent among his nobles, than they are among their followers ; from whom they receive a respect bordering on veneration. We have now no convocations at Umritsir, the sacred city

Extent of Runjeet Sing's territory.

Changes in the Seik government.

of the Seiks, where the affairs of the state were
discussed and settled, and none of the liberty
which the followers of Gooroo Govind proudly
claimed as the feature of distinction in their
tribe.   It is evident that the change will affect
the energies of the Seik nation, for they sprang
from a religion which was free from the worn-
out dogmas of Hindooism, and the deteriorated
Mahommedanism of their neighbours, the Eu-
zoofzyees : their bravery was coeval with that
religion, and based upon it ; their political greatness sprang from their change of faith, and
though that has been changed, the Seiks are yet
left with peculiar tenets, and continue to all in-
tents and purposes a distinct people.

Policy of
Runjeet
Sing, and
state of his
army.
The power which Runjeet Sing acquired has
been preserved by his policy: he has a disciplin-
ed army of infantry, with a due proportion of
cavalry and artillery.   The system is unpopular
in the country, and the Seik Sirdars view with
distrust the innovation, and the innovators.   The
French officers, when deprived of their patron,
would find it necessary to stand aloof, from
motives of personal safety ; and, if they left the
country, the wreck of their labours would soon
perish in the general tumult.   At present their
battalions manœuvre with regularity and precision : they are well accoutred and dressed, but
destitute of the most essential quality of a soldier,

— discipline.   Their payment is irregular : they undergo cheerfully the mechanical duties of the soldier, and have shown their gallantry on service ; but there is no tie between the army and the government, and the greater and more glorious victories of the Maha Rajah were achieved before he had regular troops.

The Sirdars of the Seik nation lose their power in their own feuds.   Runjeet has not failed to foment these, and turn them to advantage ; and, as a mediator of differences, he has always despoiled both parties to aggrandise himself : he considers it justifiable to profit by the vices and bad qualities of human nature, and cares not how much he promises, and how little he fulfils.   The Maha Rajah, however, has portioned out, with a liberal hand, the lands and conquests among his Sirdars, and conciliated them by this means ; few of them place any reliance on his character : they are aware of his power, and dread to give him offence. _{Seik Sirdars, or chiefs.}

The revenues of the Punjab and its dependencies amount to about two and a half crores of rupees annually : the principal item in this sum is derived from Cashmere, which furnishes thirty-six lacs of rupees.   I may add, that all the jagheers and revenues of religious persons are included in the net sum I have named.   The revenue is collected by arbitrary _{Revenues of the Punjab.}

exactions, at the will of the collector, as in other
native governments.   They are presumed, at the
outset, to be dishonest, and, aware of the fact,
rifle the peasant, and are prepared to be rifled in
return.   The exactions, as regulated by Runjeet
himself, are mild, and his late acquisitions about
Mooltan are in a most prosperous condition.
Cashmere, on the other hand, is described as the
very essence of bad government : the people are
oppressed, and the Maha Rajah is afraid to trust
other but menial servants with that valuable
ornament of his crown.

Revenues
might be
increased.
The revenues of the Punjab might be increased by annexing to it the provinces *immediately* westward of the Indus, some of which
have been subdued by Runjeet Sing; but he
has shown, in this instance, his usual foresight
and discrimination.   Across the Indus, he would
encounter a most fanatical people, the Euzoof-
zyees, who would occupy the time of his army;
he contents himself, therefore, with an annual
tribute of some horses and rice from Peshawur.
Lower down the Indus, he farms the province
of Dera Ghazee Khan to the Khan of Bhawulpoor.

Military
resources.
The military resources of the Punjab are great:
it yields more grain than is sufficient for the
consumption of its inhabitants ; but the scarcity
of population prevents the full measure of its

production.   Camels, mules, horses, and cattle abound, and all of them, except the cattle, which are small, are of a superior description.   The roads, from one extremity of the country to the other, admit of wheeled carriages, except among the mountains : the Indus, and all the other rivers are navigable, though not navigated.   They have ferry-boats in abundance, and there are also materials for their further construction ; these rivers are frequently passed on skins, but these are more in use among the mountains than the plains.

The paucity of Seiks, in a country ruled and governed by them, is remarkable.   The mother earth of the tribe is the " doab," between the Ravee and Sutlege ; but there are few of them to be found thirty miles below Lahore.   There are no Seiks westward of the Hydaspes ; and to the eastward of Lahore, where they are said to predominate, they do not certainly compose a third of the population.   The Punjab, indeed, is a poorly peopled country, in proportion to its fertility, though it is probable that it has increased in population under the present ruler.*

* A more full account of the Punjab has been given in Vol. II., which was drawn up after my last visit to that country.

300

CHAP. XIV.

THE CHENAB, OR ACESINES, JOINED BY THE RAVEE, OR HYDRAOTES.

The Chenab described.

THE Acesines is the largest of the Punjab rivers, but its size has been exaggerated. Ptolemy informs us that it is fifteen furlongs wide in the upper part of its course ; and Arrian states that it surpasses the Nile when it has received the waters of the Punjab falling into the Indus by a mouth of thirty stadia. Alexander warred in the rainy reason, when these rivers are much swollen, and when the inundation had set in for two months. We have already exposed the latter part of this amplification, in confining the Chenab to a breadth of 600 yards, and a depth of twenty feet. There is no perceptible diminution in the size of this stream, from the Sutlege upwards, for that river increases the depth without adding to the breadth ; and the Chenab, south of the Ravee, will be found, as I have before described it, only with the shallow soundings of twelve feet. Its banks are so low, that it is in some places spread as much as 1200 yards, and looks as large as the Indus. At

Mooltan ferry it was 1000 yards across, and below its junction with the Ravce, above three quarters of a mile ; but these are exceptions to the general feature of the stream.

The Chenab receives the Ravee, or Hydraotes, below Fazilpoor, under the parallel of 30° 40′ north latitude, nearly 180 miles from Ooch, by the windings of the river, and upwards of 53 miles from Mooltan ; in the neighbourhood of which city it passes on its course to the Indus, by a direction about south-west.*   The redness of its water has already been mentioned, and that of the Ravce has even a deeper tinge.   It runs quicker than the Indus, or any of the Punjab rivers, and its banks on both sides are open and richly irrigated by larger canals of running water, dug with great labour ; on the right bank, from Mooltan upwards, there is a desert of low sand-hills, which does not admit of cultivation, and presses in upon the cultivated land at the short distance of two miles from the river.   It is a mistake to believe that this desert commences so low as Ooch, and occupies the " doab " of the Indus and Acesines ; for that tract has many large villages, and is rich and fertile across from one river bank to the other.   The distance

* We performed the voyage from one junction to the other, in six days, against the stream.

between the two rivers is about twenty-five miles, nor does it become desert till it widens be-yond that space below Mooltan.

Boats of the Ace sines. At Mooltan the Acesines is navigated by the "zohruk;" but the vessel differs in some degree from that used in the Daoodpootra country: the waist is little more than a foot above water; they are much smaller, and hoist a mat-sail on a small mast.   As there is no trade, ferry-boats are only to be had, if we except the few which bring down salt from the Jelum or Hydaspes. We embarked in a fleet of ten boats, while such an additional number are not to be procured on Wood, &c. this part of the river.   These vessels are built of the dyar, or cedar wood from the moun-tains in which the Punjab rivers have their source : the supply which the inundation roots up and floats down, is sufficient for all purposes, without any one carrying on a professed trade in it.   While the boats here are constructed of this wood, they are repaired with the "talee" tree, which may be found near every village ; and, though this country is not well wooded, an army might soon procure a supply by cutting trees from the villages near the river, and float-ing them down to any place of rendezvous.

Crossing the river. The natives of this country cross the rivers without boats, on skins or bundles of reeds ; and whole families may be seen passing in this ap-

parently insecure mode. I have observed a
man, with his wife and three children, in the
middle of the stream, the father on a skin
dragging his wife and children, who were seated
on reeds, and one of them an infant at the breast:
goods, clothes and chattels form a bundle for
the head; and though alligators do certainly exist,
they are not numerous, or such as to deter the
people from repeating an experiment, to say the
least of it, not free from danger.

The greater part of the country bordering on District of Mooltan.
this part of the Acesines is included in the district of Mooltan, which, besides the city of that
name, contains the modern town of Shoojurabad.
The government, when tributary to Cabool, has
been described in the worst terms ; but Runjeet
Sing has recruited its population, repaired the
canals, and added to their number, raising it to a
state of opulence and prosperity to which it had
been long a stranger. The soil amply repays
the labour, for such is its strength, that a crop
of wheat, before yielding its grain, is twice
mowed down as fodder for cattle, and then ears,
and produces an abundant harvest. The indigo
and sugar crops are likewise rich, and one small
strip of land five miles long, which we passed,
afforded a revenue of 75,000 rupees. The total
revenue amounts to about ten lacs of rupees a
year, or double the sum it produced in 1809.

The tobacco of Mooltan is celebrated ; but, for
an Indian province, the date-tree is its most singular production.   It yields a great abundance
of fruit, which is hardly inferior to that of
Arabia ; for the trees are not weakened by ex-
tracting a liquor from them, as in Lower India.   I
imagine that they owe their maturity to the
great heat of Mooltan ; for dates seldom ripen in
India.   The mangoes of Mooltan are the best of
Upper India, and their good qualities seem also
to arise from the same cause, as the mango
is usually but an indifferent fruit beyond the
tropics.

305

CHAP. XV

THE RAVEE, OR HYDRAOTES, BELOW LAHORE.

THE Ravee is the smallest of the five Punjab The
rivers, but, in connection with them and the Ravee.
Indus, forms a navigable channel from the sea
to Lahore. It joins the Chenab in the latitude
of 30° 40′ north, near the small village of Fazil
Shah, by three different mouths, all of which have
eight feet of water. From Lahore downwards,
the Ravce preserves a breadth of about 150
yards, and, as its banks are high and firm, there
are but few places where it is more expanded.
This river is so winding, that sails cannot be
hoisted, and a day's voyage often gives but a
direct progress of three or four miles, when the
turnings of the river have been sixfold. Lahore
is only 175 miles from the mouth of the Ravee,
but, by the river, the distance exceeds 380
British miles.

The Ravce is fordable in many places during Its naviga-
eight months in the year, but its general depth tion.
is about twelve feet, and I am satisfied that a
vessel drawing four or five feet of water could
navigate this river. The boats of the country

VOL. III.   X

do not draw more than two or three, but they are the common flat-bottomed craft already described.   There is no obstruction to these vessels in any season of the year, yet the Ravce is not used by the merchants, and the boats are only built for purposes of ferrying.   Below Lahore there are fifty-two of them, we ascended in these vessels, none others being procurable. The voyage occupied twenty-one days, and was exceedingly tedious.   I am disposed to think that it is the extreme crookedness of the river which prevents its being navigated.

Peculiar-ities of the Ravee.   The Ravee is a foul river, much studded with sand banks, many of which are dangerous quicksands.   The zigzag course it pursues, bespeaks the flat nature of the country it traverses ; its banks are more firm and decided than those of the Indus, or any other of the Punjab rivers. Near Lahore, they rise sometimes to a perpendicular height of forty feet; in many places they attain half that elevation, and give to the river much the appearance of a canal.   The country bordering on the Ravee is little liable to be flooded ; and it is worthy of remark, that there are no cuts from this river, for the purposes of agriculture, below Lahore.   Its current is something less than three miles an hour.   The water is of a reddish colour, like the Chenab ; but it is liable to change, as we remarked in our voyage, from the fall of rain in the mountains. This river is sometimes called Iräoty, in which we recognise the Hydraotes of the Greeks.

The banks of the Ravee are open, and peopled from its mouth upwards; but the villages, for half the distance to the capital, are of a temporary description, the moveable hamlets of the pastoral tribe before mentioned, called Jun or Kattia. From Futtipoor they are numerous, and the country is cultivated; but the space below that town is uncultivated. The tract between the Ravee and Sutlege is of the same sterile and unproductive description as on the northern side of the river towards the Hydaspes. Saltpetre is manufactured in considerable quantities on both sides of the Ravee.

Towns, and their inhabitants.

Lahore is the only town of note on the banks of the Ravce, but the river has lately forsaken its immediate vicinity, and this ancient capital now stands on a small branch. The position of Lahore is good, in a military and commercial point of view. It is equidistant from Mooltan, Peshawur, Cashmeer, and I may also add Delhi. It stands in a most fertile country; and an army of 80,000 men has been supported on the resources of its neighbourhood, while the people assert that provisions have not increased with the increased demand. The city now contains

Lahore.

about 80,000 inhabitants.   It is surrounded by
a strong brick wall and ditch, that may be
flooded from the river.   There are twelve gates,
and as many semicircular outworks.   It could
not withstand a siege, from the density of its
population ; but might afford security against
irregular troops.   Umritoir is superior in size
and strength to Lahore : it is a mud fortification
of great thickness, and about seven miles in
circumference, and also protected by the strong
citadel of Govindghur.   It has a population of
about 100,000 souls.   Tolumba is a small town
near the estuary of the Ravee, with a population
of about 1500 people.   It has a weak brick fort
of a circular shape, and stands in a thick grove
of date trees two miles south of the river.

Engraved by E. Finden

Sindree on the Eastern branch of the Indus

SINCE SUBMERGED BY THE EARTHQUAKE OF 1819.

From a sketch taken on the spot by Capt. Grindlay in 1808.

CHAP. XVI.

A MEMOIR ON THE EASTERN BRANCH OF THE
INDUS, AND THE RUN OF CUTCH, CONTAINING
AN ACCOUNT OF THE ALTERATIONS PRODUCED
ON THEM BY AN EARTHQUAKE IN 1819, ALSO A
DESCRIPTION OF THE RUN.

[I cannot introduce more appropriately than on the
present occasion, the following paper, which was drawn
up some time since. It is necessary to mention this
circumstance, as a few of the facts communicated are
already before the public, and have been noticed by
Professor Lyell.* Of the Run of Cutch I am not
aware of any other account having been published,
though it is a tract without parallel on the globe.]

In the north-western extremity of our Indian Cutch, its
possessions, and under the tropic, is situated position.
the small and sterile territory of Cutch, important to the British from its advanced position, but of more attraction to the student of
history, from its western shore being washed by
the waters of the classic Indus.   Cutch is a

---

* See " Principles of Geology," by Charles Lyell, Esq.,
F.R.S. London, vol. ii. 1832.

country peculiarly situated. — To the west, it has the inconstant and ever-varying Indus; to the north and east, the tract called Run, which is alternately a dry sandy desert and a muddy inland lake; to the south, it has the Gulf of Cutch and the Indian Ocean, with waters receding yearly from its shores.

Alterations in its western coast by an earthquake.

The physical geography of such a province is full of interest; for, besides the alteration in its fluctuating boundaries, it is subject to earthquakes, one of which has lately produced some unlooked for changes in the eastern branch of the Indus. To particularly detail and explain these, is the object of the present memoir.

Former fertility.

Cutch at present labours under disadvantages inflicted on it by the vindictive hatred of a jealous and cruel neighbouring Government. Previous to the battle of Jarra, in the year 1762 *, the eastern branch of the Indus, commonly called the Phurraun, emptied itself into the sea by passing the western shores of Cutch; and the country on its banks participated in the advantages which this river bestows throughout its course. Its annual inundations watered the soil, and afforded a plentiful supply of rice; the

* This battle was fought near a small village of that name. The inhabitants of Cutch made a brave stand for their independence against a Sindian army led by Ghoolam Shah Kulora.

country on its banks being then known by the name of " Sayra."

These blessings, which nature had bestowed on this otherwise barren region, perished with the battle of Jarra; for the Sindian chief, irritated at the unsuccessful result of his expedition, returned to his country full of vengeance, and inflicted the deepest injury on the country which he had failed to humble. At the village of Mora he threw up a mound of earth, or, as it is called, a " bund," across that branch of the Indus which fertilised Cutch, and by thus turning the stream, which so much benefited its inhabitants, to flow into other branches of the river, and by leading it through canals to desert portions of his own dominions, he at once destroyed a large and rich tract of irrigated land, and converted a productive rice country, which had belonged to Cutch, into a sandy desert.

The mound which had been raised, did not entirely exclude the water of the Indus from Cutch ; but so impeded the progress of the main stream, that all agriculture depending on irrigation ceased.   In process of time this trivial remnant of prosperity disappeared, and the Talpoors, who succeeded the Kaloras in the government of Sinde, threw up other mounds ; and about the year 1802, the erection of one at Ali Bunder excluded the waters of the Indus, even at the period of inundation, from the channel which had once conveyed them past Cutch to the sea.   Since then, the stripe of land which once formed the fertile district of Sayra ceased to yield a blade of vegetation, and became a part of the Run of Cutch, on which it had formerly bordered.   The channel of the river at the town of Lucput shallowed* ; and, above Sindree, filled with mud, and dried up.   Lower down it changed into an arm of the sea, and was flooded at every tide.

The Raos, or Princes of Cutch, possessed at one time military stations in three different places of Sinde, — Budeenu, Ballyaree, and Rao-maka-bazar, — yet they submissively bore these indignities, as well to their own detriment as that of their subjects.   They used no exertion to recover that which nature had bestowed on their country, or to wipe off those injuries which had been offered, at variance, as they no doubt were, with the law of nations, which requires " that " different nations ought, in time of peace, to do " one another all the good they can, and in time " of war, as little harm as possible, without pre- "judice to their own real interests."†

* Captain (now Lieut.-Col.) D. Wilson, of the Bombay army, found a ford here in 1820, in a part of the river 500 yards wide.   In 1826, I found a depth of fifteen feet in the same place.

† Blackstone.

In this state of indifference, there occurred, in June, 1819, a severe shock of an earthquake, by which some hundreds of the inhabitants of Cutch perished, and every fortified stronghold in the country was shaken to its foundations. Wells and rivulets without number changed from fresh to salt water; but these were trifling alterations, compared with those which took place in the eastern branch of the Indus, and the adjacent country. At sunset, the shock was felt at Sindree, the station at which the Cutch Government levied their customs, situated on the high road from Cutch to Sinde, and on the banks of what had been once the eastern branch of the Indus. The little brick fort of 150 feet square, which had been built there for the protection of merchandise, was overwhelmed by an inundating torrent of water from the ocean, which spread on every side, and, in the course of a few hours, converted the tract, which had before been hard and dry, into an inland lake, which extended for sixteen miles on either side of Sindree. The houses within the walls filled with water, and eight years afterwards I found fish in the pools among them. The only dry spot was the place on which the bricks had fallen upon one another. One of four towers only remained, and the custom-house officers had saved their lives by ascending it, and were eventually transported to dry land by boats on the following day.*

But it was soon discovered that this was not the only alteration in this memorable convulsion of nature; as the inhabitants of Sindree observed, at a distance of five miles northward, a mound of earth or sand, in a place where the soil was previously low and level.   It extended east and west for a considerable distance, and passed immediately across the channel of the Indus, separating as it were for ever the Phurraun river from the sea.   The natives called this mound by the name of " Ullah bund," or the mound of God, in allusion to its not being, like the other dams of the Indus, a work of man, but a dam thrown up by nature.

These wonderful events passed unheeded by the inhabitants ; for the deep injury which had been inflicted on Cutch in 1762 had so thoroughly ruined that part of the country, that it was a matter of indifference whether it continued a desert, or became an inland lake.   A feeble and unsuccessful attempt was made by Cutch to establish a Custom-house on the newly raised

* Since my return to England, I have been so fortunate as to procure a view of Sindree, as it existed in the year 1808, from a sketch by Captain Grindlay, who visited it at that time.   It has been engraved for this work, and faces Chap. XVI.   Captain Grindlay's observations on Sindree follow in a note.

dam of " Ullah bund," but to this the Ameers of
Sinde objected, and Sindree being no longer
tenable, the officers were withdrawn to the main-
land of Cutch.

Matters continued in this state till the month *An over-
flow of the*
of November, 1826, when information was re- *Indus de-
stroys it in*
ceived that the Indus had burst its banks in *1826.*
Upper Sinde, and that an immense volume of
water had spread over the desert which bounds
that country to the eastward, had likewise burst
every artificial dam in the river, as well as the
" Ullah bund," and forced for itself a passage
to the Run of Cutch.   In March, 1827, I *Actual
state of the*
proceeded to investigate the truth of what I *river.*
have stated, to examine the natural mound,
and to endeavour to account for these constant
alterations in physical geography.   I journeyed
from Bhooj, the capital of Cutch, to Lucput,
a town on the north-western extremity of the
province, situated on the Koree, or eastern
branch of the Indus.   Here I embarked in a
small flat-bottomed boat, and sailed up the river.
At Lucput, and for twelve miles up, it was
about 300 yards wide, and from two to three
fathoms deep, retaining all the appearance of a
river.   At Sundo, a sand bank so called, which is
about four leagues distant from that town, the
channel shallowed to four or five feet, for two miles;
but then regaining its depth, I entered on a vast

inland lake that bounded the horizon on all sides,
amid which the remaining tower of Sindree
stood, like a rock in the ocean. At Sundo
the water was brackish, at Sundree it was quite
fresh.   Hence I proceeded to " Ullah bund,"
which I found to be composed of soft clay and
shells, elevated about ten feet from the surface
of the water, and cut through like a canal,
with perpendicular banks on either side.   The
channel was about *thirty-five yards* broad, and
three fathoms deep; and a body of fresh water,
a portion of the real Indus, rolled down it into
the lake which I had traversed, below " Ullah
bund."   Here the stream took on once more
the appearance of a river, and I found several
boats laden with " ghee " (clarified butter),
which had descended it from Wunga, and thus
corroborated all which I had heard, that the
bunds of the Indus had been burst, and that
the communication between the great river and
its eastern and long-forsaken branch was once
more restored.   I learned likewise that the far-
famed fortress of Omercote had been partially
overwhelmed in this inundation; for instead of
being an öasis in the desert, as had long been
supposed, this birthplace of the great Achar is
a small brick fort only three or four miles distant from the Indus, and between which and

Lucput, so late as May, 1829, there was a communication by water.

The " Ullah bund," which I now examined with attention, was, however, the most singular consequence of this great earthquake. To the eye it did not appear more elevated in one place than another, and could be traced both east and west as far as it could reach ; the natives assigned to it a total length of fifty miles. It must not, however, be supposed to be a narrow stripe like an artificial dam, as it extends inland to Raoma-ka-bazar, perhaps to a breadth of sixteen miles, and appeared to be a great upheaving of nature. Its surface was covered with saline soil, and I have already stated that it consisted of clay, shells, and sand. The people universally attributed this bund to the influence of the earthquake, and also assigned the shallowness of the river at Sundo to the same cause. *Ullah bund described.*

The inland lake which had been thus formed, extended for about 2000 square miles, and its limits were well defined, since the roads from Cutch to Sinde passed on either side of it. The one led from Nurra to Loonee and Raomaka-bazar, and the other from Lucput to Kotree Garee and the Jattee. I am disposed to believe that this sheet of water has collected from a depression of the country round Sindree ; for the *Opinions regarding the effects of the earth-quake.*

earthquake had an immediate influence on the
channel of the river below " Ullah bund," which
became deep enough to be navigable for boats
of 100 tons from the sea to Lucput, which had
never been the case since 1762. While the basin
of Sindree, as I may call it, was depressed, it is
evident that the mound of " Ullah bund " was
raised at the same time, as the description
already given will have satisfactorily shown.

Subsequent
alterations
in the
Indus.

In the month of August, in the year 1827, I
proceeded a second time to the eastern branch
of the Indus, to make further investigations regarding a subject on which many individuals, as
well as myself, had taken an interest.   Great
alterations had taken place in this changeable
country ; the river and lake were deeper in all
places by two feet, the channel through " Ullah
bund " was much widened, and the sheet of
water was now entirely and every where salt.
The stream which passed "Ullah bund" was
fresh, but greatly diminished in size : in the
time that had intervened between my visits,
the south-westerly winds had prevailed, and
blown the sea water in upon the fresh, which,
appeared to account for the change that had
taken place.

Besides the facts which have been recorded,
it appears clear that a portion of the waters of

the Indus have a tendency to escape by Lucput and Cutch.   We find an inundation of the river seeking an old channel which had been deserted by them for sixty-five years.*

THE RUN.

In the course of my observations on the Indus, I found myself drawn into many inquiries regarding the Run of Cutch, to which that river adjoins; for if the alterations in the river afforded room for remark, there was also much to be said on the Run, which is a tract, I believe, without a counterpart in the globe.   In length, the Run extends from the Indus to the western confines of Guzerat, a distance of about 200 British miles.   In breadth, it is about thirty-five miles; but there are, besides, various belts and ramifications, which give it an extent of about 7000 square miles.   It is accurately delineated in the map.   The whole tract may truly be said to be a " terra hospitibus ferox ;" fresh water is never to be had any where but on islands, and there it is scarce; it has no herbage, and vegetable life is only discernible in the shape of a stunted tamarisk bush, which thrives

Run of Cutch.

---

* I have suppressed various opinions which I had formed on the causes of these constant changes, deeming them of small value.   The paper has been also published at length by the Royal Asiatic Society of London.

by its suction of the rain water that falls near
it.   It differs as widely from what is termed
the sandy desert, as it differs from the cultivated plain ; neither does it resemble the steppes
of Russia ; but may be justly considered of a
nature peculiar to itself.   It has been denominated a marsh by geographers, which has
given rise to many erroneous impressions regarding it.   It has none of the characteristics
of one : it is not covered or saturated with water,
but at certain periods; it has neither weeds nor
grass in its bed, which, instead of being slimy,
is hard, dry, and sandy, of such a consistency as
never to become clayey, unless from a long continuance of water on an individual spot; nor is it
otherwise fenny or swampy.   It is a vast ex-
panse of flat, hardened, sand, encrusted with salt
sometimes an inch deep (the water having been
evaporated by the sun), and at others, beautifully crystallized in large lumps.   So much is
the whole surrounding country corrupted by
this exuberance of salt, that all the wells dug
on a level with the Run become salt.   The
depression of the Run below the level of the
surrounding country at once suggests the probability of its being a dried up lake or sea.

Mirage of   Nowhere is that singular phenomenon, the
the Run.   *mirage or surab* of the desert, seen with greater
advantage than in the Run.   The natives aptly

term it smoke*; the smallest shrubs at a distance assume the appearance of forests; and on
a nearer approach, sometimes that of ships in
full sail, at others that of breakers on a rock.
In one instance I observed a cluster of bushes,
which looked like a pier, with tall-masted vessels
lying close to it; and on approaching, not a bank
was near the shrubs to account for the deception.
From the Run, the hills of Cutch appear more
lofty, and to have merged into the clouds, their
bases being obscured by vapour. The wild ass†
is the only inhabitant of this desolate region;
they roam about in flocks, "scorning the mul-
" titude of the city, and make the wilderness
" and barren lands their dwelling." Their size
does not much exceed that of the common ass,
but, at a short distance, they sometimes appear as
large as elephants. While the sun shines, the whole
surrounding space of Run resembles a vast ex-
panse of water — the appearance it commonly
assumes — and which is only to be distinguished
from real water by those who are long habit-
uated to such visionary illusions. When the
sun is not shining, the Run appears higher at
a distance; but this has been remarked of the
sea, and other extensive sheets of water, and
is also to be accounted for in the deception of
vision.

* Dhooan.   † Called "Khur-gudha" by the natives.

The natives of Cutch, Mahommedans as well as Hindoos, believe that the Run was formerly a sea; and a tradition is in the mouth of every one, that a Hindoo saint, by name Dhoorumnath, a Jogee*, underwent penance by standing on his head for twelve years on the summit of Denodur, one of the highest hills in Cutch, which overlooks the Run.   When his penance terminated, God became visible to him, the hill on which he stood split in two, and the adjacent sea (the present Run) dried up ; the ships and boats which then navigated it were overturned, its harbours destroyed, and many wonderful events happened.   There is no race of people who have recourse to supernatural agency in their chronicles, more than the natives of India ; and, to those accustomed to enquire into them, the circumstances just recorded will appear as the graft of one of their tales on some real event which has actually occurred, and is thus trans-mitted to posterity.   Considering the frequent occurrence of earthquakes in Cutch, the volcanic appearance of its hills, and the lava which

---

* This class of people are yet numerous in Cutch : it is among them that the horrid custom called " traga" prevails. It consists in sacrificing one of their number when any injury or oppression is offered to their community, under a belief that the blood so shed rests on the head of those who oppress them.

covers the face of the country, it is to a convulsion of nature, in all probability, that we
are to attribute the foundation of such a tradition.'

The natives, however, carry their traditions   Concur-
beyond the vague legends of a saint, and point   ring tra-
                                                  ditions.
out at this day different positions, said to have
been harbours, in the Run of Cutch. At Nerona,
which is a village about twenty miles NNW.
of Bhooj the capital, and close to the Run, there
is said to have been a sea-port, which is thus
described in the poesy of the country : —

> " Nerona nuggartur
> Judhee Goontree Chitrano."

In other words, that Nerona was a sea-port (tur),
when Goontree (an ancient city in Cutch)
flourished in the neighbouring district of Chi-
trano. At Charee, a village westward of Nerona,
and on the Run, there is also a like tradition.
The people of the Puchum, the largest island
on the Run, have similar traditions, and speak
of boats having been wrecked on the hills of the
island; also that there were considerable harbours
near them, called Dorut, Doh or Dohee, and
Phangwuro, which are yet pointed out to the
westward of Puchum.   Bitaro, a small place on
the high road to Sinde, between Cutch and
" Ullah Bund," is also said to have been a sea-

port, and I could point out several others. Nor are the traditions less concurrent on the Sinde, or northern side of the Run : Veego-gud, near " Ullah Bund," is said to have been the principal sea-port, and its brick ruins are yet visible. Vingur and Ballyaree, which lie eastward, claim likewise the same privileges. This sea had the name of " Kiln ;" nor do I believe that the testimony of so many people, regarding it, can be discredited, informed as I was of these traditions by different persons, who had no communication with one another.

Effects of a late earthquake on the Run.

The effects of the earthquake of 1819 have been already mentioned, in so far as relates to the country adjoining the Indus ; but occurrences of an equally singular nature happened farther eastward. It made numerous cracks or fissures in the Run ; and I state, on the authority of eye-witnesses, that immense quantities of black, muddy water were ejected from these openings for a period of three days, and that the water bubbled out of the wells of the tract bordering on the Run, called Bunnee, till it overwhelmed the country in some place with six, and even ten feet of water. The shepherds with difficulty saved themselves and their flocks. During this time numerous pieces of iron and ship-nails were thrown up at Phangwuro, the sea-port before mentioned ; and similar things have been since found in the same neighbourhood while digging tanks. I give this fact on the authority of respectable men at Nurra, who also assured me that nothing of the kind had ever been discovered before the earthquake of 1819.

The grand Run of Cutch is that part which *Flooding of the Run.* lies between Sinde and the islands of Puchum and Khureer, the other parts being but ramifications of it. It has a communication with the sea both on the east and west, by means of the Gulf of Cutch and a branch of the Indus, and it is flooded from both these openings as soon as the south-westerly winds set in, about April each year. When local rain falls and moistens the Run, the sea enters with great rapidity, and insulates the province of Cutch for some months; but even without rain the greater portion of the Run is annually flooded. The level of the Run is obviously higher than the sea, since it requires strong winds to blow the waters of the ocean over it.

We must now attend to the configuration of *Configuration of the Run borders.* the Run. In the north-eastern extremity of Cutch, it will be observed that a chain of hills overhangs the Run at Bheyla : they are about 300 feet high, and terminate abruptly. The islands of Khureer and Puchum lie due west of this range, and are not only composed of the same sort of ironstone as the Bheyla hills, but have similar ranges running through their northern extremities, which terminate, partieu-larly at Khureer, in a bluff and abrupt outline towards the Run. Khureer is six miles west-ward of Cutch, and Puchum is about sixteen from Khureer; westward of Puchum there are a few low and sandy islets on the Run, and south of it lies the Bunnee, an extensive tract of grass land, of greater elevation than the Run, but not sufficiently so to yield grain. It has many wells, and is inhabited by a pastoral race. South of Khureer there are also many islands, the largest of which is Gangta, and covered with rocky hills. Between Guzerat and Cutch the Run is narrow; at Addysir it is but a mile and a half wide to the island of Chorar. Here there is a deposit of shells and marine matter, a car-bonate of lime mixed with other substances; it has a red and yellow petrified appearance, takes on a tolerably good polish, and from which some members of the faithful pretend to read Arabic words, or letters of the Koran. It was used in the mosaic works of all the Moghul emperors, and is commonly called Dookur-warra marble by Europeans. North of the Bheyla hills lies Parkur, a district peninsulated by the Run, having the lofty hills of Kalinjur, of a formation differing from Cutch, where they are almost all sandstone. They are primitive rocks, rising in small cones one upon another, as if they had dropped from the clouds; the summit is composed of trap, which extends for about a third of the way down, and the base is red granite, which rings when struck.   These hills are separated from Cutch by a low tract of the Run, upwards of thirty miles broad, without an intervening bush. The whole northern face of Cutch, from Bheyla on the east to Lucput on the west, presents, with a few exceptions, either a rocky or an elevated bank.   From Nurra to Lucput the rocks terminate abruptly, and form what would be called capes, cliffs, and promontories, if the water washed under them.   When the immediate vicinity of the Run is not of this description, it stretches inland, exactly as water would do when not resisted.

The sea is receding from the southern shores of Cutch; and I believe it is a generally received conclusion, that there is a depression of its level throughout the globe, though in some places it has risen.   We may, therefore, suppose the ocean to have receded from the Run of Cutch, and that that tract was at one time a navigable sea.   That the natives should attribute so great a change in a part of their country to the influence of a Jogee, is not wonderful.   A body of these persons has been long settled in Cutch.   They are a philanthropic and hospi-

Run supposed to have been an inland sea.

table body of men, who permit no one of any persuasion to leave their door hungry, and they are blessed with plenty. Like the monks in Europe in former days, these Jogees are the repository of history and traditions, and it may be their careful preservation of them, which has given rise to the belief that the alterations in the Run were accomplished in the time of Dhoorumnath, the founder of their order. In proof of this, they have a tradition that the ancestors of the present rulers of Cutch were once a class of poor shepherds from Samee (Tatta), in Sinde, and fed their flocks, till patronised by the Denodur Jogees, who raised them to be Rajahs of the country. So far is this true, the Rajpoots of Cutch did come from Tatta, and did tend herds of cattle in Cutch; but they were certainly not raised to their present elevation by the intercession of some Hindoo monks; yet such is the alteration which a story undergoes, in the course of four hundred years.*

* I have since found, in some manuscript papers of the late lamented Captain M'Murdo, written as long since as 1815, that he formed similar conclusions with myself regarding the Run of Cutch. He is treating of that part of it near Kattywar, of which I have not spoken, and the following extract is both curious and satisfactory: —

" The Runn has every appearance of the sea having
" shortly withdrawn from it. This is supported by the
" semblance and production of the neighbouring country,
" and large stones are found on the shore several miles from

" the present Runn, of a description similar to those used
" as anchors ; they have holes bored through for the cable.
" On the shore, at different places, are shown small ancient
" buildings, called Dan Derees, or houses where the dan
" or customs were collected ; and, in short, it is a tradition
" in the country, that Khor, a village two miles east of
" Teekir, was a sea-port town.   About fifty years since, the
" wreck of a vessel, of a size far beyond that of any of the
" craft now in use in the Gulf of Cutch, was discovered at
" Wawania, sunk in the mud about fifteen feet deep." —
Captain McMurdo's MS. Memoir on Kattywar, August, 1815.

NOTE ON SINDREE.

I ANNEX the following extract, describing a
journey from Lucput in Cutch, to Hydrabad in
Sinde, by way of Sindree, from the MS. of
Captain R. M. Grindlay, written in the year
1808, when with a mission to the Ameers of
Sinde, and which has been kindly furnished to
me.   It will be seen that the neighbourhood of
Sindree, which I have described to be under
water, was then dry, and that the fort of Sindree
existed at that time, as an outpost of the Cutch
Government.

" WE embarked on the creek at Lucput Bunder,
" which is about three quarters of a mile broad, and
" runs between east and north, for six or eight miles,
" when it begins to narrow very much : the shore on
" each side is a wet marsh, covered with short bushes.
    " In the evening we anchored at the turn of the tide,

" and at twelve o'clock next day we passed Sindree,
" which is about thirty miles from Lucput, and depend-
" ent on it, with a small garrison of sepoys : it is a small
" fort, with a few huts outside, and one well : the creek
" here is about a mile and a quarter broad, and has a
" ferry across.   The travellers who take this route to
" Sinde are not numerous, and leave no vestige of a
" road in the light sand, of which the dry part of the
" Run is composed.   The heat of the meridian sun is said
" to be so intense, that they generally travel in the
" night.   From Sindree, by land, the next stage is about
" twenty-four miles to Baura, after which the Run ends,
" and water becomes tolerably plentiful.

   " We passed Sindree, and observed several inferior
" branches leading through the Run, among which we
" saw a few straggling men and women; about twenty
" miles beyond Sindree, we reached Aly Bunder, at
" eight o'clock at night, and came to anchor close to the
" mound which confines the fresh water : when the day
" appeared, we observed it to be a poor mud village, of
" about fifty huts, and a tower of the same unsub-
" stantial materials. Here we encamped for the purpose
" of collecting the boats from the freshwater side of the
" mound, and not finding a sufficient number, several
" of those we brought with us were dragged over : this,
" however, was a work of three days ; and, during that
" time, from the nature of the soil, we were annoyed by
" the dust in such a manner as would scarcely be
" believed by those who had not been in a similar
" situation : the sun was completely obscured by it,
" an object at the distance of 100 yards was invisible;
" and the natives moving about were so disguised, that
" their colour was not distinguishable.   The soil of the
" Run is a mixture of fine sand and the salt deposited

" by the inundation. This, dried by several months' sun,
" becomes a most impalpable powder. The Run, which
" ceases about a line with Aly Bunder, from north-east
" and north, is covered with aquatic bushes and a few
" shells : the sand entangled amongst these bushes forms
" hillocks of various heights, from five to fifteen feet,
" according to the size of the bush. It does not ap-
" pear that any of the side channels lead beyond the
" Run, or that any of them are navigated by boats,
" except those which again join the main stream : that
" by which we came is certainly by far the most con-
" siderable.

" On the 10th we embarked again on the freshwater
" river, which is there about 400 yards broad, and soon
" after widens very much, with high sand-hills on the
" banks, and a few huts with a little cultivation. The
" river here takes the name of Goonee.

" At the distance of about twelve miles from Aly
" Bunder, the river divides, and soon after becomes so
" narrow, that our boats, though not large, had difficulty
" in passing through the large bushes which overhang
" the bank, and has great appearance of a cut canal, or
" at least of a channel cleared out and deepened ; the
" banks are irregular in their height, and the land
" immediately beyond them low, and in several places
" swampy. We passed the mouth of a creek on the
" west, said to lead to Tatta, besides several other in-
" ferior streams which run through the country, and are
" cut into a variety of channels, for the purposes of
" cultivation.

" About ten miles beyond Aly Bunder, on the west
" bank, is Chuttee Thur (or ferry), opposite to which is
" the mouth of a considerable stream, with a dam across,
" which we understood to be the Phoran. This was

" formerly a very large branch of the Indus, and ran
" past Nusserpoor, which I learn is to the south-east.
" Many of the inhabitants of that place recollect a
" remarkable change in the river : the inundation swal-
" lowed up a great part of the town, and altered the
" course of the river, which since then has had much
" less water in it. The whole of Sinde, from the nature
" of its soil, is subject to these alterations by the annual
" floods, many striking instances of which the inhabit-
" ants are well acquainted with, particularly that which
" I have already mentioned, and the great alterations in
" the branches below Tatta."—*See Captain Grindley's
Journal in MS.*

THE END.

LONDON :
Printed by A. SPOTTISWOODE,
New-Street-Square.